D1087779

**Rural Policy
Problems:
Changing
Dimensions**

Rural Policy Problems: Changing Dimensions

Edited by
William P. Browne
Central Michigan University
Don F. Hadwiger
Iowa State University

HN
90
.C6
R82
1982

LexingtonBooks
D.C. Heath and Company
Lexington, Massachusetts
Toronto

INDIANA
PURDUE

WITHDRAWN

FORT WAYNE

Library of Congress Cataloging in Publication Data

Main entry under title:

Rural policy problems.

Includes index.
1. United States—Rural conditions—Addresses, essays, lectures.
2. Rural development—Government policy—United States—Addresses,
essays, lectures. I. Browne, William Paul, 1945-   . II. Hadwiger, Don F.
HN90.C6R82   307.7'2'0973   81-48069
ISBN 0-669-05242-6   AACR2

Copyright © 1982 by D.C. Heath and Company

All rights reserved. No part of this publication may be reproduced or
transmitted in any form or by any means, electronic or mechanical,
including photocopy, recording, or any information storage or retrieval
system, without permission in writing from the publisher.

Published simultaneously in Canada

Printed in the United States of America

International Standard Book Number: 0-669-05242-6

Library of Congress Catalog Card Number: 81-48069

pd
8-8-83

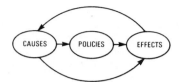

Organization Series
Policy Studies

General Approaches to Policy Studies

Policy Studies in America and Elsewhere
  edited by Stuart S. Nagel
Policy Studies and the Social Studies
  edited by Stuart S. Nagel
Methodology for Analyzing Public Policies
  edited by Frank P. Scioli, Jr., and Thomas J. Cook
Urban Problems and Public Policy
  edited by Robert L. Lineberry and Louis H. Masoti
Problems of Theory in Policy Analysis
  edited by Philip M. Gregg
Using Social Research for Public Policy-Making
  edited by Carol H. Weiss
Public Administration and Public Policy
  edited by H. George Frederickson and Charles Wise
Policy Analysis and Deductive Reasoning
  edited by Gordon Tullock and Richard Wagner
Legislative Reform
  edited by Leroy N. Rieselbach
Teaching Policy Studies
  edited by William D. Coplin
Paths to Political Reform
  edited by William J. Crotty
Determinants of Public Policy
  edited by Thomas Dye and Virginia Gray
Effective Policy Implementation
  edited by Daniel Mazmanian and Paul Sabatier
Taxing and Spending Policy
  edited by Warren J. Samuels and Larry L. Wade
The Politics of Urban Public Services
  edited by Richard C. Rich
Analayzing Urban Service Distributions
  edited by Richard C. Rich
The Analysis of Policy Impact
  edited by John Grumm and Stephen Washby
Public Policies for Distressed Communities
  edited by F. Stevens Redburn and Terry F. Buss
Implementing Public Policy
  edited by Dennis J. Palumbo and Marvin A. Harder
Evaluating and Optimizing Public Policy
  edited by Dennis J. Palumbo, Stephen B. Fawcett, and Paula Wright
Representation and Redistricting Issues
  edited by Bernard Grofman, Arend Lijphart, Robert McKay, and
  Howard Scarrow
Administrative Reform Strategies
  edited by Gerald E. Caiden and Heinrich Siedentopf

Specific Policy Problems

Analyzing Poverty Policy
  edited by Dorothy Buckton James
Crime and Criminal Justice
  edited by John A. Gardiner and Michael Mulkey
Civil Liberties
  edited by Stephen L. Wasby
Foreign Policy Analysis
  edited by Richard L. Merritt
Economic Regulatory Policies
  edited by James E. Anderson
Political Science and School Politics
  edited by Samuel K. Gove and Frederick M. Wirt
Science and Technology Policy
  edited by Joseph Haberer
Population Policy Analysis
  edited by Michael E. Kraft and Mark Schneider
The New Politics of Food
  edited by Don F. Hadwiger and William P. Browne
New Dimensions to Energy Policy
  edited by Robert Lawrence
Race, Sex, and Policy Problems
  edited by Marian Lief Palley and Michael Preston
American Security Policy and Policy-Making
  edited by Robert Harkavy and Edward Kolodziej
Current Issues in Transportation Policy
  edited by Alan Altshuler
Security Policies of Developing Countries
  edited by Edward Kolodziej and Robert Harkavy
Determinants of Law-Enforcement Policies
  edited by Fred A. Meyer, Jr., and Ralph Baker
Evaluating Alternative Law-Enforcement Policies
  edited by Ralph Baker and Fred A. Meyer, Jr.
International Energy Policy
  edited by Robert M. Lawrence and Martin O. Heisler
Employment and Labor-Relations Policy
  edited by Charles Bulmer and John L. Carmichael, Jr.
Housing Policy for the 1980s
  edited by Roger Montgomery and Dale Rogers Marshall
Environmental Policy Formation
  edited by Dean E. Mann
Environmental Policy Implementation
  edited by Dean E. Mann
The Analysis of Judicial Reform
  edited by Philip L. Dubois
The Politics of Judicial Reform
  edited by Philip L. Dubois
Critical Issues in Health Policy
  edited by Ralph Straetz, Marvin Lieberman, and Alice Sardell
Rural Policy Problems
  edited by William P. Browne and Don F. Hadwiger

Contents

Acknowledgments

The editors gratefully acknowledge the assistance of three organizations. Economic Research Service, U.S. Department of Agriculture, provided the funding for this symposium. The Farm Foundation helped direct the policy focus by funding a national rural-policy conference related to farm structure at the inception of this project. The Policy Studies Organization served as an important sponsor. Within those organizations, thanks go to John Lee, J.B. Penn, Susan Sechler, David Brewster, Wayne Rasmussen, Garth Youngberg, Jim Hildreth, and Stuart Nagel.

The Policy Studies Organization thanks the U.S. Department of Agriculture for its financial aid to the symposium on which this book is based. However, no one other than the individual authors is responsible for the ideas advocated here.

Special thanks also go to Linda Browne for research assistance, to Judy Neely for superb clerical aid in assembling a final manuscript, and to Susan J.S. Lasser of Lexington Books for keeping the editors prompt and their manuscript complete.

Introduction

We have been convinced for some time that rural policies need more attention, particularly at the level of their interrelationships. Rural policy merits a large audience, within agriculture and within the rural United States, as well as among the nation's informed public.

Research efforts on the rural United States have been fragmented and unevenly distributed. Many natural scientists are devoted to improvement of agricultural technology. Agricultural economists have studied the organization of agricultural production, and some have studied price and income policies. Rural social patterns, community organization, and social change have been studied by many rural sociologists. Natural and social scientists have examined soil and natural-resource conservation. Rural families as consumers have been one major focus of home economists.

Other distinct fields have been studied by small groups of researchers from these fields and from others, including political science. For example, a few scholars have studied counties, cities, townships, special districts, and other rural governments. A few others have studied federal policy in one functional area as it relates to rural areas—education, health, housing, community facilities, industrial development, and the like.

In no way do we mean to degrade the work of those scientists who have studied one or another aspect of agriculture and rural society. By and large their research is of proved value and merits high respect. What we as political scientists understand of rural needs and rural policy comes largely from these sources.

However, we do object to the fact that rural policy is so fragmented. An isolation has been imposed on the work of rural social scientists. There have been efforts to remedy this difficult problem, efforts symbolized in the Rural Development Act of 1972. But these efforts have been too easily discounted and too quickly ended for lack of quick success.

We object to the fact that rural problems and policy do not have mainstream status. In the past, policymakers for U.S. society have habitually ignored their vital interests in the social, economic, and resource pathologies of rural regions.

As scholars and teachers of rural policy, we are unhappy that our fragmented research findings are, understandably, in a scattered pattern of publication. Too few attempts are made to bring findings in different fields together in one book.

These conditions must be remedied. The problems of the rural United States, in general, need be recognized. They are many. Levels of government services are consistently lower in rural areas. Rural residents, on the average, still have lower incomes and greater developmental need than their counterparts elsewhere. The countryside and its natural resources frequently suffer from misuse and depletion. In various rural states can be found sprawling mine spoil, eroding fields, and thousands of cases of groundwater contamination. Rural local governments lack the funding and expert personnel to solve these and other escalating problems.

Several ongoing factors mandate attention to developing a healthy rural United States and protecting its resources. They can be summarized as follows:

1. It is abundantly clear that events in rural regions have an impact on occurrences elsewhere. For example, rural unemployment in agriculture precipitated the urban migration of midcentury, with its resulting urban crisis.

2. The nation as a whole is becoming increasingly dependent on rural regions in ways other than just the extraction of food, fiber, and natural resources. Agriculture sustains the U.S. balance of trade internationally. States such as Michigan, faced with a sharp manufacturing decline, find themselves compelled to look to rural regions for economic gain. Michigan's second and third largest industries, respectively, are agriculture and tourism. Both are rural centered.

3. A rural in-migration of population has occurred during the 1970s. This increase in population has somewhat changed the nature of rural areas and has undoubtedly strained the already tight demand for local services and resources.

4. Many natural resources—including soil, land, and minerals—are being converted, polluted, or removed. As in the past, this is often done with some local support from those citizens who gain financially, although little compensation or trade-off goes to the community or area as a whole.

5. Finally, the cutbacks in federal programs under the Reagan administration further undermine rural regions' ability to deal with their own problems. With budgets already strapped, cutbacks mean greater neglect, less service, and ever-increasing need as local rural governments adjust to increased program responsibilities.

Rural America is not simply an untapped resource waiting to be used to alleviate the nation's economic and population problems. Although rural areas have much to offer, they have a distinctly limited capacity to deal with present— let alone new—problems. We believe that this is reason to emphasize the need for comprehensive rural policy aimed at developing, allocating, maintaining, and preserving rural resources.

The research and analysis collected for this book offer some informed observations that can be directed toward the development of rural policy. Although chapters are not perfectly integrated or sequential, they are more than first cuts in that each of the authors has attempted to apply specialized expertise to the common problems of rural conditions. This interdisciplinary collection combines the work of sociologists, demographers, economists, political scientists, public administrators, and political theorists. Authors come from both land-grant and non-land-grant schools. They have been, variously, professors, researchers, consultants, and administrators in academia, federal agencies, and the White House. One contributor is a part-time local official.

The fifteen chapters that follow are divided into four sections. Part I deals with general rural problems. In chapter 1, Ted K. Bradshaw and Edward J. Blakely examine some present, and largely recent, characteristics of rural America. Bradshaw and Blakely see the emergence of new patterns of population and economic dispersal that explain recent rural growth. They attribute that growth—where it occurs and where it is likely to occur—to technological innovation, improvements in the capacity and quality of community life, and intercommunity linkages. Under such conditions they see indigenous economic development as a distinct possibility for many rural regions.

William L. Flinn adds a significant warning in chapter 2, however. Not only do communities vary, Flinn notes, but they also differ internally in terms of community values and the ideology of the residents. Conflicting values present a concerted effort to improve rural communities' welfare, despite some supportive public sentiments. In chapter 3 John Dinse builds on Flinn's concerns, examining the general nature of the forces that represent rural interests in government. In terms of expenditures, rural policy has translated into agriculture policy, which today means farm-income support. From the perspective of the rural interest, Dinse argues, this produces and maintains policies for the few at the expense of the many.

Part II examines the meaning of population changes that have been evident in recent years, especially during 1970s. Calvin L. Beale, the most prominent of the sociologist/demographers who study rural population trends, interprets the continuing rural in-migration patterns seen in the 1980 census. Chapter 4 is Beal's second look at the emerging census data; it contains some definitive comments on the trends of the 1970s.

Chapter 5 by William P. Browne reports on the attitudes and expectations residents have toward government and its services in one rural community subjected to intense in-migration. This short chapter was included because it makes some important observations about the politics of escapism. These residents, rather than being primarily interested in better services, more jobs, modern government, and a sense of community cooperation, were oriented toward the enjoyment of rural isolation with a few friends and neighbors. They had a broad view of services rather than a more disjointed concern with bad roads or intermittent police services.

In chapter 6 Lynn M. Daft, a veteran rural specialist who worked on the Carter administration's rural policy, turns to the progress made on behalf of the rural poor in the 1970s. Daft finds that, as a result of federal social programs, rural poverty has lost much of its harsh personal impact. This factor may in large part account for another trend now being noted about rural in-migration, the influx of sizable numbers of low-income residents maintaining themselves on income-transfer supports.

A less optimistic group of chapters is included in part III. These chapters deal with the difficulties faced by local governments in handling new residents, new work loads, expanded services, and escalating problems. Each chapter emphasizes the same theme: the limited professional and technical capacity of these governments. Paul M. Green, in chapter 7, presents a case study detailing changes in service demand and delivery programs for policy, roads, and schools in Will County, Illinois. In chapter 8 Alvin D. Sokolow examines those variables that explain the change to more professional management in a sample of several small, rural California cities.

Substate regionalism and the prospects of declining federal support are addressed by Lewis G. Bender in chapter 9. Bender compares and evaluates the operations, tasks, and opinions of local officials about regional organizations. He finds—unfortunately for some of the hopes expressed earlier by Bradshaw and Blakely—that the future of regional organizations is far less than promising by any of his measures.

In part IV the book moves from government operations to specific policy concerns. Four conventional and often discussed rural subjects are addressed: land use by Jan E. Dillard in chapter 10, housing by Daniel M. Ebels and Harriet Newburger in chapter 11, law enforcement by Fred A. Meyer, Jr., and Ralph Baker in chapter 12, and rural education by Daryl J. Hobbs in chapter 13. Each of the topics is handled from different perspectives and methodologies, a fact that makes the chapters all the more interesting and useful in a section intended to illustrate specific rural problems. Dillard produces a state-by-state comparison of land-use policies. Ebels and Newburger conceive a rural housing strategy based on a national voucher plan. Meyer and Baker analyze rural law enforcement and crime trends. Finally, Hobbs examines the prospects of a new approach to rural education.

The last of the specific policy chapters, chapter 14 by Sydney Duncombe, turns away from the routine policy concerns of rural residents and analysts. What, Duncombe asks, will happen to rural America in the event of nuclear war? According to existing government plans, it is to be a repository for evacuated urban residents. Yet neither the federal government nor local units have made minimal arrangements to care for what could be this final wave of rural in-migrants. Given all the other defense preparations for nuclear disaster, this presents a serious shortcoming. Duncombe's example, more than any other chapter, best emphasizes the inescapable role rural regions play in any set of policy circumstances. That which is rural, he shows, always must be seen as part of the national whole.

In the concluding chapter of this book, Frederick H. Buttel examines the linkages between rural policy and agricultural policy. He argues forcefully and carefully that the two can never be seen as separate and distinct. Rural regions still usually rest on an agricultural base. In reviewing and explaining the relationships found in a large amount of rural development, rural sociology, and farm-structure research, Buttel maintains that a healthy and productive agriculture that successfully employs large numbers of local residents for local purposes best meets the needs of the rural population. Departures from that structural arrangement, in terms of either agriculture or rural activities, present serious problems.

Buttel both challenges and confirms many of the introductory points made by Bradshaw and Blakely as well as by some of the other authors. Most important, he brings the entire book back to the question of the purpose best served by a sound rural environment. Despite the fact that many types of workers would like to live a rural life, despite the economic emergence of a number of "silicon valleys," despite efforts to provide multiple government services in the country, rural America follows a rural pattern that must be in large part adapted to the public interest through the production of food and fiber. To the extent that any rural specialists forget about national agricultural needs, they do us all a serious injustice.

Part I
General Rural Problems

1 The Changing Nature of Rural America

Ted K. Bradshaw and
Edward J. Blakely

The recent reversal in rural population trends from decades of decline to substantial increases is significant for two reasons.[1] First, the vast, depressed, sparsely settled nonmetropolitan parts of the country are experiencing both population and economic growth.[2] This growth is bringing jobs, commercial services, diversity, and a general improvement in the quality of life,[3] despite some evidence that growth is also associated with ecological imbalances,[4] increasing crime rate, congestion, and social and economic inequalities among both old and new residents. Increasingly, it is suspected that population growth and economic change may not necessarily equal progress and benefits for all rural people.

Second, the recent rural growth phenomenon defies and disconfirms an earlier premise of major modern theories of social and economic development, which depicted technological progress as *urbanism* and forecasted the continued growth of megacities along the nation's perimeters. Current rural growth cannot be explained or easily understood by the earlier models, which fail to account for nonmetropolitan population growth, economic development, and the rural community in explaining this recent phenomenon.

The purpose of this chapter is to review what is being learned about the source of recent rural growth, to identify the new problems emerging from this growth, and to point to some policy directions for effective rural development. Three forces that have combined to make new patterns of population and economic dispersal possible and attractive help to explain why rural growth has occurred now rather than before. These three forces now stimulating rural development do not derive from agriculture and the rural heritage, but rather reflect the opportunities of an advanced industrial society, which finds rural places a compatible venue for its development. From this perspective the three most crucial components of recent rural development are as follows:

1. Technological innovation and the expansion of employment in service industries have made possible the emergence of a new economic base to replace agriculture in rural communities.

This chapter was made possible by a grant from the Ford Foundation to support the Rural Development Policy Project. The assistance of Philip Shapira and Nancy Leigh-Preston is gratefully acknowledged.

3

2. The improving capacity and quality of community life brought about by improved physical and social services makes rural areas attractive for technological and social development.
3. The ability of rural areas to develop links with each other and with urban centers makes it feasible for rural areas to attract people, business, and industry.

These three forces of rural change thus provide mutually reinforcing opportunities for rural development built not on old rural characteristics but on new ones. This suggests that rural areas are no longer "rural" in the sense of agricultural, backward, isolated, and conservative. In many ways they are finding themselves at the frontier of change and development.[5] As with any pioneering venture, new sets of problems have emerged, requiring new policy mechanisms. The most significant policy directions involve a shift in development strategies: from attracting industry to stimulating local-based businesses, from public-works projects to human-resource activities, and from local-capacity development to regional voluntary, shared-power arrangements for service delivery to small communities.

Rural Areas and Advanced Industrial Society

It is no longer an anomaly to describe rural areas apart from the central urbanizing forces shaping most of the industrialized world. The forces of change creating the postindustrial, or advanced industrial society are altering the way rural areas are developing.[6] Indeed, some rural areas represent not bastions of traditionalism, but, rather, vanguards of the emerging socioeconomic order.[7]

Hage notes that rural areas have entered a "postindustrial" stage that is "so qualitatively different that one must look for quite different causal laws or hypotheses."[8] The expansion of advanced industrial characteristics into rural areas provides an alternative view of the future and of the role of rural areas in an evolving society. The growth of rural society is a significant development of advanced industrial society because it is made possible by new economic and organizational possibilities. In this way, rural development may be at the frontier of change rather than in the backwater.[9]

But despite improved conditions in many rural parts of the United States, significant areas continue to experience stagnation, decline, and isolation. Many of these areas have little prospect ot taking advantage of the new opportunities associated with an advanced industrial society. There is a great deal of variation in how, and how much, the forces of advanced industrial society influence rural America. This chapter builds on our new research in the rural areas of four states (California, Wisconsin, North Carolina, Vermont), which is part of the Rural Development Policy Project; but it does not attempt to present the project's preliminary empirical findings.

The states surveyed have different economic structures and levels of human-resource services. California's rural areas, which are experiencing the greatest level of service employment and high-technology development, benefit from a well-developed social and institutional infrastructure. Vermont is developing a high-technology economy with significant tourism and small-business components, but it has a weak delivery system for human services. Wisconsin has a traditional rural economy that now faces the influx of large plants and insurance companies, but it has a well-developed human-resource infrastructure. Finally, North Carolina has a rural economy marked by many low-skill manufacturing plants, coupled with a poorly developed service and institutional infrastructure.

The Possibility of Rural Growth:
Technology and Services

Since World War II the major agricultural impact of technological development on rural areas has been the reduction in the difficulty and costs of spatial separation. Low-cost telecommunications, particularly with satellite technology, have put the whole country—indeed, most of the world—within reach of the telephone. Increasingly, this means connection to such computer resources as teleprocessing, data files, and graphics. Innovations in media have made television available to most of the remote corners of the country, and the distribution of national news has broadened. Electronic control of processes in manufacturing and information management has allowed the dispersion of plant locations throughout small communities in the Midwest and South. A larger share of the value in many products now comes from the kind and quality of technical input they embody, rather than from their raw materials or energy-consuming processes, making transportation costs less crucial. Services, especially education, insurance, and government, are easily dispersed for similar reasons, as numerous studies have noted. In short, the impact of these developments for rural society is that the economic base is now linked to the most progressive parts of the national and world economy, as an adjunct to metropolitan production rather than a distant supplier of materials, workers, and life-style.

The Changing Shape of Rural Employment Opportunities

Three trends are significant for the changing rural economy (see figure 1-1). First, in virtually every section of the country, agriculture is no longer the dominant employer; most important, it has nearly reached a stable low employment level, halting its century-long decline. Second, manufacturing employment has grown in rural areas, especially those with branch plants and factories connected to growth industries. Finally, services have expanded to employ

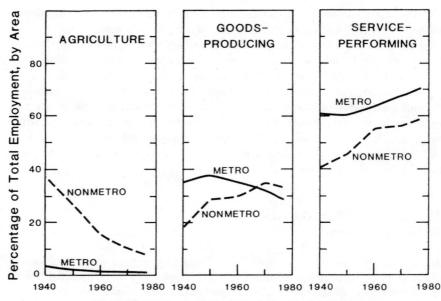

Figure 1-1. Comparative Employment, by Sector

nearly 60 percent of the rural labor force and to provide the new basic economy for the growing rural population.

Employment in agriculture is very close to stability, meaning that there will be few new displaced farm workers available to work in rural factories or to continue to migrate to urban areas. Bureau of Labor statistics data for 1980 show that from the mid-1950s to the mid-1960s agriculture lost about 200,000 employees per year. By the 1970s the loss was reduced to one-tenth of the previous total, about 20,000 employees per year. Agricultural employment dropped from 7.2 million in 1950 to 3.5 million in 1970. By 1979 agriculture still employed 3.3 million (see table 1-1). These data suggest that a major qualitative change is occurring in the character of the labor force in rural areas as the huge impact of displaced agricultural workers disappears.[10]

Manufacturing industry is a growing and powerful force in many regions of the United States. From 1962 to 1978 manufacturing employment grew by 3.2 million, with 1.8 million (56 percent) in nonmetropolitan areas. From 1962 to 1970 nonmetropolitan manufacturing employment grew 30.8 percent, compared with only 15.2 percent in metropolitan areas; but in the 1970s nonmetropolitan manufacturing employment increased by a much more modest 12.1 percent, and metropolitan employment actually declined by 3.5 percent.[11] The slower growth of manufacturing employment in the 1970s reflected more difficult economic times, but the distribution of that growth indicated clearly

Table 1-1
Agricultural Employment in the United States

Year	Agricultural Labor Force (Thousand)	Change from Previous Period	Average Annual Change	Average Annual Change (%)
1950	7,160	–	–	–
1955	6,450	– 710	-142	-2.0
1960	5,458	– 992	-198.4	-3.1
1965	4,361	-1,097	-219.4	-4.0
1970	3,462	– 899	-179.4	-4.1
1975	3,380	– 82	– 16.4	-0.5
1979a	3,297	– 83	– 20.8	-0.6

Source: Bureau of Labor Statistics, 1980.

aFour-year period

that there has been a significant shift in manufacturing to rural areas. During this period the South added 966,000 manufacturing jobs, 53 percent of the national manufacturing-job growth.

There are a number of factors associated with the growth of rural manufacturing employment. The first is the declining importance of proximity to natural resources. Spengler estimates that today only 7 percent of the labor force needs to be located close to natural resources, whereas thirty years ago nearly 30 percent of the labor force was locationally determined.[12] This spatial freedom in part reflects the lighter weight per dollar value of new products such as electronics, and in part the greater ease of transportation. Hansen argues that "economic opportunity is associated with capital and human skill, and not with land and natural resources."[13] A second reason is that growth industries are choosing rural locations because there they find skilled workers and a life-style that is considered essential.[14] Bradshaw and Blakely have shown that between 1965 and 1976 rural California acquired over 5,000 new high-technology jobs, 26 percent of all new nonmetropolitan manufacturing jobs in the state.[15]

A final reason for rural manufacturing growth is that corporations can find a low-wage, nonunion work force in rural areas. In times of declining productivity and profits, and increasing international competition, firms are seeking labor advantages wherever they can. Rural areas offer these opportunities.

Service employment has become the largest and most significant component of the rural labor force in recent decades. From 1962 to 1978 nonmetropolitan counties gained 6,232,000 new service jobs, 73 percent of the total new nonagricultural-job growth during that period.[16] Manufacturing, by comparison, gained 21 percent. It is important to note that trade and government each gained more new jobs than did manufacturing, and personal and professional services gained nearly as many.

The strongest sector of rural service-industry growth is professional services. Based on 1977 *Current Population Survey* data, professional service-industry employment grew 43.1 percent from 1970 to 1977, whereas overall employment in nonmetropolitan areas grew by 24.4 percent. Business services grew by 41.0 percent. The implication is that the new growth in rural parts of the country is very service oriented and that a major part of it employs the most skilled segments of the labor force.

Evidence is also accumulating to suggest that services play a more catalytic role in rural economies than has previously been assumed. Smith and Pulver have shown that service industries contribute significantly to the basic income of an area; that is, they bring income into the area from outside.[17] For example, in trucking, insurance, wholesale trade, construction, and computer services, major income flows were from outside the community.

Rural Dual Labor Market

Research on the quality of jobs in rural areas has consistently found the manufacturing jobs relatively poor and characterized by considerable amounts of unemployment and such poor wages that often they were attractive only to female labor. Averitt describes this as a characteristic of the dual economy in rural areas.[18] Some rural states even advertise their nonunion status by promising firms persistent lower wages. Many of the high-technology electronics and similar firms moving to rural areas characteristically have a sharply bifurcated labor force: large numbers of very low skill workers, and a significant number of managers, scientists, and technicians—but few medium-skilled workers between, and little opportunity for job mobility.[19]

Despite the growth in rural employment, rural earnings still lag considerably behind those in urban areas. The data show that metropolitan earnings are about 20 percent higher than nonmetropolitan.[20] These data also show that from 1968 to 1975 the total per-capita personal income of nonmetropolitan residents increased from 76.8 percent of the average per capita for the entire United States to 82.8 percent. The improvement of rural incomes by 6.0 percentage points during this short period indicates that the gap between rural and urban areas may be closing rather rapidly. Moreover, the nonmetropolitan South depresses these figures. The rural West is over 90 percent of the national average, but still almost 20 percentage points behind the metropolitan West. Further, the rate of increase of nonmetropolitan areas was double or nearly double the rate of increase per capita in every region except the South. But the South had the highest overall rate of increase and the highest metropolitan increase rate.

The Attractiveness of Rural Growth:
Human Resources and Quality of Life

The second force for rural development has been a broad-based improvement in the level of human services and amenities that has transformed rural areas from intimidating and inconvenient hinterlands into attractive and advantageous sites for new technological development. The interstate highway system primarily links cities to each other, but along the way it gives easy access to vast rural areas. Government intervention has paid off in rural areas in rural electrification, improvement of schools, availability of public services, increases in government capacity, and modernization of sewer and water systems. More recently, medicine, higher education, regional planning, and similar activities have reduced the disadvantages of rural life in many parts of the nation, permitting people to live out their preferences for a rural life-style. In short, the second component of the model suggests that recent improvements in organizational capacity, physical infrastructure, and quality of life have made rural areas attractive to the potentials offered by advanced industrial technology and services

The extent to which this organizational development has occurred is documented by Webster and Campbell, who studied the various service agencies in sixteen predominantly rural counties in East Tennessee.[21] They discovered 919 different agencies in these counties and, even more significantly, showed that nearly every local service was made available to rural residents. The crucial predictors of agency growth were median income, median education, and the rate of immigration. In short, the services were most available in those communities with the strongest connections to the socioeconomic resources of the wider society.

Human Resources and the Changing Rural Demography

There are essentially two ways to show that rural growth is responsive to the changing attractiveness of rural areas. The first is to document that population change precedes economic change, and the second is to show that the most highly skilled are the most likely to choose to migrate. Evidence supports both points, suggesting that rich human-resource bases are the foundation for rural development.

A recent study by Zuiches and Price has shown that rural population growth in Michigan preceded economic development, with jobs a *response* to recent population growth.[22] Equally applicable are the findings from a number of surveys of recent newcomers to rural areas. These have found that the majority of the newcomers arrive for life-style reasons, or because they like the particular rural area in contrast to their urban residence. Most do not have jobs when they arrive but are soon able to find or create jobs. In a recent study of 533 newcomers to six northern California communities. Bradshaw and Blakely found that a high proportion of newcomers started their own businesses.[23] Over all, 42 percent were involved in starting a business during the first few years of their residence in rural communities. Self-employment is the major source of income for 31 percent of the newcomers; another 5.3 percent are partially self-employed. The final 2.5 percent either have not yet completed their plans or have failed. These businesses ranged from small retail outlets to professional consulting firms. In any case, the resources of the newcomer were crucial in making the opportunities available.

National data further support these findings on the role of small business in rural employment. Data from the Survey of Income and Education indicate that there is double the proportion of self-employment in nonmetropolitan areas (17.4 percent) as in metropolitan areas (8.9 percent).[24] Self-employment in nonmetropolitan areas exceeds self-employment in metropolitan areas in every industrial sector except recreation and entertainment services; moreover, many of the largest self-employment industries, such as agriculture, are found in higher proportions in rural areas than in urban.

A second source of evidence of the attractiveness of rural areas lies in the types of people who are arriving in those areas. Data show consistently that these migrants are also more likely to be highly skilled, educated, and resource-rich. Although this is the pattern of many migrant streams, the attractiveness of rural areas to these migrants is a recent development. Beale computed the employment patterns of nonmetropolitan workers from the 1975 survey of income and education.[25] These data showed that 22.9 percent of the recent migrants (nonmetropolitan residents who were metropolitan residents in 1970) were employed in professional services, the highest category of employment. In contrast, only 17.0 percent of the old-timers (nonmetropolitan residents in both 1970 and 1975) worked in professional services. Trade was the second most common source of employment (21.3 percent of the newcomers), followed by manufacturing (18.1 percent). Newcomers equaled or exceeded old-timers in proportion of employment in every field except manufacturing, agriculture, and transportation/public utilities. Clearly, newcomers are a major force shaping the growing sector of the economy.

Persisting Inequalities

The main finding that emerges from the analysis of these data on the migration into rural areas is that the newcomers are bringing both significant human resources and the economic base that relies on these skills. On the other hand, minorities, women, and youth are losing out. By 1977 only 3.1 percent of nonmetropolitan black men over 25 had completed four years of college or more, compared with 8.3 percent of metropolitan blacks; in comparison, 6.8 percent of nonmetropolitan white men had completed this much college, compared with 23.4 percent of white metropolitan men. Similar figures show the disadvantages of rural Hispanic men. Moreover, minorities are greatly over-represented among the functionally illiterate. As a consequence, nonmetropolitan minorities lag in salary and suffer greater rates of unemployment.

Data on female earnings suggest that there may be a deterioration in wage equivalency between rural female and male workers. In 1969 women overall earned 48.5 percent of male nonmetropolitan earnings. By 1976 this factor had dropped to 47.5 percent, a slight decline. More telling, the female wage dropped in every occupational category except operatives, laborers, and service workers, where gains were noted. The disparities were significant in some occupations. For example, in sales, females earned 31 percent of male salaries in 1969; this figure dropped to only 28.5 percent in 1976.[26]

Facilitating Low-Density Development Patterns of Regional Coordination

The third force shaping the recent growth of rural areas is a new pattern of community structure that makes possible truly dispersed rural growth, in contrast to growth focused in medium-sized growth centers. Despite the continued significance of rural population nodes such as Burlington, Vermont, or Stevens Point, Wisconsin, smaller rural communities throughout the nation are becoming more specialized, differentiated from one another, linked into regional business and employment networks, and organized into new and innovative regional service-delivery ventures. Without these changing forms of regional community ecology, rural areas would not be as attractive. Rural areas are rapidly converging with urban in terms of many characteristics, such as the economy and overall quality of life; but rural areas remain distinctive in that they must overcome the disadvantages of low population density. Specialization and regional linkage enable many communities to overcome the disadvantages of low population concentrations while taking advantage of the flexibility rural environments provide.

Community Diversity

A major tenet of rural regional studies is that the various communities are relatively independent of each other, each providing basic services for its residents, with larger regional nodes providing specialized services. Thus it is often assumed that all small rural towns are very much alike; and that within a region the social and economic structure of one town is similar to that of the others. This pattern is breaking down rapidly; under the new growth patterns, rural communities are just as clearly differentiated as urban neighborhoods. However, each community in a rural region contributes something to the whole; thus an explicit organic network of relations is evidence of the communities' greater interdependence. Hage argues this thesis most succinctly: "Nonmetropolitan areas are becoming like wheels in communications networks rather than like trees."[27]

Rural growth has created a number of interdependent types of community that are often linked to each other in a regional network. Each type of community reflects a different history and different patterns of resource development; each attracts a different migratory stream from the urban areas. Together, these community types describe the variety of change occurring in rural areas.

Six types of rural growth community have been identified. There are other types that describe declining or stagnant communities.[28] Each type is not found in every region, although most are distributed throughout the country. These are ideal types, whereas in reality more than one may combine to characterize a particular community.

Government-Trade Communities. The prototypical service communities, these communities are often the larger county seats and have both government and trade growth. Regional shopping centers are located here, as are the offices of an impressive array of social services.

University-Professional Communities. These communities are usually centered around state colleges and universities. They have become the backbone of the sophisticated technological development occurring in rural areas. The key to the economy of these places is the regional provision of expert advice in accounting, engineering, law, business services, and similar professional activities. Health care is usually more specialized and prevalent in these locations.

Industry-Dominated Communities. These communities have a large manufacturing plant or office complex that employs many rural residents. Manufacturing plants are the backbone of the economy in some areas and provide considerable employment, as is often seen in many states in the South. Often the jobs in these plants are poor and working conditions less than ideal. The plants have often been located there because of significant tax incentives and the promise of an undemanding and nonunion rural labor force. Large insurance companies and the offices of other service industries are found throughout the Midwest and serve many of the same functions in communities as do manufacturing plants.

Tourism Communities. The growth of tourism in recent years has provided a partial base for many rural communities. However, most tourism is highly seasonal and employs people only in minimum-wage jobs in restaurants and motels. Moreover, tourist communities are increasingly attracting a cadre of well-educated, economically independent permanent residents who bring portable professional businesses with them from the urban areas. In the small communities around Stowe, Vermont, or Mendocino, California, newcomers can afford the high cost of the tourist setting while remaining economically active in their investment, writing, art, consulting, and similar occupations. The remotely located computer programmer is prototypical.[29] A variant is the counterculture communities of the West and many other areas, which are in relatively attractive places, though away from the high prices of the tourist centers.

Retirement Communities. The retirement-dominated community is becoming noticeable in many rural areas, such as northern Wisconsin, Florida, and California. The prevalent trend is for retired people either to enter into largely retirement subdivisions (often buying mobile homes) or to take up full-time residence in summer cottages. Retired people usually constitute about half the population; the other half provide services for them.

Resource-Based Boom Towns. Though not a new phenomenon, these communities have recently become common along the eastern slope of the Rockies, in the Appalachians, and in the oil-rich parts of the South. The drive for new natural resources continues to subject many areas to considerable growth.

Isolated and Declining Communities

In contrast, 485 nonmetropolitan counties in the nation lost population during the 1970–1980 decade.[30] These counties reflect the lack of a successful accommodation to the pressures of the growing society. For the most part they are in the Midwest and the South, are still dependent on agriculture for their economic life, and have not been successful in turning their agriculture into a more viable economic base. They also reflect the problems of declining resource industries such as mining and logging, the closing of railroads and other transportation networks, and the closing of factories (as in the New England area). Finally, the declining communities are generally less attractive to the new migrants and new business in terms of physical amenities.

Policy Directions

The major efforts of most federal, state, and regional agencies have treated rural America in terms of its agricultural-industrial base, working to improve its backward economy, deprivation of social services, emigration drain, and limited community capacity. Only now is a rural-policy framework being formulated that takes into account the growth and potential for growth in large sections of the nonmetropolitan country side. There are two reasons for the neglect of growth as a component of rural policy. First, few policymakers have been convinced that small-town growth is important to the nation. Some view it as a temporary condition that could be quickly altered by the energy crisis or merely as the extension of urbanization beyond the suburbs. Second, most policymakers do not understand the mechanisms by which the opportunities and capacities of growing rural areas may be enhanced. As a contribution to the creation of a more sensitive policy framework, we suggest three directions that capture the potential of the major forces posited in this chapter.

Economic Development versus Industrial Attraction

The strong bias of past policy initiatives has been toward attracting industry in the hope of creating a stronger rural economy. Recently, a considerable amount of research has suggested that successful economic development projects may come from a local base instead of externally controlled branch plants. For example, Smith suggests that community-based economic development is very effective in creating jobs, to the extent that (1) projects have adequate start-up money and financing during their early growth phases, (2) community leadership is present, and (3) coordinated human-resource-development programs are able to link job training with necessary human services.[31] In short, the economic-development potential of community-based organizations may be more effective than industrial attraction, especially in the growing service sector.

Another direction for rural economic development is to break out of the centralized grip that large nonlocal firms have on raw materials and food production. Efforts to link resources and end-product development in rural communities may pay off on a broad scale. For example, Vermont is attempting to do more in-state cheese production rather than shipping milk products elsewhere for processing; many rural states are attempting to produce more of their own table vegetables rather than importing them from California. The leadership and markets for these types of product development are increasingly in place in growing rural areas.

Human-Resource Development

The pervasiveness of poverty and depleted community structures in rural America has long dominated the policy concerns of most rural initiatives. Although these concerns persist and service-delivery systems still need improvement in rural areas, it is time for an effective effort to complete the upgrading of the rural human-resource base. Newcomers are bringing new skills into rural areas, and the institutional framework is largely in place. What is needed, however, is a better appreciation of the full range of human-resource-development activities that need to be coordinated in a rural region.

Less advantaged indigenous rural residents need to be introduced to the opportunities associated with rural growth. Traditional training programs probably will no longer work. Coordinated training, placement, and enterprise development efforts need to be undertaken.

Increasing Regional Capacity

The third policy direction builds closely on the themes of regional interdependence articulated earlier. Although capacity development has been a consistent small-town policy theme at the national level for several decades, it is becoming clear that capacity development in thousands of the smallest communities and counties is no longer sufficient, and that providing duplicate services in each community is wasteful. Yet regional coordination of rural communities is still an ad hoc relationship for which there are few guidelines and little experience.

In the past, most efforts have established regional planning and coordinating bodies that either have no power, and so cannot get things done, or are unpopular because they have power at the expense of local communities. On the other hand, a number of communities in several regions have voluntarily developed joint-powers arrangements that provide waste removal, transportation, water, or social services for several geographically contiguous communities and counties. The mechanisms for such entities are only now emerging, but some of the outlines are becoming clear: the regional body has a specific limited focus; it has joint powers shared among cities, counties, or their specific agencies; and it has day-to-day independence in running its program. These arrangements promise to be an effective means for communities to formalize their interdependence without becoming bogged down in another layer of bureaucracy.

Conclusion

Rural America is rapidly departing from its heritage based on agriculture and resource-dependent industries, and it is developing alternatives to low-skill industry and perpetually depressed local economies. The changing conditions present opportunities as well as constraints. Although the situation in many rural communities remains difficult because of extreme physical isolation, unattractive physical surroundings, or lack of leadership, it is clear that new approaches are needed in establishing effective rural policy in the coming decades. Moreover, as recent cuts in federal programs are felt in rural areas, some of the capacity for dealing with emerging problems will surely be lost. The crucial issue will be to devise ways for growing communities to have the resources to deal intelligently with their situation, both to their benefit and to the benefit of all parts of their region.

Notes

1, Calvin L. Beale, "The Revival of Population Growth in Nonmetropolitan America" (Washington, D.C.: U.S. Department of Agriculture, Economics Statistics, and Cooperative Service, ERS-605, 1975); Peter A. Morrison with Judith Wheller, "Rural Renaissance in America?" *Population Bulletin* (October 1976).

2. Claude C. Haren and Ronald W. Holling, "Industrial Development in Nonmetropolitan America," in Richard Lansdale and H.L. Seyler, eds., *Nonmetropolitan Industrialization* (New York: Halsted Press, 1979), pp. 13-45; Calvin L. Beale, "The Changing Nature of Rural Employment," in David L. Brown and John M. Wardwell, eds., *New Directions in Urban-Rural Migration* (New York: Academic Press, 1980), pp. 37-50.

3. Paul R. Eberts, "Growth and the Quality of Life: Some Logical and Methodological Issues," in Gene F. Summers and Arne Selvik, eds., *Nonmetropolitan Industrial Growth and Community Change* (Lexington, Mass.: Lexington Books, D.C. Heath and Company, 1979), p. 180.

4. Eugene A. Wilkening and Lowell Klessig, "The Rural Environment: Quality and Conflicts in Land Use," in Thomas R. Ford, ed., *Rural USA: Persistence and Change* (Ames: Iowa State University Press, 1978).

5. Ted K. Bradshaw and Edward J. Blakely, *Rural Communities in Advanced Industrial Society* (New York: Praeger, 1979).

6. We prefer the term *advanced industrial* rather than *postindustrial* to describe these developments. First of all, the data do not support the notion that there is a decline of industry (meaning manufacturing) as part of the modern economy. Virtually all the growth in services has been proportionate to the decline of agriculture and other extractive industries, with manufacturing remaining fairly constant over the last sixty years. We also use advanced industrial to signal our skepticism of the urban/progress bias of past work, allowing us to focus more evenly on the problems these changes generate. See Bradshaw and Blakely, *Rural Communities*; Jerald Hage, "A Theory of Nonmetropolitan Growth," in Gene F. Summers and Arne Selvik, eds., *Nonmetropolitan Industrial Growth and Community Change* (Lexington, Mass.: Lexington Books, D.C. Heath and Company, 1979).

7. Frank M. Bryan, *Politics in the Rural States: People, Parties, and Processes* (Boulder, Colo: Westview Press, 1981); Ted K. Bradshaw and

Edward J. Blakely, *Resources of Recent Migrants to Rural Areas for Economic Development: Policy Implications* (Berkeley: Cooperative Extension Service, University of California, September 1981).

8. Hage, "Theory of Nonmetropolitan Growth," p. 98.

9. A number of recent views of the future present an alternative to the postindustrial thesis; rural life is seen as a decentralized option for the future. Ted K. Bradshaw, "Trying Out the Future," *Wilson Quarterly* (Summer 1980): 66-82; Alvin Toffler, *The Third Wave* (New York: Morrow, 1980); William I. Thompson, *Darkness and Scattered Light* (Garden City, N.Y.: Anchor Press/ Doubleday, 1974); Theodore Roszak, *Person/Planet* (Garden City, N.Y.: Anchor Press/Doubleday, 1978).

10. The end of massive agricultural labor displacement in the 1970s corresponds closely to the rapid turnaround of rural population and economic growth. It is not clear whether or not this is a causal relationship.

11. Haren and Holling, "Industrial Development."

12. Joseph Spengler, "Some Determinants of the Manpower Prospect, 1966-1985," in Irving Siegal, ed., *Manpower Tomorrow: Prospects and Priorities* (New York: August Kelley, 1967), p. 91.

13. Niles N. Hansen, "How Regional Policy Can Benefit from Economic Theory," *Growth and Change* (January 1970):23, 20-27; Robert Wrigley, Jr., "Small Cities Can Help to Revitalize Rural Areas," *Annals* 405(January 1973):59.

14. M.F. Petrulis, "Growth Patterns in Nonmetro Manufacturing Employment" (U.S. Department of Agriculture, Economics, Statistics, and Cooperatives Services, Rural Development Research Report no. 7, 1978), p. 15.

15. Bradshaw and Blakely, *Rural Communities*, p. 43.

16. Haren and Holling, "Industrial Development."

17. Steven M. Smith and Glen C. Pulver, "Characteristics of Nonmanufacturing Businesses in Nonmetropolitan Wisconsin" (Madison: University of Wisconsin Research Bulletin R2879, 1980).

18. Robert F. Averitt, "Implications of the Dual Economy for Community Economic Change," in Gene F. Summers and Arne Selvik, eds., *Nonmetropolitan Industrial Growth and Community Change* (Lexington, Mass.: Lexington Books, D.C. Heath and Company, 1979).

19. Annalee Saxenian, "Silicon Chips and Spatial Structure," Working Paper no. 345 (Berkeley: Institute of Urban and Regional Development, University of California, 1981).

20. Herman Bluestone, "Income Growth in Nonmetro American, 1968-75" (Washington, D.C.: U.S. Department of Agriculture, Economics, Statistics, and Cooperative Services, Rural Development Research Report no. 14, 1979), p. 18.

21. Stephen A. Webster and Paul M. Campbell, "The 1970s and Changing Dimensions in Rural Life—Is a New Practice Model Needed?" in *Social Work in Rural Areas* (Knoxville: University of Tennessee, 1976).

22. James T. Zuiches and Michael L. Price, "Industrial Dispersal and Labor Force Migration: Employment Dimensions of the Population Turnaround in Michigan," in David L. Brown and John M. Wardwell, eds., *New Directions in Urban-Rural Migration* (New York: Academic Press, 1980), p. 356.

23. Bradshaw and Blakely, *Resources of Recent Migrants.*

24. Bureau of the Census, *Survey of Income and Education* (1976).

25. Calvin L. Beale, *Rural and Small Town Population Change, 1970–1980* (Washington, D.C.: U.S. Department of Agriculture, Economics and Statistics Service, ESS-5, February 1981).

26. Bureau of the Census, *Social and Economic Characteristics of the Metropolitan and Nonmetropolitan Population: 1977 and 1980, Current Population Reports*, Special Studies Series P-23, no. 75 (Washington, D.C.: U.S. Department of Commerce).

27. The classic form of a "tree" in the language of set theory is a bureaucratic organization chart wherein connections are as few as possible and hierarchially organized; on the wheel, everything connects to everything else. See Hage, "Theory of Nonmetropolitan Growth," p. 95.

28. Bradshaw and Blakely, *Resources of Recent Migrants.*

29. Toffler, *The Third Wave.*

30. Beale, *Rural Population Change.*

31. Hubert L. Smith, "Non-Agricultural Rural Development: Four Case Studies" (Boston: Institute on Employment Policy, Boston University, 1980), pp. 263-277.

2

Communities and Their Relationships to Agrarian Values

William L. Flinn

The rural community is usually imagined as a village or small town—a trade center—surrounded by farms and open country. One traditional view sees the rural community as a good place to live, a homogeneous crossroads community where the population is small and the system simple. Periodicals and newspapers have lately seized on the "back to small-town" movement, attributing "the special allure of small towns" to lower crime rates, friendlier atmospheres, lower levels of pollution, and a host of other features.[1] This reborn appreciation of the virtues of small-town life is also represented, perhaps, in the spate of newspaper stories headlined "The Sale of Podunk Center,"[2] "George Washington Is Up for Sale,"[3] and "Small Town for Rent."[4]

Favorable interpretations of small-town life were first questioned in Howe's *Story of a Country Town* in 1884.[5] Later, Anderson's *Winesburg, Ohio* in 1919 and Lewis's *Main Street* in 1920 and *Babbitt* in 1922 focused on small-town hypocrisies and the follies of boosterism.[6] Today, television often perpetuates this harsher view of rural communities in the United States.[7]

Residential Preferences

Zuiches argues that all surveys of public preferences—from the Harris and Gallup polls to the more detailed multidimensional surveys at national, regional, state, or local levels—show that small towns and rural areas would be the first choice, and large cities the last choice, if respondents could live where they wanted.[8] Fuguitt and Zuiches add that proximity to a large city is also important; especially desirable residential locations are small in size but lie within the periphery of a more populous place.[9] These researchers also demonstrate an association between agrarian values and residential preference for small-town and rural sites in Wisconsin, whether or not this preferred site is within thirty miles of a central city. Dillman notes that all residential-preference surveys carried out since 1970 show that most Americans prefer residential locations more rural than their present ones.[10] Two recent national surveys—Gallup in 1977 and Harris in 1978—continue to show a modal preference (at 38–39 percent) for rural areas. The high value placed on noneconomic amenities in the quality of life a rural communities—less crime, better air and water quality, greater community spirit, and more friendliness—probably indicates well-respected attributes of small-town life. Beale suggests that the pattern of population movement since 1970 consists to a considerable extent of people implementing a preference for rural or small-town life.[11] Research by Beale and Fuguitt indicates that emigrants from the big cities have moved to rural residences in the open country in larger proportion than they have to small towns.[12]

Farm-Structure Preferences

All recent public-opinion polls have consistently documented a widespread belief that the family farm should be preserved.[13] A recent Harris poll shows that 60 percent of the public feels that the United States should strive to retain a relatively large number of small farms, whereas only 19 percent feel that the nation should rely on a relatively small number of large farms. On the other hand, respondents did recognize that most of the food in the United States is not grown on smaller family farms. In light of these values, one wonders why the general public has not been more vocal about the issue of farm structure, especially since recent censuses have shown a continuing decline in the number of small farms. Data from other studies reveal, however, that favorable attitudes toward preservation of family farms are not strongly held; on Likert scales, most respondents tend to "agree" rather than "strongly agree" with pro-family-farm statements.[14]

Community Welfare

Studies of small towns leave little doubt that rural trade centers have lost many of their service functions. Newspaper stories such as "Iowa Mayor Selling Town" exemplify the death of rural communities as trade centers.[15] Wisconsin studies indicate that concern over lack of services is higher among upper-middle-class rural residents (educated, politically liberal, and young) than it is among older, more politically conservative rural residents; those living within thirty miles of the central city were more dissatisfied with local services than those living further from the city.[16] Chenaut and Voss also indicated that recent migrants to nonmetropolitan areas are dissatisfied with the services offered by their rural community.[17]

Rodefeld shows that population change in trade centers is directly related to the number and variety of retail businesses and to the volume of retail trade.[18] A national sample of incorporated places with populations of less than 2,500 in 1960 shows that they had fewer retail and service businesses and fewer business functions in 1970 than in 1960; the average number of establishments decreased from twenty-three to eighteen.[19] The same study concludes that small towns have become less and less important as retail service centers but cautions that increasing distance from larger business centers mediates against this trend.

In general, however, farm and nonfarm shoppers, now able to travel greater distances with improved transportation, tend to bypass smaller trade centers in favor of the more specialized goods and services offered in larger places. The result has been consolidation and concentration of all functions—trade and service—in larger (and still expanding) centers. In addition, the minimum population level at which a trade center can exist is increasing. Although changes in the number of farms are often postulated as direct or indirect causes of these changing patterns of small-town business, other factor receive as much or more attention—loss of industry, changes in transportation, changing attitudes, and metropolitan dominance. Larson, however, has noted that the smaller the community, the greater the influence of the farming component and farm structure.[20]

Public Concern

Research clearly suggests that there is a public concern for the welfare of small farms and small towns and for rural life in general. The general public, as well as the residents of rural communities, do not see these issues as related to each other. Instead, overarching social-class contours within the ideological issues of farm structure and community welfare—especially in the heterogeneous rural community—divide attitudes between urban and rural residents, and among rural residents themselves.

It is not surprising that farm operators are even more likely than the general public to express values favorable toward the family farm.[21] However, farmers are not a homogeneous class. Older, less well educated, smaller-scale farmers (with scale measured in number of acres and gross farm income) are most likely to agree with statements supporting agrarianism and the family farm: rugged individualism, the virtue of family farming as a way of life, and faith in farming as the one occupation on which all others depend. These small farmers (and low-income segments of the general public) are more sympathetic to preserving the family farm and blocking corporate penetration of agriculture than are relatively privileged farmers and nonfarmers. In addition, there is evidence that positive attitudes toward the family farm and small-scale agriculture are tied to a general critique of the social order in terms of alienation, powerlessness, and political cynicism.[22]

Unpublished Ohio data indicate that there are also class differences between those holding so-called small-town values and those holding agrarian values. [Small-town ideology is the belief that the small town is the mother of society— the natural life (as opposed to the artificial life of the city and farmstead) and the natural home of democracy.] Believers in small-town values tend to be older, middle-class residents of small trade centers. Although scoring higher on a scale of agrarian values than their city cousins, small-town believers were not highly supportive of subsidy payments to farmers. Because small towns are dominated by small businessmen, political leaders are concerned about taxes first and services second; the small town usually seeks to avoid innovation, strongly opposes the "social-service state," and tries to postpone as many decisions as possible.

Wisconsin data suggest a competition between agrarian ideology, small-town ideology, and *ruralism*—a back-to-nature or antiurban philosophy only faintly related to the pattern of thought called agrarianism.[23] Ruralism was most prevalent among the upper middle class, whereas no such correlation was observed for agrarianism. Perhaps believers in ruralism are the people most likely to be involved in the rural turnaround of the 1970s.

Social scientists have often been unclear about what they mean by rural values and have mistakenly tended to assume these values to be homogeneous within the total community. Rural values might better be portrayed as pertaining to at least three distinct dimensions of sentiment—agrarianism, small-town ideology, and ruralism—that roughly correspond to class positions. Heterogeneity of the rural population means that there cannot be a single strategy or a single policy to deal with issues of farm structure and community welfare. Instead there are, implicit in public views, a farm problem, a rural nonfarm problem, and/or a small-town problem. At the risk of oversimplification, ruralism (with its links to the upper middle class) is likely to be a set of environmentally aware attitudes that favor country life—but not farming—because it offers more room, better health and closer relations with nature. The farmer, sometimes seen as an exploiter of nature and a miner of natural resources in his land-use policies, disrupts the ruralist's tranquil environment.

Ideological proponents of small-town sentiments, especially middle-class businessmen, suffer from diseconomies of scale; they want to grow without suffering the problems of growth. They decry the development of highway systems that spread the "community" over vast distances and cost them their monopoly over local business in groceries, dry goods, hardware, and the like. New residents in and around the small town—the ruralists—often trade in the big city, not in "town." Those same ruralists often oppose the local growth or industrialization that could help the businessman, but simultaneously want higher taxes to provide better schools and more services. Farmers are likewise unhappy with the ruralists, who compete for land and then drive land prices higher. Small farmers may be unhappy with larger, more prosperous farmers for the same reasons; and large farmers worry about increasing the scale of their operations to remain competitive, while realizing at the same time that bigness cannot assure success.

In some respects, separate territorial bases help perpetuate separate class identities. The upper-middle-class ruralist lives in the country but interacts with peers in the city, not with people in the rural community who consider "newcomers" outsiders.[24] The middle-class businessman lives in the small town and sees himself as a pillar of society and protector of the community's institutions. Farmers may have a range of class interests. The larger ones tend to identify with urban residents of similar financial status.[25] The small farmers, in their own view, remain poor, hard-working, law-abiding yeomen who provide cheap labor and food in exchange for agrarian virtue.

Consequences of Agricultural Structure for Rural Communities

Rural sociologists have long been interested in changes in farm structure and their effects on community life. Much of this interest was the result of an increase in landownership by nonfarmers between 1900 and 1940, as the number of acres operated by hired managers and various tenants rose from 280 million in 1910 to 397 million in 1935.[26] Early studies in various parts of the United States showed that the participation of farm tenants in community affairs tended to be more restricted than that of owner-operators.[27] Kolb and des Brunner advanced the opinion that the social effects of high rates of tenancy are usually undesirable.[28] Landis pointed out that it is difficult to convince the absentee landlord that better community facilities for other people are sufficiently important to him to offset the cost of higher taxes.[29] These early studies exposed the "evils" of tenancy as a "menace" to the social life of the rural community.[30] The agrarian ideal of owner-operated farmsteads no doubt had some influence on these early researchers in land-tenure issues. World War II, however, soon "solved" the tenancy problem with higher farm prices, mechanization, and bigger farms. Acres in owner-operated farms increased from 391 million in 1935 to 419 million in 1950; acreage farmed by hired managers and tenants declined from 397 million to 319 million acres.[31]

During the 1940s the structure of large-scale, corporate-capitalist or industrial farms and their influence on community welfare became a focus of researchers. In 1944 Goldschmidt's anthropological study of Arvin (a community characterized by large farms with hired labor forces) and of Dinuba (a community in which family farms using family labor predominated) showed that the structure of farming was apparently related to welfare of the community.[32] Dinuba ranked higher than Arvin on a number of measures of community service and participation, including family income, level of living, social and physical amenities, social and religious institutions, and degree of local control of politics. The controversy surrounding this study and the problems of case-study methodology led to an effective moratorium on community studies for nearly fifteen years.

Ploch examined contract poultry production in Maine and showed that contract, as compared to independent, table-egg producers, participated less in community organizations.[33] Since then a number of studies and restudies on the relation between farm structure and community welfare have been completed. This handful of studies is quite familiar to students of the changing structure of agriculture and its consequences for community welfare. Heffernan finds it significant, however, that a dozen studies spanning four decades and all parts of the nation, performed by different researchers using different methodologies, have rather consistently showed that a shift toward corporate agriculture will have negative consequences for community welfare.[34] Despite this consistency of findings, more precise longitudinal studies are needed to document and refine that general conclusion.

The extent to which the structure of U.S. agriculture has shifted toward corporate or industrial farms cannot be determined definitively because of changes in census definitions and categories. Rodefeld, using data from 1959 to 1964, indicated that industrial farms were the only type that grew in absolute numbers in that time.[35] He urges that the census of agriculture reestablish the classification of farms by tenure of operator, as in censuses before 1969. Trend data on changes in the structure of agriculture could then be extracted.

Despite the lack of sound data, a number of writers have argued that there has been an increase in farm ownership by nonfarm persons.[36] Barlowe and Libby say that it is "common knowledge that doctors, lawyers, bankers, and other urban investors have acquired considerable tracts of valuable and productive farmland around urban areas and in prime agricultural and ranching areas."[37] The rapid rise of farmland values coupled with poor returns on other investments has made capital gains in farmland ownership attractive. Other features of investment in land—deductions of interest payments on mortgages, cash versus accrual accounting systems, and deductions for farm operating losses from taxable income, to name a few—make farm ownership profitable for nonfarm interests.

A recent survey by the U.S. Department of Agriculture (USDA) provides some trend data on the extent of absentee ownership when the figures are compared with a similar survey from 1946.[38] The earlier survey estimated that about 3 percent of the owners hold about 48 percent of the farmland and ranch land. Of the 6 million owners in 1946, 70 percent were farm operators; in 1978 only about one-third of the 6 million farmland owners were farm operators. Farmers, who represent about one-quarter of all farm and ranch landowners, own 56 percent of the farmland and ranch land. White-collar workers constituted approximately 31 percent of farmland and ranch owners and owned 14 percent of the land. Blue-collar workers represented another 21 percent of the owners but held only 7 percent of the land. Retirees accounted for approximately another 25 percent of the owners, owning 17 percent of the farmland and ranch land.[39]

Farms are likely to continue to increase in size and decline in number, and these changes will adversely affect the business sectors of rural communities. Schreiner estimates that in North Dakota the annual loss of 3,700 on-farm workers because of farm enlargement and reorganization reduced nonfarm employment by 5,772 persons.[40] If an increase in absentee ownership of farms accompanies continued change in the size and number of farms, some owner-operators will be replaced by hired labor. Past research has suggested that agricultural change of this last sort will exacerbate the consequences for rural communities.

Heady and Sonka used a value-of-sales model to project the effect of farm-size alternatives on the number of farms, farm employment and economic activity in rural areas in 1980.[41] The small-farm alternative (gross farm sales of less than $10,000) yielded an average acreage of 232. The large-farm alternative (gross farm sales of at least $40,000) predicted an average acreage of 1,603. Other results indicated that increased farm size would reduce total farm employment and net income to the farm sector, but would produce advantages for those who operated large units. In contrast, a structure of small farms would tend to produce greater income generation in rural communities, but net income from farming for the families operating these small farms would be near the poverty level. Outcomes under either alternative seem likely to widen the cleavages among large farmers, small farmers, and townspeople of rural communities.

Impact on Small Rural Communities

The effects of changing agricultural structure have not been and cannot be confined to the farm or the farm population. Rural communities, especially relatively small communities in the nonurbanized "agricultural interior," also will unavoidably feel the impact of changing farm structure.[42] Declines in the size of the on-farm work force usually yield declines in the population of rural communities and trade centers greater than the initial loss of farm people,[43] because larger farms and increased mechanization tend to undermine the sales and eventually the survival of retail merchants and other small businesses.[44] The trend is aggravated by the constantly increasing level of sales necessary to support small business operations in rural communities.[45]

Although the causes of any one phenomenon are too complex and interrelated to permit the pinpointing of one single aspect of farm structure as *the* cause, data on incorporated and unincorporated small towns in Ohio between 1930 and 1970 will be presented in order to attempt to quantify some of these effects. A small town is here defined as a place recognized by name by local residents; it must also have a built-up section. This population nucleus—both the town itself and its population, excluding people living on farms and other outlying residences—was required to have more than 75 and fewer than 2,300 inhabitants in 1930 in order to qualify as a small town. Furthermore, the named place must have been listed in 1930 and/or 1970 in *Rand McNally's Commercial Atlases*. The cutoff points of 75 and 2,500 people were chosen because the latter figure is often used as the upper limit for a "small town" and because a town with fewer than 75 people will seldom have a well-defined nucleus. The span from 1930 to 1970 was selected for study because the watershed between growth and decline in number of farms and number of farm workers was 1935.[46]

Table 2-1 shows the percentages and numbers of small towns with declining populations between 1930 and 1970 for incorporated and unincorporated places in Ohio in various population categories in 1930. The distribution of the population changes in places grouped by initial size is given for both metropolitan and nonmetropolitan areas. The data indicate that 9 percent of the incorporated places in metropolitan areas lost population between 1930 and 1970. However, 52 percent of the unincorporated places in metropolitan areas and 75 percent of the unincorporated places in nonmetropolitan areas lost population between 1930 and 1970. Table 2-1 also demonstrates that population declines were greatest for the smallest of the small unincorporated towns in nonmetropolitan areas.

The difference between the problems of unincorporated and incorporated places is evident from their patterns of decline. Many small incorporated places are growing in size, but quite the reverse is true for unincorporated places. Data on unincorporated places that do not appear independently in the census present a picture of small towns very different from that of the census—a picture of much greater population decline. It must be remembered, however, that figures on unincorporated places are self-reported by local residents and thus are subject to error.

The data in table 2-1 suggest that regional and occupational differences may also be important for rural communities. A breakdown of Ohio counties into cornbelt and noncornbelt regions indicated that 76.6 percent of the unincorporated places in the cornbelt lost population, compared with 74.7 percent of the unincorporated places outside the cornbelt. A similar difference between the unincorporated places was noted for farm and nonfarm counties (farm counties were defined as those with a 1974 farm population of 18 percent or more). It is interesting to note that fewer incorporated cornbelt and farm places lost population between 1930 and 1970 than their respective non-cornbelt and nonfarm counterparts. Most interesting, however, is the influence that intensive agriculture, such as dairy farming, has on small communities. Fewer unincorporated places (70.7 percent) in the eight leading dairy counties had population declines than cornbelt places (76.6 percent) or farm places (77.1 percent).

Differences in the extent of decline, though small, do suggest the continuing importance of cornbelt and farm centers as trade and service centers and also suggest that further structural change could alter these patterns substantially. In fact, a recent study of incorporated towns in the Ohio cornbelt shows that 70 percent *grew* during the decade of the 1960s; however, more than

Table 2-1
Percentage and Number of Incorporated and Unincorporated Small Towns in Ohio that Declined in Population between 1930 and 1970, Metropolitan, Nonmetropolitan, and Regions

				Nonmetropolitan							
Size in 1930	Ohio	Metropolitan Areas[a]	Nonmetropolitan Areas	Cornbelt Counties	Noncornbelt Counties	Farm Counties[b]	Nonfarm Counties	Dairy Counties	Nondairy Counties	Appalachian Counties	Nonappalachian Counties
Incorporated											
75–149	22.2 (36)	9.1 (11)	28.0 (25)	8.3 (12)	46.1 (13)	16.7 (12)	38.5 (13)	– (9)	43.7 (16)	(8)	5.9 (17)
150–299	20.1 (144)	6.9 (58)	29.1 (86)	16.2 (37)	38.8 (49)	25.0 (32)	31.5 (54)	– (17)	33.3 (69)	57.1 (35)	9.8 (51)
300–499	11.2 (143)	4.7 (64)	16.5 (79)	0.0 (25)	24.1 (54)	15.0 (20)	17.0 (59)	– (13)	18.2 (66)	40.0 (30)	2.0 (49)
500–749	15.3 (118)	10.4 (48)	18.6 (70)	3.1 (32)	31.6 (38)	15.8 (19)	20.0 (51)	– (14)	21.4 (56)	37.0 (27)	7.0 (43)
750–999	13.0 (77)	10.8 (37)	15.0 (40)	6.7 (15)	20.0 (25)	8.3 (12)	17.9 (28)	– (6)	14.7 (34)	29.4 (17)	4.3 (23)
1,000–2,499	10.8 (157)	11.5 (78)	10.1 (79)	2.9 (34)	15.6 (45)	3.6 (28)	13.7 (51)	– (15)	9.4 (64)	22.2 (27)	3.8 (52)
Total	14.5 (675)	8.8 (296)	19.0 (379)	6.45 (155)	27.7 (224)	14.6 (123)	21.1 (256)	9.5 (74)	21.3 (305)	41.0 (144)	5.5 (235)
Unincorporated											
75–149	69.1 (495)	57.5 (193)	75.6 (302)	75.5 (106)	77.0 (196)	75.5 (98)	76.9 (204)	71.1 (45)	77.4 (257)	78.2 (133)	75.2 (169)
150–299	65.8 (403)	47.7 (153)	76.8 (250)	77.6 (67)	76.5 (183)	79.6 (54)	76.0 (196)	77.1 (48)	76.7 (202)	76.9 (121)	76.7 (129)
300–499	61.5 (174)	50.7 (67)	68.2 (107)	76.7 (30)	64.9 (77)	80.0 (20)	65.5 (87)	55.0 (20)	71.2 (87)	72.0 (50)	64.9 (57)
500–749	59.3 (27)	– (11)	– (16)	– (2)	71.4 (14)	– (2)	75.6 (14)	– (2)	71.4 (19)	– (9)	– (7)
750–999	55.6 (9)	– (5)	– (4)	– (0)	– (4)	– (1)	– (3)	– (1)	– (3)	– (3)	– (1)
1,000–2,400	60.0 (10)	– (9)	– (1)	– (0)	– (1)	– (0)	– (1)	– (0)	– (1)	– (1)	– (0)
Total	66.3 (118)	52.3 (438)	75.3 (680)	76.6 (205)	74.7 (475)	77.1 (175)	74.6 (505)	70.7 (116)	76.2 (564)	77.0 (317)	73.8 (363)

[a]Standard metropolitan statistical area (SMSA) is any county or group of contiguous counties that contains at least one city of 50,000 inhabitants or more and any contiguous counties that are socially and economically integrated with the central city. There were thirty-one SMSA Ohio counties in 1970.

[b]The rural farm counties are defined as those Ohio counties with a farm population of 18 percent or more. Seventeen counties were in this category. The farm population for the state was 12 percent in 1974.

50 percent of the cornbelt towns *lost* population in the 1970s.[47] The 1970s were a time of major changes in Ohio agriculture. Although these data imply a negative relationship between community welfare and the changing structure of agriculture, the assertion of a causal connection is clearly beyond this analysis. In any case, the data show heterogeneity among regions and imply difficulty in formulating public policies that deal equitably and appropriately with incorporated, unincorporated, farm, and cornbelt communities.

Discussion

The heterogeneity represented and probably reinforced by the various ideologies in rural communities has hindered the formulation of a comprehensive rural policy. The various segments of the rural community—farmers, small-town inhabitants, and open-country residents—act and react in their own interests. These residents of rural communities give little emphasis to the commonality of their problems.

The rural turnaround and back-to-the-land issues may further obstruct any attempt at a comprehensive rural policy. Newspapers, magazines, and television are filled with articles about a rural renaissance. The general public is being informed, at least by implication, that the welfare of many rural communities is greatly improving. Although this implication may be correct for some types of communities—especially rural nonfarm communities—those counties that showed a population loss from 1970 to 1975 continue to be concentrated in areas heavily dependent on agriculture and remote from large urban centers.[48] That pattern repeats the contours of population losses in other recent decades. The general public, however, may see little need for additional aid to rural areas because of the favorable publicity given to the growth of some rural communities. A mistaken view of rural communities as homogeneous units will discourage a comprehensive policy that recognizes differences among and within farming communities, mining communities, vacation villages, and mill towns.[49]

Factors other than the mistaken image of widespread rural prosperity may hinder effective policies for dealing with rural problems. As the feature article headlined "She Fell in Love with a Farm" implies, the image of romance among the soybeans is pervasive. A trip through the countryside or real-estate ads finds hundreds of retirement minifarms, rural condominiums, backyard pastures and weekend farms.[50] Ownership of a "farm" and spending a weekend "at the farm" are status symbols in urban America.[51] "Schools for greenhorns" have sprung up to educate the *nouveaux rurals*. Small-farm ownership has a social value quite apart from any economic benefits that may acquire to its urban absentee owner. The urbanite simply cannot believe that men who drive $65,000 tractors and live in an idyllic environment have problems. Their problems must be fictitious.

Another factor—size of farm population—works against policies to improve community welfare. The 1980 census indicates that fewer than 3 percent of the population is engaged in farming, and that small proportion continues to decline. The general public may wonder why anything should be done for such a small minority of the population. The linkage of the farm sector with the small-town business sector, of course, has important multiplier effects. Raup notes that changes since 1940 have narrowed the service base of smaller rural towns and made them even more dependent on their functions as supply centers for farm-production inputs.[52]

In any case, a policy concerned with community welfare should take into account the type of community and its heterogeneity. This is unlikely to happen; Americans will continue to look at values as motivators rather than preservers of the status quo.

Notes

1. *Newsweek*, 11 January 1974, p. 53; *Wisconsin State Journal*, 30 March 1975, p. 4; *The Columbus Dispatch Magazine*, 3 August 1975, p. 3.

2. *The New York Times*, October 21, 1969, p. 28:3.

3. *Wisconsin State Journal*, 30 March 1975, p. 3:5.

4. *The Columbus Dispatch*, 10 April 1976, p. 3:10.

5. E.W. Howe, *Story of a Country Town* (Atchison, Kansas: Howe and Company, 1883).

6. Sherwood Anderson, *Winesburg, Ohio* (New York: B.W. Huebsch Publishers, 1919); Sinclair Lewis, *Main Street* (New York: P.F. Collier, 1920); idem, *Babbitt* (New York: P.F. Collier, 1922).

7. Benjamin Stein, "Whatever Happened to Small-Town America?" *The Public Interest* 44(Summer 1976):17-26.

8. James G. Zuiches, "Residential Preference of Americans," in Daryl J. Hobbs and Don A. Dillman, eds., *Rural Society: Research Issues for the 1980's* (Boulder, Colo.: Westview Press, 1982).

9. Glenn V. Fuguitt and James J. Zuiches, "Location Preference of Contemporary Americans: Research and Implications" (Unpublished paper, Department of Rural Sociology, University of Wisconsin–Madison).

10. Don A. Dillman, "Residential Preference, Quality of Life and the Population Turnaround," *American Journal of Agricultural Economics* 61 (December 1980):960-966.

11. Calvin L. Beale, *The Revival of Population Growth in Nonmetropolitan America* (Washington, D.C.: Economic Research Service, U.S. Department of Agriculture, ERS-605, 1975).

12. Calvin L. Beale and Glenn V. Fuguitt, "Demographic Perspectives on Midwest Population Redistribution During the 1970's" (Paper presented at Conference on Issues and Consequences of Population Redistribution, Urbana, Ill., March 1979).

13. O. Bill Martinson and William L. Flinn, "Preserving the Family Farm: Persistence of Rural-Urban Differences" (Department of Agricultural Economics and Rural Sociology, Ohio State University, Columbus, 1975).

14. William L. Flinn and Frederick H. Buttel, "Sociological Aspects of Farm Size: Ideological and Social Consequences of Scale in Agriculture," *American Journal of Agricultural Economics* 62(December 1980):946-953.

15. *The New York Times*, 1 March 1978, p. 39:4.

16. Frederick H. Buttel, Oscar B. Martinson, and Eugene A. Wilkening, "Ideologies and Social Indicators of the Quality of Life," *Social Indicators* 4:353-369; and J. Gary Linn, "Residential Location, Size of Place and Community Statistics in Northwestern Wisconsin," Series on Quality of Life, Report no. 13, Department of Rural Sociology, University of Wisconsin-Madison (August 1976).

17. Maria V. Chenaut and Paul R. Voss, "Determinants of Community Satisfaction among Recent Nonmetropolitan Migrants" (Paper presented at the Conference on Small City and Regional Community, University of Wisconsin-Stevens Point, March 1980).

18. Richard D. Rodefeld, *The Direct and Indirect Effects of Mechanizing U.S. Agriculture* (Monclair, N.J.: Allenhold, Osmun and Company, 1982).

19. Harley E. Johansen and Glenn V. Guguitt, "Population Growth and Rural Decline: Conflicting Effects of Urban Accessibility in American Villages," *Rural Sociology* 44(Spring, 1979):24-38.

20. Olaf F. Larson, "Farming and the Rural Community," in A.H. Hawley and Vincent Rock, eds., *Rural Renaissance and Urban Phenomena* (Chapel Hill: University of North Carolina Press, 1982).

21. William L. Flinn and Donald E. Johnson, "Agrarianism among Wisconsin Farmers," *Rural Sociology* 39(Summer 1974):187-204.

22. Frederick H. Buttell and William L. Flinn, "Sociopolitical Consequences of Agrarianism," *Rural Sociology* 41(Winter 1976):473-483.

23. Frederick H. Buttell and William L. Flinn, "Conceptions of Rural Life and Environmental Concern," *Rural Sociology* 42(Winter 1977):545-555.

24. Lowe Crew, "Thriving as an Outsider, Even as an Outcast, in a Small Town" (Paper presented at the Conference on Small City and Regional Community, University of Wisconsin-Stevens Point, March 1980).

25. Denton Morrison and Allen Stevens, "Social Movement Participation," *Rural Sociology* 32(December 1967):414-434.

26. Richard D. Rodefeld, "Farm Structure and Structural Type Characteristics: Rural Trends, Implication and Research Needs" (Unpublished paper, Department of Rural Sociology, Pennsylvania State University, College Park, 1981).

27. Carl C. Taylor, *Rural Sociology*, rev. ed. (New York: Harper and Brothers, 1933), pp. 256-257.

28. John W. Kolb and Edmund des Brunner, *A Study of Rural Society* (New York: Houghton Mifflin, 1952).

29. Paul H. Landis, *Rural Life in Process* (New York: McGraw-Hill, 1948).

30. Taylor, *Rural Sociology*, p. 258.

31. Rodefeld, "Farm Structure."

32. Walter Goldschmidt, *As You Sow* (Montclair, N.J.: Allanhold, Osmun and Company, 1978).

33. Louis A. Ploch, "A Comparison of the Social Characteristics of Maine's Contract and Independent Table-Egg Producers," Publication no. 670, Maine Agricultural Experiment Station, University of Maine (November 1965).

34. William D. Heffernan, "Sociological Dimensions of Agricultural Structure in the United States," *Sociologia Rurales* 12(1972):481–499; Bruce L. La Rose, "Arvin and Dinuba Revisited: A New Look at Community Structure and the Effects of Scale of Farm Operations," in *The Role of Giant Corporations in the American and World Economics*, part 3: *Corporate Secrecy: Agribusiness*, Hearings before the Subcommittee on Small Business, U.S. Senate, 92nd Congress, First and Second Sessions (Washington, D.C., U.S. Government Printing Office, 1973); Jan L. Flora, Ivan Brown, and Judith Lee, "Impact of Type of Agriculture on Class Structure, Social Well-Being and Inequality" (Paper presented at the Annual Meeting of the Rural Sociological Society, Madison, Wisconsin, 1977). Iaso Fujimoto, "The Communities of the San Joaquin Valley: The Relation between Scale of Farming, Water Use and Quality of Life," Testimony before the Federal Task Force on Wetlands, Sacramento California, 4 August 1977; Walter Goldschmidt, "Large-Scale Farming and Rural Structure," *Rural Sociology* 43(Fall 1978):362–366; William D. Heffernan and Paul Lasley, "Agricultural Structure and Interaction in the Local Community: A Case Study," *Rural Sociology* 43(Fall 1978):348–361; Graig K. Harris and Jess C. Gilbert, "Large-Scale Farming, Rural Social Welfare and Agrarian Thesis: A Re-examination" (Paper presented at the Annual Meeting of the Rural Sociological Society, Burlington, Vermont, August 1979); Jerald C. Wheelock, "Farm Size, Community Structure and Growth: Respecification of a Structural Equation Mode" (Paper presented at the Annual Meeting of the Rural Sociological Society, Burlington, Vermont, August 1979); and William D. Heffernan, "Structure of Agriculture and Quality of Life in Rural Communities," in Daryl J. Hobbs and Don A. Dillman, eds., *Rural Society: Research Issues for the 1980's* (Boulder, Colo.: Westview Press, 1982).

35. Rodefeld, "Farm Structure."

36. Ibid., p. 56.

37. Richard Barlowe and Lawrence Libby, "Policy Choices Affecting Access to U.S. Agriculture," in H.A. Ginther, ed., *Who Will Control U.S. Agriculture*? North Central Regional Extension Publication 31 (Champaign–Urbana: University of Illinois, College of Agriculture, Special Publication 27, 1971).

38. James A. Lewis, *Landownership in the United States, 1978*, Agricultural Information Bulletin no. 43b (Washington, D.C.: U.S. Department of Agriculture, Statistics, and Economics, Cooperative Service, 1980).

39. Ibid.

40. Dean F. Schreiner, "Rural Community Service in a Dynamic Economy," in A. Gordon Ball and Earl O. Heady, eds., *Size, Structure and Future of Farm* (Ames: Iowa State University Press, 1972).

41. Earl O. Heady and Steven T. Sonka, "Farm Size, Rural Community Income, and Consumer Welfare," *American Journal of Agricultural Economics* 56(1974):534–542.

42. David L. Brown, "Farm Structure and the Rural Community," in *Structure Issues in American Agriculture*, Agricultural Economic Report no. 438 (Washington, D.C.: U.S. Department of Agriculture, Economics, Statistics, and Cooperative Service, 1979).

43. Kevin Goss and Richard D. Rodefeld, "Consequences of Mechanization in U.S. Agriculture" (Paper presented at the Rural Sociological Society Meetings, Madison, Wisconsin, September 1977).

44. Heady and Sonka, "Farm Size."

45. Bert L. Ellenbogen, "Service Structure of Small Community: Problematic and Options for Change," in L.R. Whitney, ed., *Communities Left Behind: Alternatives for Development* (Ames: Iowa State University Press, 1974), pp. 82–90.

46. Kevin Goss and Richard D. Rodefeld, "Farming and Place Population Change in Michigan, 1930–1970" (Paper presented at the Annual Meetings of the Rural Sociological Society, Madison, Wisconsin, August 1977).

47. Donald McCloud, Dale W. Wimberley, and William L. Flinn, "Small Town Growth and Decline in Ohio, 1960, 1970 and 1980" (Paper delivered at the Annual Conference on the Small City and Regional Community, University of Wisconsin-Stevens Point, March 1981).

48. Peggy J. Ross and Bernal Green, *Impact of Rural Turnaround on Rural Education*, Education Resource Information Center, Clearing House on Rural Education in Small Schools, New Mexico State, Las Crucas, March 1979.

49. Allen A. Edwards, "Types of Rural Communities," in Marvin B. Sussman, ed., *Community Structure and Analysis* (New York: Thomas Y. Crowell, 1959), pp. 92–108.

50. *Wisconsin State Journal*, 18 August 1974, p. 4:1; *Milwaukee Journal*, 22 July 1973, p. A:1, 14.

51. *U.S. News and World Report*, 14 February 1977, pp. 37–38.

52. Phillip M. Raup, "The Impact on Trends in the Farm Firm on Community and Human Welfare," in John R. Brake, ed., *Emerging and Projected Trends Likely to Influence the Structure of Midwest Agriculture, 1970–1985* (Iowa City: University of Iowa, College of Law, Monograph no. 11, 1970, pp. 104–115.

3 Toward the Public Interest: Redefining Rural-Policy Needs

John Dinse

This chapter addresses rural public policy from the standpoint of the public interest. Although this theme is an old one, present circumstances require its renewed examination.

The prevalence of clientelism in national-government subsystems has brought us to a point where normative reorientation is necessary. *Clientelism,* as an operational code in policymaking, encompasses elements of both praxis and belief. It is expressed in public policies that selectively provide benefits that predictably accrue to specifically assignable individuals.

A possible alternative to clientelism is a shared-interest concept of the public interest that can serve as a standard in normatively assessing public policy. In order to arrive at this, the chapter first analyzes and critiques traditional patterns of clientelism as it has directed policy benefits to rural America primarily through agricultural programs. It then moves on to a more philosophical section based on Brian Barry's substantive concept of the public interest.[1] The conclusion attempts to offer some general implications of Barry's concept for redirecting rural public policy.

The Nature of Clientelism

Political analysts have been scrutinizing policymaking subsystems within the national government for many years.[2] Although some variations in their conclusions are apparent, a relatively coherent picture emerges. Subsystems evidence characteristic patterns in terms of structure, actors, and processes. The structure of subsystems is triangular, incorporating the relevant congressional committees, bureaucratic agencies, and interest groups. The actors are politicians, administrators, and lobbyists, who have intense concerns within the policy domain of the subsystem. Processes involve exchanges among the actors that generally result in decisions to their mutual benefit. According to Redford, subsystems pervade our national political process: "There is probably some kind of subsystem for every major activity of government."[3] Through them, stability is provided for traditional balances of interests, and continuous access and superior opportunities for influence are insured for so-called high-quantity interests.[4]

To understand the impact of subsystems on the distribution of public-policy benefits, look briefly at the U.S. Department of Agriculture (USDA). The USDA's original mission was twofold: to encourage agricultural productivity and assist rural development. Thus it serves as the overall agent of public policy for the nonurban United States. Its operations have not reflected its total mission, however. Since the 1933 passage of the Agricultural Adjustment Act, the greatest amount of federal dollars directed to rural areas have been through commodity programs. Not surprisingly, these have been the key forms of what developed as agricultural—as opposed to rural—subsystems.

By 1977 government payments for commodity programs alone had accounted for $55 billion.[5] The USDA, congressional subcommittees, and interest groups are organized along commodity lines, (for example, wheat, corn, feed grains, cotton, rice, peanuts, tobacco, dairy products, wool, and sugar). Particular political actors seek benefits for the particular commodity with which they are identified. For example, Senator Robert Dole (R-Kansas) is known as a "wheat senator"; the National Association of Wheat Growers is the "wheat lobby"; and USDA officials responsible for wheat programs are "in-house advocates" for wheat.

Although commodity programs structure benefits in complex ways, the basic idea is simple—to subsidize farm income through price supports and assistance, nonrecourse loans, supply control, or a combination of these. In fiscal 1978 total government outlays to support farm income were estimated to be $7.8 billion.[6] As substantial as this sum is, it still does not take into account other, less traceable benefits delivered by agricultural subsystems. These include USDA research such as advisory and educational programs, disaster payments, and tax breaks for farmers.

The dynamics of subsystem politics throw some light on the reasons that commodity programs and other forms of government aid to farmers have persisted over time. The best-organized and most united rural-oriented groups tend to be commodity organizations, of which there are well over a hundred. Because of their unity of purpose, commodity lobbies have become increasingly effective relative to other interest groups, such as general farm organizations. They are able to pinpoint their influence in both legislative and administrative arenas and to maximize their impact on narrow issues of greatest concern to them.

Agricultural special interests also have a variety of other political advantages. They have information and expertise about the economic value of their products that is superior to that of other interests. U.S. political culture, with its supportive attitude toward farmers as custodians of rural America, usually ensures a relatively quiescent attitude on the part of the mass public. All these factors provide real incentives to legislators and USDA administrators to emphasize commodity supports.

Scholars have often appraised this subsystem positively, even concluding that it operates in the public interest. Cochrane and Ryan suggested that:

A public interest point of view emerged from struggles and compromises among the varied and differing contending interest groups.

The action and interaction of the varied, contending, and conflicting interest groups . . . tended to wash out the most crass demands of those interest groups and to push the public interest into the foreground.[7]

Agricultural Clientelism: A Critique

A primary original intention of agricultural programs was to provide a healthy rural economy in the context of market instability. There were many farmers, the principal rural residents, with many small farms. Their supply chronically exceeded demand. These factors, coupled with other uncertainties of production such as weather, led to government intervention.

Yet the conditions of agricultural production have changed dramatically since the inception of the Agricultural Adjustment Act, as has the demographic makeup of rural America. By 1979 farm population was less than 3 percent of the national total and only about 11 percent of the rural total.[8] Even among those who do farm, their aggregate nonfarm income exceeded farm income.[9]

The tendency is toward fewer farms and larger farm operations. The number of farms declined from 5,803,000 in 1948 to 2,370,000 in 1978.[10] A mere 1 percent of farmland owners own 30 percent of all farmland and ranch land in the Central States.[11] Over half of all crops and livestock are produced by 6 percent of U.S. farmers, whereas 46 percent produce only 3 percent of crops and livestock.[12]

Markets, land prices and values, and technology have also changed dramatically. Farmers are now a rural minority, possessing immense capital resources in comparison with their neighbors. They serve an international market through capital-intensive production. In short, they no longer hold the rural United States together, nor are they even its primary employers.

There exists an important historical lag between the traditional assumptions of farm policy, which are rooted in a former decentralized agricultural economy with many similar units of production, and the actual conditions of today's agricultural sector, which is dominated by a few large farms. The continued existence of various support and subsidy programs is difficult to explain empirically in terms of economic necessity, and especially in terms of serving rural America. Agricultural clientelism appears to be the sole maintaining factor.

The essence of clientelism is the selective provision of benefits to producers. As with all selective programs, the benefits of commodity programs can be predicted in advance. Those engaged in the production of covered commodities make up a relatively stable and enduring assignable group of U.S. citizens. Entry into this group is less than fluid because of the high costs of starting a viable farm and other limiting factors.

The structure of farm programs is also regressive because payments accrue to the rather static group with the largest acreage and production. John E. Lee

Table 3–1
Percentage of Total Payments Received by Different Groups of Farmers

Commodity	Smallest 50% of Farmers	Largest 50% of Farmers	Largest 10% of Farmers	Number of Farmers
Wheat	10.9	89.1	50.5	38.734
Cotton	6.2	93.8	53.3	5,045
Rice	7.0	93.0	39.8	1,658
Feed grain	13.3	86.7	39.5	62.037
Total	9.7	90.3	46.0	73,635

Source: John E. Lee, Jr., "Some Economic, Social, and Political Consequences of the New Reality in American Agriculture." Paper presented at Symposium on Farm Structure and Rural Policy (Ames: Iowa State University, October 1980).

provides recent data showing the distribution of direct payments by commodity in 1978.[13]

These data indicate that in 1978 almost half of the $2 billion spent on deficiency payments went to the 10 percent of farmers who are the largest producers. Yet these farmers already earn incomes well above the median income of the total nonfarm population. Farms with $20,000 or less in sales (about two-thirds of the total in the United States), receive "little benefit" from commodity programs.[14] Thus one can conclude that the redirection of USDA programs has led to a most inequitable situation for the department's total constituency. Rather than contributing to any development of rural America, USDA programs primarily serve to allow prosperous farmers to farm with little or no risk during bad times, while still making profits during good times.

The case of sugar deserves special mention. In 1978, "Americans paid more than a billion dollars in higher sugar prices to support a sugar program which transferred more than $300 million additional income to some 16,000 beet and cane producers whose average income and wealth were greater than the average non-farmer's."[15] The average benefit to growers was about $18,750.[16] It is clear that clientelism in agriculture has contributed to the creation of an assignable group of farmers who benefit from a regressive redistribution of public monies.

The consequences of clientelism go beyond this, however. Agricultural experts often claim that commodity programs are a primary cause of:

increased intensive specialization in supported crops and decline in crop rotation leading to soil erosion;

increased land prices as a result of program benefits being capitalized into higher asset values;

further decline in the number of farms and increased difficulty of access
to farm ownership;

growth in farm consolidation by wealthy farmers and landowners;

higher prices for U.S. farm products to consumers at home and abroad.[17]

There are also less tangible political costs imposed by traditional farm
programs. As emphasized by U.S. political thinkers from James Madison to
Theodore Lowi, the very legitimacy of the political order suffers when assignable groups gain benefits from government.[18] The general citizenry resents
seeing their tax dollars targeted for "special interests." Madison, for example,
argues that the greatest threat to democracy comes from "factions" whose
interests are "adverse to the rights of other citizens or to the permanent and
aggregate interest of the community."[19]

Although Madison was an empirical pluralist in recognizing the inevitability
of interest groups, he was not a normative one because he saw them as potentially dangerous to the public interest. Madison's perspective is relatively uncommon today, however. Instead, we find views stressing the convergence of the
public interest with satisfaction of intense minority interests. Such arguments
are facilitated by process conceptions of the public interest, of which Frank
Sorauf's is typical: "Instead of being associated with substantive goals or
policies, the public interest better survives identification with the process of
group accommodation."[20]

Though appealing in its realism, Sorauf's process definition lends normative support to clientelism and thus to the neglect of general rural problems.
According to Sorauf, commodity programs—but not rural-development programs—are in the public interest because they are a product of the "process
of group accommodation."

Yet given the costs and consequences of emphasizing commodity-based
agricultural policies as they have detracted from a general rural concern, this
conclusion is less than satisfying. In fact, Sorauf's "public interest" can become
a mere stamp of approval for almost any government policy, regardless of its
impact. The same can be said of Michael Harmon's formulation that: "The
public interest is the continually changing outcome of political activity among
individuals and groups within a political system."[21]

The problem here is not so much with the idea of the public interest as
with the faulty nature of process conceptions. What is needed is reorientation
to a substantive conception of the public interest that is consistent with
normal usage of the term and that can serve as a viable normative standard
for considering and evaluating public policy in general and agricultural/rural
policy in particular.

Raising the Alternative: Barry's Concept
of the Public Interest

Brian Barry proposes a definition of the public interest as "those interests which people have in common *qua* members of the public."[22] Used adjectivally, *public* refers to "that which has no immediate relation to any specified persons, but may directly concern any member or members of the community without distinction."[23] When *the public* is employed as a noun, "the emphasis is upon an 'indefinite number of nonassignable individuals'."[24] Because "the public" primarily refers to people as consumers, it can vary from one context to another. The public for theaters is theatergoers; for universities, students; for airlines, air travelers. In all such cases, consumers are publics that comprise indefinite groups of people. Even though not everyone will actually go to the theater or attend a university or travel by airplane, these services are accessible to all without distinction. It is impossible to predict accurately who will benefit from them.

In the realm of agricultural/rural policy, various actual publics are perceptible. For example, there is the vast public that consumes food produced by farmers and has an interest in the maintenance of the natural environment of agriculture. Those who reside in rural America are also an indefinite group of nonassignable persons who have an obvious stake in this policy domain.

"Interest," according to Barry, is a "want-regarding concept." To say something is in someone's interest is to say that a person wants it. Thus, " 'the public interest' tends to be restricted to contexts where the means of general want-satisfaction are at stake. . . ."[25] Examples of general wants include food, housing, roads, sewers, and insurance of various kinds.

When "interest" is used in a public-policy context, it often incorporates a comparative dimension. "If you ask whether a certain policy is in someone's interest this requires expansion into 'Is this policy more in his interests than that policy?. . . . 'Being in someone's interest' is at least a triadic relation between a person and at least two policies."[26] A certain policy can be 'in so and so's interest' when compared with one alternative and 'contrary to so and so's interest' when compared with another alternative."[27]

The secret comparison in all statements about interest is often a source of confusion in discussions of the public interest. Arguments about what the public interest is stem not so much from the difficulty of the concept (as Barry formulates it) as from the tendency of people to judge policies in light of other policies. "For any given proposal, there is nearly always at least one that, compared to it, is in someone's interest and at least one that, compared to it, is contrary to someone's interests."[28] Controlling for this, however, it is not uncommon in actual choice situations to find shared interests among nonassignables on specific policies that achieve general want-satisfaction. These policies can be said to be in the public interest.

The nonassignable nature of the "public" means that policies are most oriented to it when "the incidents of benefits and losses arising from them cannot be accurately predicted in advance."[29] Such is the case, for example, with the USDA's food-stamp program because, given the vicissitudes of a free-market economy, it is impossible to predict in advance who might be eligible for benefits.

On the other hand, when government policy serves the utilities of specific assignable individuals in their roles as producers, especially when market entry is restricted, this diminishes its public orientation. Commodity programs primarily help an enduring group whose recipient status can be nearly perfectly predicted. The category of large agricultural producers, to which the bulk of the payments go, is not a fluid group.

Objections may be raised that traditional farm policies are in the public interest because, even though they aid assignables, they *also* have the effect of facilitating general want-satisfaction of nonassignables. That is, they provide plentiful supplies of food at low prices. The problem here is that it has not been empirically demonstrated that today's commodity programs serve that purpose. At any rate, subsystems operate on the basis of clientelist dynamics and values without primary reference to nonassignables' interests.

A case in point was the USDA's lowering of milk-price supports during Nixon's second term. Although the decision was clearly in the interest of milk consumers, a nonassignable public, it was later reversed because of pressure from a clientele group, the Associated Milk Producers Incorporated (AMPI).[30] AMPI no doubt hailed the USDA's reversal as being in the public interest. Yet the reinstitution of higher price supports resulted mainly from clientele pressures and not from a serious attempt to achieve the public interest.

It is apparent that there is a contrasting distinction between *clientele* and *public*. A clientele is an assignable group of producers whose benefiting members can be predicted in advance. A public is a nonassignable group of indefinite number whose members are consumers and whose benefits cannot be predicted. Milk producers fall in the first category, milk consumers in the second.

To sum up to this point: Barry's conception of the public interest offers three interrelated criteria for assessing the degree to which government policies are in the public interest. Policies in the public interest provide benefits that: (1) accrue to nonassignable individuals, (2) cannot be accurately predicted in advance, and (3) achieve general want satisfaction. On the basis of these criteria, it is doubtful that agricultural commodity programs are in the public interest.

Clientele groups no doubt would be affected adversely if public policies were reoriented along the lines of the public interest. Yet such adversity would be relative, not total. Let us assume that only a portion of funds utilized for milk subsidies were transferred to the establishment of needed rural medical clinics. As members of the rural public, former recipients of milk subsidies would benefit from the medical clinics, although they would be required to make a net sacrifice. In other words, the previously subsidized milk producer would be asked "to place those elements in his own good which he shares with others above those elements, the pursuit of which, benefit only him."[31] Public-interest policies thus may impose a net sacrifice on some but still have the quality of providing benefits to the sacrifiers.

The Public Interest: The Implication
for Rural Policy

In order to derive concrete policy proposals for rural America based on Barry's concept of the public interest, attention must be focused on the needs of the rural nonassignable public. As architects of the Rural Policy Development Act of 1979 observed, these needs are all too apparent:

> The median income of rural and small town families is a fifth lower than that of metropolitan families, ... substandard housing and poverty are still disproportionally rural, ... the incidence of chronic illnesses and disabilities is greatest among rural people, as is the frequency of underemployment. And nowhere is the condition of ethnic minorities so far below that of the general population as in the rural setting.[32]

These comments suggest various directions for public-interest-oriented rural policy.[33] The resource base of rural America requires protection and development, both on the farm and in small communities. Conservation policies for water, soil, and farmland preservation need to be considered in terms of their importance for maintaining the productive capacity of rural America. The impact of herbicides and pesticides and their application practices on rural residents needs evaluation. The viability of small towns and villages, which have traditionally serviced agriculture, is in question as farms are consolidated and the number of farmers declines.

Service programs relative to the quality of rural life are no less important. Rural crime plagues all areas, but rural law enforcement suffers from inadequacies. Schools, health care, and fire protection all have facility and program problems unique to their local rural constituency. Social-service programs need upgrading to handle the disproportionate number of rural needy. There are, in summary, a tremendous array of nonassignable interests requiring attention.

These problems exist for many reasons. There is no simple, clear-cut explanation. Such factors as the industrialization of metropolitan areas has helped bring higher incomes and some better quality-of-life measures there. Yet that does not explain the general policy neglect of rural America. Urban conditions have been the specific focus of general public policy for thirty years; and, as Edward C. Banfield concludes, urban conditions have improved over that period.[34] Rural observers report no such general improvement. In rural

America, as if to confirm Barry's criticism, policy advances have been note-worthy in those limited program areas where recipients come from assignable publics. In this book, chapter 6 by Lynn Daft outlines progress made in the battle against rural poverty. At least a considerable portion of the lack of pro-gress in other areas, such as economic development and environmental improve-ment, results from the structural features of politics that provide rural programs. These can be summarized in three points:

There exist no specific support groups for general rural programs.

As a result, general rural issues cannot compete for attention with agricul-tural-support issues within the same department, the USDA.

The designation of vast numbers of federal service programs, from health to housing, earmarked for urban areas ignores the need factor evident in rural America.

No clearer indicator of rural America's disadvantaged state exists than the government's own efforts to allocate program benefits to rural residents. There has been nowhere near a consensus on even the definition of *rural* for program delivery. The Census Bureau, the Office of Management and Budget, the Admin-istration on Aging, and the Rural Development Policy Act all use different ones. The USDA has several definitions. The Farmers Home Administration within the department has three of its own for various programs. Little wonder that the 1980 Rural Policy Act was designed with the twin notions of rural neglect and noncomprehensive program efforts in mind.

No matter how hard rural advocates may try, however, they will not satis-factorily address the inequities by replaying the urban crisis to a rural tune. Yet this seems to be precisely what they 1979 extension of the Rural Develop-ment Act of 1972 was all about. It badly missed the boat, if one would judge from Barry's work. By adding another bureaucratic layer at the USDA under-secretary level, rural America gains only a cosmetic touch. Urban programs gained continued support through local coalitions, including large-city mayors and the national political efforts of groups like the U.S. Conference of Mayors and the National League of Cities. This was classic clientelist politics, and the 1979 act offered neither a powerful rural substitute nor a strategy for ensuring representation of the public interest in a broad rural sense.

Even a casual observer would find it necessary to conclude—especially in an era of fiscal austerity and program retrenchment—that rural America will continue to suffer at least relative, and perhaps absolute, neglect. It will not be through misguided programs, nor will it be because rural residents are less visible and hence less obviously in need as the rest of society. That rather easy prediction of neglect rests solely on the grounds that the cards are stacked strongly against any consideration of the actual rural interest in policymaking circles. Rural development must start with that condition as a given; and those who work for it need to go on from there, recognizing their disadvantage.

Notes

1. Brian Barry, *Political Argument* (London: Routledge and Kegan Paul, 1965).

2. J. Leiper Freeman, *The Political Process: Executive Bureau-Legislative Committee Relations* (Garden City, N.Y.: Doubleday, 1955); Theodore Lowi, *The End of Liberalism* (New York: Norton, 1969); Emmett S. Redford, *Democracy in the Administrative State* (New York: Oxford University Press, 1969).

3. Redford, *Democracy*, p. 18.

4. Ibid., pp. 102-105.

5. Don Paarlberg, *Farm and Food Policy: Issues of the 1980's* (Lincoln: University of Nebraska Press, 1980).

6. Ibid., p. 40.

7. Willard W. Cochrane and Mary E. Ryan, *American Farm Policy, 1948-1973* (Minneapolis: University of Minnesota Press, 1976).

8. Thomas McDonald and George Coffman, "Fewer, Larger U.S. Farms by Year 2000—and Some Consequences," Agriculture Information Bulletin 439 (Washington, D.C.: U.S. Department of Agriculture, Economics, Statistics, and Cooperative Service, 1980).

9. Paarlberg, *Farm and Food Policy*, p. 29.

10. McDonald and Coffman, "Fewer, Larger U.S. Farms," p. 6.

11. U.S. Department of Agriculture, *Who owns the Land?* ESCS-70 (Washington, D.C.: U.S. Department of Agriculture, Economics, Statistics, and Cooperative Service, 1979).

12. Paarlberg, *Farm and Food Policy*, pp. 221-222.

13. John E. Lee, Jr., "Some Economic, Social, and Political Consequences of the New Reality in American Agriculture" (Paper presented at Symposium on Farm Structure and Rural Policy, Iowa State University, Ames, 20-22 October 1980).

14. Ibid., pp. 11-12.

15. Ibid., p. 12.

16. Ibid.

17. James D. Johnson, Milton H. Erickson, Jerry A. Sharples, and David H. Harrington, "Price and Income Policies and the Structure of Agriculture," *Structure Issues of American Agriculture*, Agricultural Economic Report 438 (Washington, D.C.: U.S. Department of Agriculture, Economics, Statistics, and Cooperative Service, 1979), pp. 174-184.

18. Lowi, *End of Liberalism*; James Madison, in Ray P. Fairfield, ed., *The Federalist Papers*, no. 10 (Garden City, N.Y.: Anchor Books, 1966).

19. Madison, *Federalist Papers*, no. 10, p. 17.

20. Frank J. Sorauf, "The Public Interest Reconsidered," *Journal of Politics* 19(1957):616–639.

21. Michael Harmon, "Administrative Policy Formation and the Public Interest," in Joseph A. Uveges, Jr., ed., *The Dimensions of Public Administration* (Boston: Holbrook Press, 1975).

22. Barry, *Political Argument*, p. 190.

23. Ibid.

24. Ibid., p. 192.

25. Ibid., p. 202.

26. Ibid., p. 192.

27. Ibid., p. 194

28. Ibid., p. 195.

29. Ibid., p. 197.

30. Carol S. Greenwald, *Group Power* (New York: Praeger, 1977).

31. Barry, *Political Argument*, p. 204.

32. U.S. Department of Agriculture, *Implementation of the Small Community and Rural Development Policy* (Washington, D.C.: Office of the Under Secretary for Small Community and Rural Development, 1981).

33. William P. Browne, Don F. Hadinger, David Brewster, and Garth Youngberg, "Toward Comprehensive Rural Policy," *Policy Studies Journal* 8(1980):969–977.

34. Edward C. Banfield, *The Unheavenly City Revisited* (Boston: Little, Brown, 1974).

Part II
Rural Population Changes

4

The Population Turnaround in Rural Small-Town America

Calvin L. Beale

In what must surely have been the earliest recorded expression of urban fundamentalism, the Greek dramatist Euripides is said to have declared in the fifth century B.C. that, "The first prerequisite to happiness is that a man be born in a famous city." Since then, views of the relative merits of rural and urban life have varied over the centuries. The United States began on a distinctly agrarian note, with Thomas Jefferson the most noted proponent of the rural-is-good, urban-is-bad philosophy. The industrial and agricultural revolutions, however, urbanized the United States to such an extent that by the early twentieth century the country appeared to have become unremittingly metropolitan urban in character and trend. With each census the proportion of people living in large cities and their environs (metro) grew, fed by a continued exodus from the countryside. As late as 1970, forecasts of the future confidently predicted further urban concentration. Euripidean perceptions of the first prerequisite to happiness seemed clearly borne out in American residential choices.

However, if one looked closely enough, there were hints of a topping out of the urbanization process by the late 1960s. In the early 1970s a renewal of rural and small-town (nonmetro) growth of thoroughly unforeseen dimensions began. Most startling of all was the realization that the rate of nonmetro population increase had come to exceed that of metro areas—a phenomenon unknown in the modern era—and that more people were moving into nonmetro counties than out of them. Acceptance of the reality and nonephemeral nature of the trend was gradual at first, for a preponderance of rural-to-urban movement had come to be taken for granted. As the decade progressed, however, evidence coerced belief.

This chapter updates and reevaluates the rural turnaround with the benefit of data through 1980, noting the amount and location of the trend, the circumstances under which it has occurred, the characteristics of the migrants, and some implications of this major redirection in the course of U.S. demographic history.

The Trend

In the period 1970-1980 the population in nonmetro territory increased by 15.8 percent, compared with growth of 9.8 percent in metro counties (see table 4-1).[1] By contrast, from 1960 to 1970 the nonmetro population increased by just 4.4 percent, barely one-quarter of the metro growth of 17.0 percent.

Table 4-1
Population Change by Metropolitan Status and Size of Largest City

Characteristic	Number (Thousands)			Population		Percentage Change	
	1980	1970	1960		1970–1980	1960–1970
Total	226,505	203,301	179,323		11.4	13.4
Metro[a]	163,503	148,877	127,191		9.8	17.0
Nonmetro	63,002	54,424	52,132		15.8	4.4
Nonmetro						
Adjacent counties[b]	32,901	28,031	26,113		17.4	7.3
Nonadjacent counties	30,101	26,394	26,019		14.0	1.4
With city of 10,000 or more[c]	13,642	11,910	11,132		14.5	7.0
With no city of 10,000	16,458	14,484	14,887		13.6	−2.7

Source: Compiled from the *U.S. Census of Population*, 1960, 1970, and 1980.

[a]Metro status as of 1974.

[b]Nonmetro counties adjacent to standard metropolitan statistical areas.

[c]Counties with a city of population 10,000 or more in 1970.

This major change resulted from an unprecedented shift in migration. Whereas a net of 2.8 million more people left nonmetro communities in the 1960s than moved into them, the rural and small-town counties had a net in-migration of at least 3.5 million from 1970 to 1980 (precise data not available). Metro areas continued to receive some net in-migration of people because of immigration from abroad, but their combined growth from domestic and international migration dropped from 6 million in the 1960s to about 1 million from 1970 to 1980.

Metro people outnumbered those in nonmetro areas by nearly 3 to 1 in 1970. Therefore, the higher growth rate of nonmetro areas in the 1970s does not mean that an absolute majority of population growth occurred in the rural areas and small towns. However, the nonmetro counties did acquire 37 percent of all U.S. growth from 1970 to 1980, although they had less than 27 percent of the total population at the beginning of the decade.

A look at the characteristics of nonmetro counties by their growth trend provides insights into the nature of the turnaround that has taken place in rural and small-town population change.

Proximity to Metro Areas

Adjacency to metro areas was an important determinant of nonmetro growth in the 1960s. Rural and small-town counties that adjoined a metro area had moderate growth as a class, although they experienced some out-migration. However, counties that were not adjacent to a metro area were nearly stationary in population and had substantial out-movement. In the 1970s the adjacent nonmetro counties continued to grow more rapidly than those farther from the metro centers, but not by very much (17.4 percent versus 14.0 percent). Both types of counties have participated in the revival of nonmetro growth, but the degree of change from the past has been greater in the nonadjacent counties. Through sheer proximity, adjacent counties are in a better position to acquire the spillover of settlement from metro areas, but that advantage has not resulted in a much greater margin of recent growth and has not been the principal source of increase in nonmetro growth.

Income Levels

In the 1960s (and also in the 1950s), people moved toward high-income counties and away from low-income counties. The metro growth of that period was itself a manifestation of this trend, inasmuch as family incomes in metro areas have typically been a good bit higher than those in nonmetro areas.[2] However, the same pattern of movement was also evident in nonmetro areas. Thus the data in table 4-2 show that during the 1960s there was a strong positive association between nonmetro-county income levels and population growth. The high-income counties had substantial growth (including in-migration), middle-income counties had minor growth, and low-income counties experienced population loss and heavy out-migration.

In the 1970s this pattern was broken. Differences in growth rates by income level were minor among the various counties, and the degree of change from the 1960s was actually greatest in the lowest income classes. Other research has shown that population increase has also not been particularly related to county growth of income.

Thus people have been moving to or remaining in nonmetro communities in a manner essentially undetermined by either income levels or income trends of the counties concerned. Everyone needs a source of income, and opportunities for earning money in rural and small-town areas are, indeed, better than they used to be. However, for many who have chosen nonmetro residence in recent years, money seems not to have been the principal objective of the decision about where to live. Either they have chosen not to maximize income; or they depend on transfer payments, especially if retired, and can live where they wish or where their money will go furthest without concern over availability of work or wage levels.

Density of Population

Density of settlement, like income, was strongly related to rural and small-town population change in earlier years. The counties with relatively higher density—which often meant that they contained small cities—had the highest population increase. More sparsely settled counties—especially those with fewer than twenty-five people per square mile—had mild population loss as a group and a good bit of out-migration. In the 1970s this pattern ended. When nonmetro counties are grouped by density levels, their growth rates are very similar to one another's. Many of the sparsely settled counties are in the West, and their new growth reflects the rapid development of rural areas in that region.

Retirement

Retirement seems to be the only social characteristic of nonmetro counties that was positively related to growth in the 1960s and earlier that is also found to be as strongly related in the 1970s. During the 1960s there was considerable in-movement of people 60 years old and over into a number of nonmetro counties that had not formerly served as retirement havens. Many areas in

Table 4–2
Nonmetro Population Trends, by County Characteristics, 1960–1980

County Characteristic	Population (Millions)			Percentage Change		
	1980	1970	1960	1970–1980	1960–1970	
	(1)	(2)	(3)	(4)	(5)	(4) – (5)
Population density per square mile, 1970						
150 or more persons	5.9	5.1	4.5	13.7	13.4	0.3
100–149	7.4	6.4	5.7	15.6	11.4	4.2
75–99	6.8	6.0	5.6	14.2	7.0	7.2
50–74	9.6	8.4	8.0	13.9	4.5	9.4
25–49	17.7	15.2	14.8	16.1	2.9	13.2
10–24	10.1	8.7	8.8	16.5	−1.0	17.5
Less than 10 persons	5.6	4.6	4.7	20.9	−1.4	22.3
Percentage of blacks in population, 1970						
50 or more	1.8	1.7	1.9	3.2	−9.8	13.0
40–49	2.0	1.8	1.8	10.3	−2.5	12.8
30–39	3.5	3.1	3.0	14.4	1.0	13.4
Less than 30	55.8	47.9	45.4	16.5	5.5	11.0
Net migration rate, persons 60 years and over, 1960–1970 (retirement indicator) (%)						
15 or more	6.6	4.5	3.5	47.5	26.5	21.0
10–14	3.8	3.1	2.8	23.0	10.0	13.0
Less than 10 or negative	52.6	46.9	45.8	12.3	2.3	10.0
Percentage of employment in manufacturing, 1970						
40 or more	9.7	8.6	8.1	12.6	7.0	5.6
30–39	12.0	10.6	10.1	12.4	5.0	7.4
20–29	15.2	13.3	12.9	14.7	3.2	11.5
10–19	15.1	12.7	12.0	18.9	6.1	12.8
Less than 10 percent	11.0	9.2	9.1	19.8	1.0	18.8
Percentage of employment in agriculture, 1970						
40 or more	0.4	0.4	0.5	−5.8	−13.4	7.6
30–39	1.6	1.6	1.8	0.5	− 9.9	10.4
20–29	5.2	4.7	4.9	10.6	− 3.5	14.1
10–19	15.4	13.3	13.1	16.5	1.3	15.2
Less than 10	40.3	34.4	31.9	17.2	8.0	9.2
Median family income, 1969						
$10,000 and over	3.3	2.8	2.4	16.9	18.6	− 1.7
$9,000–9,999	9.1	7.8	6.9	15.8	12.7	3.1
$8,000–8,999	14.8	12.8	11.9	15.7	7.1	8.6
$7,000–7,999	13.7	11.9	11.5	15.1	3.1	12.0
$6,000–6,999	11.3	9.6	9.4	17.5	2.3	15.2
$5,000–5,999	7.1	6.1	6.3	15.8	− 2.5	18.3
Under $5,000	3.8	3.4	3.7	12.3	− 8.2	20.5

Table 4-2 Continued

County Characteristic	Population (Millions)			Percentage Change			
	1980	1970	1960	1970-1980	1960-1970		
	(1)	(2)	(3)	(4)	(5)	(4) –	(5)
Presence of four-year state college							
With college	9.9	8.4	7.5	17.0	13.0		3.9
Without college	53.1	46.0	44.7	15.5	3.0		12.5
Military personal as percentage of population 1970							
10 percent or more	1.4	1.2	1.0	12.3	24.3		-12.0
5–9 percent	1.3	1.1	1.0	16.8	14.2		2.6
Less than 5 percent	60.4	52.1	50.2	15.8	3.8		12.0

Source: Compiled from the *U.S. Census of Population*, 1960, 1970, and 1980.

Florida, Arizona, and California had long attracted older people, but during the 1960s there was an approximate tripling in the number of counties outside of these states in which high rates of net in-migration (15 percent or more) were observed for persons 60 and over. By 1970 about three-quarters of all counties showing this level of attractiveness to older people were outside the three states mentioned, with many of them far removed from the Sun Belt.

From 1970 to 1980 the 200 nonmetro retirement counties of the 1960s accelerated their rate of growth, becoming the most rapidly growing of all classes of counties. From 1970 to 1980 they experienced a remarkable overall growth in total population—47 percent—and had more than twice the annual volume of in-migration they had received in the 1960s. In other words, these retirement counties acquired one-quarter of all net nonmetro growth even though they had only 8 percent of the nonmetro population at the beginning of the 1970s.

It should be stressed that many of these counties also grew from other factors not specifically related to retirement, and in most of them a majority of the in-movement came from people not of retirement age. However, the retirement migration has been the most visible and important indicator of their growth. About twice as many people of retirement age move from metro areas into nonmetro counties as elect to move in the opposite direction. There are indications that even more nonmetro counties became destinations for older people in the 1970s.

Reasons for the great increase in retirement as a source of rural and small-town growth must come largely from inference. However, it seems certain that the improved income of many retired people has given more of them freedom of movement. In addition, the younger average age at retirement has released people from work when they are still likely to be physically vigorous, married, and willing to try life in another location.[3] This trend, together with a positive attraction to rural areas or small towns, a negative reaction to problems in the major cities, and perhaps a desire to move to an area with lower costs of living, has resulted in a much greater and more widespread movement of older people into nonmetro communities than was anticipated.

Presence of State Colleges and Military Installations

Two factors that were associated with instances of substantial nonmetro growth in the 1960s—at a time when there was very limited nonmetro growth overall— lost their special growth influence in the 1970s. These are the presence of senior state colleges and of military installations. In the 1960s, a period of expanded college attendance, nonmetro counties containing a senior (four-year) state college averaged 13-percent population growth and acquired about two-fifths of all nonmetro growth, even though they had only about one-seventh of the nonmetro population at the beginning of the decade. In the 1970s senior-college enrollment leveled off as the military draft for men ended, as the impact of the post-World War II baby boom lessened, and as most enrollment growth shifted to nonresidential two-year schools. State-college counties managed to retain their overall growth rate—apparently from other sources of growth—but no longer grew at a much faster pace than all other nonmetro counties as a group.

Counties dominated by military installations are not numerous, but in the 1960s—a period of military expansion—they tended to have rapid population growth. In part, this stemmed from the high birth rate caused by the presence of so many young families. During the 1970s many nonmetro military bases were closed or sharply cut back. In consequence, counties in which 10 percent or more of the population consisted of military personnel in 1970 had net out-migration and below-average population growth in the 1970s. They appear to form the only identifiable class of counties in which the trend has been directly counter to the general revival of growth in nonmetro population.

Dependence on Manufacturing

The substantial amount of decentralization of manufacturing that took place in the 1960s was a major factor in providing alternatives to farming, a diversified job mix, and job opportunities for rural and small-town women. Population growth in that decade was not strongly associated with the percentage of workers engaged in manufacturing but counties with a near absence of such work (less than 10 percent of employment) had almost no overall population growth (1 percent). In the 1970s, however, such counties had the highest growth rate of any manufacturing dependency class; and there was a basically negative association between demographic growth and manufacturing dependence. Thus nonmetro growth in the 1970s moved heavily into the least industrialized rural and small-town areas. Manufacturing provided 31 percent of all nonmetro nonfarm wage and salary job growth in the 1960s, but only 15 percent in the 1970s. As in the metro sector, service-performing industries have become the leading source of job growth.

Dependence on Agriculture

High dependence on agriculture has for a good half century now been a cause of out-migration from rural areas. The modernization of farming brought such drastic reductions in labor requirements per acre of land that farm employment has fallen by about three-fifths since 1940, at a time when the number of workers in most other industries has expanded rapidly. Under these conditions, counties with a high relative dependence on farming have generally either lost population or have obtained other types of employment and ceased to be primarily agricultural. Table 4-2 shows that counties that had at least 30-40 percent of their employed people in agriculture in 1970 declined heavily in population in the 1960s, whereas counties with lower dependence either had minor losses or gained in population where the farm economy was least important.

From 1970 to 1980 the pattern of relationship between population change and farming continued. However, counties of every degree of farming concentration greatly improved their retention of people, whether still losing, reverting to growth, or increasing previous growth. Although farming is still not a growth industry in employment, its losses are far less than in the past and are no longer numerically large enough to control overall rural change as used to be commonly the case. Primary agricultural employment dropped by 2 million people in the 1960s but only by 150,000 in the 1970s.

Presence of Black Population

In recent decades the outpouring of blacks from the rural South was one of the major forces of rural loss and urban growth. The greater proportion of these people came from agriculture, as Southern crop farmers abandoned the tenant system and modernized. From 1960 to 1970 a net of 16 percent of all nonmetro blacks moved elsewhere, compared with only 1 percent of whites. As a result, overall nonmetro change by counties was strongly associated with the percentage of blacks in the population.

In the 1970s the association of population change with presence of blacks continued, but in a much diminished way. The amount of black out-migration is not yet known, but the predominantly black counties had a small collective increase in residents from 1970 to 1980, and those with 40 percent or more of blacks also reverted from loss to growth. Although these counties are having much smaller growth than most other types of nonmetro counties, they clearly are very much a part of the rural turnaround. Racial data from the 1980 census reveal that much of this change has come from greater retention of the nonmetro black population, and not just growth of whites. By 1970 only a few of the counties with black majorities or near majorities were any longer those with high percentages of employment in agriculture. Thus the somewhat common trends occurring in the 1970s in black counties and high-farm-dependence counties are essentially independent of each other. Although most of the black counties once had an overwhelming dominance of farm employment, this was so reduced in the 1950s and 1960s that it was no longer true of many black counties by 1970.

Regional Trends

To obtain a picture of the geographic trend in nonmetro population, the country was divided into twenty-six subregions, based on such factors as homogeneity of topography, climate, economy, settlement, history, and culture. These identify such well-known areas as the Southern Appalachian Coal Fields, the Southern Piedmont, the Florida Peninsula, the Mississippi Delta, the Lower Great Lakes Industrial Belt, the Dairy Belt, the Corn Belt, the Great Plains, and the Rio Grande Subregion.

Tabulations for these areas show that all but one had increased growth of the nonmetro population in the 1970s, including a turnaround from decline to increase in nine subregions. The only subregion to have had a lower rate of growth of nonmetro people in the 1970s than in the 1960s was the Lower Great Lakes Industrial Belt, stretching from northwestern Ohio to southeastern Wisconsin. In this part of the country, a number of the nonmetro counties have small industrial cities of about 20,000–40,000 people, which have had the same basic difficulty in retaining or expanding their employment base that many of the metro areas in the subregion have had. The nonmetro population here has not declined as a whole and is not experiencing the heavy out-movement characteristic of its metro neighbors, but it does not show the enhanced growth seen elsewhere.

The sharpest change from the 1960s has been evident in the Southern Appalachian Coal Fields. Here a population decline of 11 percent in the 1960s was replaced by an increase of 21 percent from 1970 to 1980, and only one of the seventy-six nonmetro counties in this subregion declined in the latter period. Revival of coal mining did much to reverse the former trend, but return of former residents—many of them retired—and increased industrialization and service employment added to the trend.

The most rapid nonmetro growth has occurred in the Florida Peninsula, where a remarkable increase of 71 percent took place from 1970 to 1980. Almost none of the Florida growth stemmed from natural increase, for so many older people moved in that deaths almost equaled births. The other most rapidly growing nonmetro populations in the 1970s were those in the West. The Rockies, the Southwest, the Pacific Coast, Alaska, and Hawaii each increased by 30 percent or more. Mining, recreation, retirement, relatively high birthrates, "back-to-the-land" settlement, and manufacturing and public-service employment all played roles in the growth.

The Migrants

Although there is some selectivity in the migration of people into nonmetro areas, the broadness of the groups involved is impressive. All age, education, occupation, and income classes are found. A national survey in 1975 showed that 23 percent of the migrants from metro to nonmetro areas were children and youth under the age of 15, 46 percent were young adults 15–34 years, 25 percent were middle-aged (35–64), and 6 percent were 65 and over (table 4–3). However, there is still much movement of people in both directions, especially of young adults. As a result, the large influx of young adults into rural and small-town communities was all numerically offset by outflow of people of the same age. From the standpoint of net in-movement, the largest share of the migration is still children and youth, but because of the comparative lack of offsetting outflow, older persons amounted to 16 percent of the net movement, more than double their share of gross inflow.

The education attainment of the new migrants is, on average, higher than that of the longer-term nonmetro residents, and about the same as that of all metro residents. The inmigrants are found in all occupations but provide a disproportionate supply of professional and technical workers, salespeople, and managers and administrators. They are substantially underrepresented among farmers, factory operators, and vehicle operators.

The median income level of the migrants to nonmetro areas was intermediate between the higher income levels of metro residents and the lower typical incomes of longer-term nonmetro residents. Some income sacrifice was undoubtedly incurred by the typical rural and small-town in-migrant.

White people made up 94 percent of the gross inflow to nonmetro areas. However, with the direction of black migration still toward the cities, whites accounted for all the net growth of nonmetro areas from migration.

Conclusion

In its broadest aspect, the new trend appears to have been economically facilitated and socially motivated. Not nearly as many people were displaced from

Table 4-3
Characteristics of U.S. Nonmetropolitan Population in 1975, by Migration Status since 1970

Characteristics	Total 1975 (Thousands)	Nonmetro in Both 1970 and 1975	Metro in 1970 and Nonmetro in 1975 — Number	Metro in 1970 and Nonmetro in 1975 — Percentage of Total Nonmetro
Total, 5 years old and over	53,295	47,078	6,217	11.7
White	48,183	42,318	5,865	12.2
Black and other races	5,113	4,761	352	6.9
Male	25,902	22,837	3,065	11.8
Female	27,393	24,241	3,152	11.5
South	22,231	19,606	2,625	11.8
North and West	31,064	27,472	3,592	11.6
5-14 years	10,677	9,270	1,407	13.2
15-24 years	20,644	9,388	1,256	11.8
25-34 years	7,398	5,809	1,589	21.5
35-44 years	6,014	5,272	742	12.3
45-64 years	11,890	11,059	831	7.0
65 years old and over	6,673	6,280	393	5.9
Median age	31.9	33.4	27.3	—
Total, 18 years old and over	38,928	34,449	4,479	11.5
Elementary school	9,805	9,234	571	5.8
High school				
1-3 years	6,778	6,046	732	10.8
4 years	14,495	12,841	1,654	11.4
College				
1-3 years	4,408	3,662	746	16.9
4 years and over	3,442	2,666	776	22.5
Median years	12.2	12.2	12.6	—
Civilian employed, 16 years old and over	21,586	19,130	2,456	11.4
Agriculture	2,039	1,911	128	6.3
Mining	428	378	50	11.7
Construction	1,388	1,216	172	12.4
Manufacturing	5,042	4,598	444	8.8
Transportation and public utilities	1,256	1,116	140	11.1
Trade	4,217	3,694	523	12.4
Finance, insurance and real estate	753	621	132	17.5
Professional services	3,819	3,256	563	14.7
Services other than professional	1,615	1,430	185	11.5
Public administration	1,032	912	120	11.6
Median income				
Male	$ 7,072	$6,954	$7,850	—
Female	$ 2,620	$2,611	$2,650	—

Source: Data from Bureau of the Census, *Current Population Survey*, March 1975, retabulated for the Department of Agriculture.

agriculture in the 1970s as in the past, and mining—the other major rural extractive industry—had an increase in jobs following an earlier decline. Decentralization of much manufacturing and the growth of trade and services in rural and small town areas provided numerous job alternatives for rural natives and urban newcomers alike.

The effect of these economic changes was enhanced by the social fact that a large reserve of people had developed negative views about life in major or older metro areas, and/or a positive image of the quality of life in rural areas or small towns. Surveys of metro-origin newcomers to the smaller communities have found that the majority of them give noneconomic reasons for wanting to live in these communities.

Other keys to understanding what has taken place are:

1. The population turnaround has been greater in the open country than in incorporated small towns.
2. Many of the most rapidly growing rural counties are resort-retirement areas, reflecting in part the large number of comparatively young retirees who have incomes large enough to enable them to move where they want to.
3. Rural and small-town counties that adjoin metro areas have grown only modestly faster than those that are more remote. This trend is not merely metro sprawl.
4. Low-income counties have shown just as high population growth as have other counties, with the exception of those that were predominantly black racially.

The changes that have occurred since 1970 have been in accord with national policy objectives for a more balanced distribution of people, such as those expressed in the Rural Development Act of 1972. In the process they have:

1. diversified the mix of employment in rural and small-town communities;
2. given several million additional people the opportunity to live where they want to, rather than only where they feel they have to;
3. helped to normalize the age composition of the population in hundreds of nonretirement counties that the young had been leaving.

However, the trend has undesirable consequences as well. For example:

1. Some rural areas are growing so fast in population that comunities are disrupted and local government cannot keep pace in planning or provision of services.
2. The rural economy is now more vulnerable to general recessions in goods-producing industries.

3. Dispersed settlement is more expensive for provision of utilities and other services, even if it does accord with residential preferences. It also impinges on preservation of farmland.

In sum, the events of the 1970s produced far-reaching and unexpected changes in the economy and demography of rural and small-town America. On balance, these changes are largely beneficial and are likely to continue in the 1980s. They do not solve all rural problems any more than city growth created urban utopias in earlier years. However, they have muted many conditions that led to urban acceptance and support of rural-development programs. It is difficult to continue to appeal to urban self-interest when the flow of population is now into nonmetro areas. But great diversity within the rural United States remains. From a policy point of view, it is necessary to focus simultaneously on small agricultural communities of continued demographic decrease at one extreme, and on nonagricultural rural areas of rapid growth at the other.

Notes

1. In general, metropolitan (metro) areas are defined by the federal government wherever there is an urban aggregation of at least 50,000 people. The areas are generalized to county lines, and adjoining counties are added to them if certain conditions of metro character and worker commuting are present. In this chapter the metro delineations are those in effect after the full results of the 1970 census became available, but before any additional areas were created based on post-1970 special censuses or estimates.

2. In 1959 the median income of metro families was 41 percent above that of nonmetro families; in 1969 the difference was only 23 percent.

3. From 1970 to 1978 the population 60 years of age and over increased by 17 percent, whereas the total population grew by only 8 percent. In the same period the percentage of people 60-69 years old who were in the labor force declined from 42.5 to 35 percent. From 1970 to 1977 the average monthly retirement benefit from Social Security, federal retirement, and private pension plans doubled, whereas only a 56-percent increase would have been required to keep pace with the reduced value of the dollar.

5 Political Values in a Changing Rural Community

William P. Browne

One of the major population shifts evidenced in the 1970s was the influx of new residents to rural communities having access to small cities.[1] In a great many instances these rural communities are recreational or of a semiresort nature, with lakes, forests, and/or ski facilities. Usually their population growth clusters around older, established villages that previously served agricultural producers.

Several problems are attendant on such shifts and the resulting rapid population increases.[2] First, rural government institutions are strained to produce services to meet increased demand. Second, long-time residents resent the newcomers' demands on increasingly scarce services and the increased tax rates brought by area expansion. Third, this resentment leads to perceptions of conflict by both old and new residents. Finally, there are increasing demands to restructure local government in order to update and modernize its ability to provide more and better services, especially to those residential areas that are, in effect, urbanizing.

This pattern of strain, tension, and demand suggests that moves toward conflict resolution will be forthcoming—that is, if accepted theories of politics hold true.[3] In the rural United States that means that either counties will have to expand and provide specific services to unique population centers within their boundaries, or townships will be elevated to new status as service providers, or new municipalities and villages will be incorporated. Of those options, the first two seem unlikely means of resolution in most instances. Counties would need far more funds to comply, and user taxes on specific residential areas would be difficult to implement given present structures.[4] Townships likewise are limited because the new residential areas often overlap the boundaries of two or more of these units. Thus incorporation, following the pattern of suburban governments, is left as the major vehicle for meeting the need for increased local services in these changing rural communities.

However, municipal incorporation demands support from residents, not simply wishful thinking from those who identify problems. This chapter examines the likelihood of gaining support of that kind among citizens who have sought and found a rural life-style. It provides a useful commentary on how effectively we can hope to manage rural change.

The Study

This chapter results from a detailed examination of the Weidman area of western Isabella County in north-central Michigan, in particular the urbanizing cluster composed of the unincorporated village of Weidman and the recreation areas of Lake Isabella, Coldwater Lake, and Ojibwa.[5] This area and its approximately 1,000 residents were selected for analysis because of a developing population density and the reported prevalence of the kinds of environmental and political problems that such growth brings. But the project began at the request of the Weidman Business Association and the leaders of the area's various property owners' associations, all of whom were anxious to know more about the attitudes of area residents and the prospects for future community change for their own planning purposes.

For the most part, these sponsors were interested in the feasibility of and need for municipal incorporation. Accordingly, the project addressed two basic questions: (1) Are existing governments adequately servicing area problems? (2) What support is there for change in the operation of existing governments?

To answer these questions, a three-part study was organized, including a land-use survey, elite interviews, and a public-opinion survey. The land-use survey first mapped the area of population density and then plotted patterns of residency and commerce. An inventory of environmental problems and substandard public and private facilities was also included.[6]

The elite interviews were done to complement the land-use inventory of problems. Selected community leaders were asked to note what troubled them most about conditions in the area; develop a comprehensive inventory of specific problems found there; and then propose whatever action, if any, they considered necessary regarding future area governance. These leaders were identified as any public officials residing in the area, owners of large businesses located there, or any other residents regularly featured in regional newspapers as active in community affairs. These individuals were then asked to suggest additional residents as leaders.[7] Anyone not previously on the list was added to the final group of twenty-two interviewees if mentioned at least twice.

The inventory of problems and the sentiments of the leaders were used to aid in constructing a questionnaire for surveying the opinions of the area's general population. Residents were asked to determine the area's most serious problems, evaluate the quality of specific services, assess the benefits of municipal incorporation, and state their degree of satisfaction with other units of government. An additional series of questions was asked to develop some measures of community integration and to determine how attitudes about local conditions were formed by individual residents. Personally conducted interviews were held with 204 of the 340 heads of household in the area.[8]

Area Problems

The initial finding of greatest consequence to the study dealt with the distribution of area residents. Although the entire kidney-shaped zone around the area's several lakes was urbanizing, present development centered on four distinct locations. Therefore, the area appeared to be socially fragmented, and public services were provided individually to each of the four subareas rather than uniformly to the whole community. The less populated connecting links between the population centers, in turn, were important because their presence meant that the overall density rate for the area was legally insufficient for incorporation.

Not unexpectedly, given the unevenness of their distribution within the area, public services were found to be inadequate. With rural crime generally on the increase, about half the area's residents received almost no routine patrol, whereas other groups of residents who chose to pay additional service fees received daily patrol through the sheriff's department. Roads that were not hard surfaced—that is, most of the area's roads—were generally maintained at a substandard level. Fire protection was left to volunteers and, because of township contributions, was hampered by the question of jurisdictional responsibility. The other major service directly provided in the area, exclusive of education, was for county programs for the elderly. Despite the fact that the area's percentage of the elderly was approximately 60 percent more than the national average and more than 40 percent greater than for the county as a whole, those services fell below the average for the county both on a per-capita-expenditure basis and with regard to the variety of programs available.[9]

The area suffered from the lack of government attention in other ways as well. Some sections had no zoning; in others, present zoning regulations were unable to prevent an accumulation of junkyards and residential mixes of mobile homes located alongside expensive permanent dwellings. In addition, two areas of excessively blighted housing were completely ignored by public officials. Environmental problems were also severe. The water supply in Weidman was periodically too contaminated for safe human consumption. Area waters were subject to direct discharge and, more often, to contamination from inadequate septic tanks. Finally, drainage ditches were often blocked and filled, and other stagnant bodies of water were able to form in residential areas.

The last problem detailed in the inventory related to the economic viability of the area. For the most part, jobs were twenty or more miles away, with some residents traveling fifty miles or more to work. There were only about three jobs for every twenty residents; many of these—perhaps one-third—were held by nonresidents. This factor limited growth and, thus, the immediate prospects for future incorporation; it also inhibited the overal integration of the area by divorcing economic ties from related social and political ones.

In assessing these problems, there was general agreement between the observations of the planning team and the opinions of local leaders. Diversity and a lack of integration within the community, poor services, major environmental problems, and the limited ability of government to control area problems were noted by planners and by a majority of local leaders. If nothing else, this incidence of agreement indicates that all of these are real problems affecting area residents. However, it also led both groups to the conclusion that change in local government was necessary.

Public Opinion

Agreement between planners and leaders notwithstanding, the general public within the area failed to acknowledge the severity of these problems. On the contrary, residents registered real contentment with the status quo. When asked about municipal incorporation, as can be seen in table 5-1, area residents are overwhelmingly opposed. They clearly do not favor the alternative form of government suggested by planners and local leaders as a solution to existing problems. In fact, if leaders are removed from the resident survey, less than 10 percent of the population supports incorporation. On the contrary, residents who have an opinion about township government express satisfaction with its present operation. As indicated in table 5-2, nearly twice as many people are satisfied as dissatisfied. As shown in table 5-3, this satisfaction leads a strong plurality of area residents to conclude that townships can better meet the needs of the area than can either the county government or any future municipality.

However, support for township governments is not premised on the belief that they provide the best services for the area. The evidence suggests that they are viewed as most appropriate to the area rather than as better service providers. For example, as noted in table 5-4, a majority of residents feel that a municipality would provide more and better-quality services. In addition, the present level of services, as judged in table 5-5, gained less than the most enthusiastic support of recipients.

Table 5-1
Percentage of Residents Favoring Municipal Incorporation

Favor	Oppose	Do Not Know	Total
17	77	6	100
N = 204			

Table 5-2
Percentage of Residents Satisfied with Township Government

Satisfied	Not Satisfied	Do Not Know	Total
38	22	40	100
N = 204			

Table 5-3
Percentage of Residents Selecting One Form of Government to Best Meet Area Needs

Townships	County	Municipality	Do Not Know	Total
39	20	10	31	100
N = 204				

Table 5-4
Percentage of Residents Assessing Benefits of Municipal Incorporation

	Improved Quality of Services	Increased Number of Services
Would occur with incorporation	51	55
Would not occur with incorporation	49	45
Total	100	100
N = 204		

Table 5-5
Percentage of Residents Satisfied with Present Level of Public Services in General

Entirely Satisfied	Somewhat Satisfied	Not at All Satisfied	Uncertain	Total
16	59	10	15	100
N = 204				

Despite the strong tendency to be only somewhat satisfied with the general level of services, specific public services drew little opposition. When asked to rate individual services, the great percentage of area residents found each of them adequate. Even the major services that troubled planners and leaders were supported by the general population. The breakdown in table 5-6 shows that some of the most potentially irritating acts of government caused few complaints. Despite a proliferation of potholes and rapidly rising taxes, most individuals are content with the work of those who repair roads and assess property.

When asked separately to note specific problems needing additional government attention within the area, residents were even less critical of public services than they were when rating them. In fact, only one of the service arenas (road maintenance) evaluated in table 5-6 was volunteered by as many as 10 percent of the respondents to be a specific problem. Thus the adequacy of major services

Table 5-6
Percentage of Residents Rating Present Level of Specific Public Services

	Adequate	Inadequate	Total
Police protection	71	29	100
Fire protection	89	11	100
Road maintenance	63	37	100
Welfare, social service	87	13	100
Other[a]	67	33	100
N = 190			

[a]Includes sanitation, health, ambulance service, services for the aging, and tax assessment.

was not as irritating to the public as were certain services ignored as problems by both planners and local leaders. Dog control and the disposal of waste were the most frequently cited of these; but a few others, such as a lack of park equipment, were mentioned repeatedly. And even these sorts of problems with local services did not draw the critical attention that was directed to two problems generally beyond the scope of government itself: a lack of jobs and a lack of leaders (see table 5-7). In explaining their responses to those two concerns, most residents asserted that the major difficulties affecting the area resulted from the fact that the majority of the population was composed of either inactive retirees or workers employed elsewhere. These circumstances, they concluded, lead to a lack of interest in promoting area needs.

Paralleling their belief that area services are adequate, residents saw little likelihood of future potential conflict within the area except over property taxes. Excluding taxation, 57 percent of the area residents anticipated none of the conflict that might be predicted for the area. Thus, since some conflict between a few area interests already existed in each of the categories noted in table 5-8, it might be more appropriate to claim that resident perceptions of conflict were not closely attuned to reality. That finding, in turn, suggests that the satisfaction with present conditions registered by the residents might not be indicative of the quality of these services.

An analysis of the interaction of area residents does much to confirm the impression that citizen attitudes do not reflect the quality of services. As the evidence in table 5-9 shows, friends and neighbors are the single most important source of information about specific local issues. Their impact is nearly twice that of any of the sources in which most informed opinions might be found—local newspapers, organizations, or officials and leaders. Furthermore, even though only 48 percent of the residents have extended family within the area, the family was claimed as a reference nearly as often as were any of these other sources.

Table 5-7
Percentage of Residents Identifying Specific Problems of Area Needing Additional Government Attention

Lack of employment	45
Lack of leadership	38
Dog control	12
Cleanliness of area; garbage	17
Road maintenance	18
$N = 175$[a]	

[a]Includes only affirmative responses to one or more items.

Table 5-8
Percentage of Residents Expecting Areawide Conflict over Selected Issues

Inadequate public services	29
Unavailable public services	22
Municipal incorporation	34
Taxation	58
Industrial development	30
Recreational development	27
Environmental problems	22
$N = 136$[a]	

[a]Includes only affirmative responses to one or more items.

Table 5-9
Percentage of Residents Identifying Source of Political Information on Local Political Issues

	Used as Reference	Not Used as Reference	Total
Family	29	71	100
Friends and neighbors	56	44	100
Local officials and leaders	30	70	100
Local newspapers	30	70	100
Local organizations	32	68	100
$N = 200$			

Evidence to support the influence of family, friends, and neighbors as opinion sources can be found by additional analysis of the specific problems volunteered by respondents. When the three most frequently noted problems are broken down by subareas in which the respondents reside, as they are in table 5-10, it becomes clear that the problems cluster within these divisions.

However, no specific clustering of problems was noted by either the planners or the local leaders in the initial stages of the project.[10] Furthermore, when planners were sent back to secure additional information about these subareas, they detected little or no difference between these and other sections of the area with respect to any of these three problems.[11] This leads to the conclusion that opinion leaders, through the two-step flow of communication, do much more to structure opinions in this area than do direct personal experiences with the local services.[12] There is additional support for this conclusion back in table 5-6. The most frequently contacted service, road maintenance, is the least adequate, whereas the least contacted, fire protection (less than one fire per month in the area), is rated more adequate.

There is at least one important explanation for the influence of friends and neighbors as well as families on the political opinions held by area residents. Unlike most established towns and cities, the area has few other integrating institutional arrangements binding residents together.[13] Most respondents, as shown in table 5-11, have their most personal social ties with friends or family in the area. Church affiliation and voluntary membership in other organizations within the area is low, however. Few people shop in the area, except for groceries, and even fewer work there. Because of this low level of interaction, which leads to little social or economic integration within the area, residents have few reasons to seek out information from more informed sources. They rely instead on those who are truly "significant others."[14]

Table 5-10
Number of Residents Identifying Specific Problems, by Section

	Dog Control	Road Maintenance	Garbage
Section A	0	5	29
Section B	23	13	0
Section C	1	18	0
Other sections	1	2	5
Total complainants	25	38	34
$N = 82$[a]			

[a]Includes only those responding to one or more of these items.

Table 5-11

Percentage of Residents Having Social and Economic Ties within the Area

	Yes	No	Total
Closest friends residing in area	58	42	100
Extended-family members residing in area	48	52	100
Church affiliation in area	37	63	100
Voluntary-club or group membership in area	19	81	100
Comparative shop for major purchases in area	28	72	100
Usually shop for groceries in area	53	47	100
Work in area	20	80	100

$N = 204$

Conclusion

Those interested in rural development should be most interested in the differences that separate the values and opinions of planners and local leaders from those of the general population. If local groups of residents are to organize to deal with the problems they face in their changing residential environment, some realistic sense of the nature of these problems must be developed. Only then will they see the need to pay the price for restructuring local units of government. Without such a realization, referenda will not pass, charters will not be granted, and funds will not be raised for the extension of county services.

The evidence presented here suggests that such a realization will be difficult to bring about. The type of growth seen in rural areas like the one studied in this chapter discourages the development of an integrated community, the emergence of informed opinion leaders, and the attentiveness of most residents toward local problems. To correct this situation, interaction within rural communities must be more than casually social. Economic and political ties need also be developed in order to encourage areawide communication and a sense of common purpose. When the residents of the Weidman area were asked to identify the area in which they lived, 63 percent responded by noting one of the four specific subareas rather than the area as a whole. Less than 30 percent of the population—and most of these were residents who worked in the area—identified with the area as a whole.

Any attempts to correct situations of this kind must include additional development. Although residents strongly support more jobs and job opportunities, others of their preferences militate against economic growth. The most striking data in the residential survey indicate that the rural character of the area is what attracted and holds 75 percent of the population. Moreover, by more than a 3-to-1 margin, area residents do not favor new industries or businesses that will change that rural character. Just as residents reject better services because they find township government more appropriate, so they are prepared to live without a solution to what they see as the area's most identifiable problem.

Apparently the development of rural communities results from the politics of escapism. People are unlikely to emulate voluntarily the structures from which they are escaping. Therefore, it seems that the task for rural developers is to convince new residents that they cannot succeed in maintaining a pleasing environment by ignoring conditions that might destroy it.

Notes

1. Calvin C. Beale, *Rural and Small Town Population Change, 1970–80* (Washington, D.C.: U.S. Department of Agriculture, Economics and Statistics Service, February 1981).

2. U.S. Department of Commerce, Bureau of the Census, *Current Population Reports*, Series P-25, no. 620 (Washington, D.C.: U.S. Government Printing Office, 1972).

3. Primarily, but not exclusively, systems theory.

4. L.L. Ecker-Racz, *The Politics and Economics of State-Local Finance* (Englewood Cliffs, N.J.: Prentice-Hall, 1970); James A Maxwell. *Financing State and Local Government*, rev. ed. (Washington, D.C. Brookings Institution, 1969).

5. The study was undertaken by myself and several Central Michigan University students enrolled in my advanced-level course in local government and politics during the spring of 1976.

6. This methodology was derived from F. Stuart Chapin, *Urban Land Use Planning*, 2nd ed. (Urbana: University of Illinois Press, 1965); William I. Goodman and Eric C. Freund, *Principles and Practice of Urban Planning*, 4th ed. (Washington, D.C.: International City Manager's Association, 1968); William R. Lassey, *Planning in Rural Environments* (New York: McGraw-Hill, 1977). This work was carried on by a team of planners enrolled in the local-government-administration curriculum, planning option.

7. Nelson W. Polsby, *Community Power and Political Theory* (New Haven, Conn.: Yale University Press, 1963). In the end leaders were selected on a reputational basis, even though every attempt was made to identify the broadest possible base of leaders.

8. An attempt was made to interview each head of household, but time allowed for only three return visits to each housing unit. Therefore, 136 were not interviewed.

9. This controls for the likelihood that elderly residents were more likely to appear in our survey since they are more likely to stay at home. It also controlled for their greater likelihood of being in Florida during the interview schedule.

10. That is, on these and related problems, some environmental problems were noted to be unique to individual sections.

11. This finding is reported even after reflecting on Robert Goodman, *After the Planners* (New York: Simon and Schuster, 1971). It also calls to mind the confrontation between citizen views of police performance and the recommendations of area police officials reported by Ostrom and Smith, Elinor Ostrom and Dennis C. Smith, "On the Fate of 'Lilliputs' in Metropolitan Policing," *Public Administration Review* (March–April 1976):192–200.

12. Scott Greer, *The Emerging City: Myth and Reality* (New York: Free Press, 1962).

13. Elihu Katz, "The 'Two-Step Flow of Communication': An Up-to-Date Report on an Hypothesis," *Public Opinion Quarterly* (1957):76–77.

14. Manford H. Kuhn, "The Reference Group Reconsidered," *The Sociological Quarterly* (Winter 1964):6–21.

The Rural Poor

Lynn M. Daft

This chapter addresses the issue of rural poverty as it has been treated through public policy in the United States. It begins with a look at some of the causes of rural poverty and the evolution of public-policy responses. This is followed by a review of poverty trends, including key characteristics of the current rural population ,living in poverty. Trends in overall income distribution are also discussed. The chapter concludes with a discussion of the outlook for future policy.

Historical Perspective

The transformation of the United States from an agrarian to an industrial society and then to a postindustrial society placed an enormous strain on the economic and social fabric of the rural economy. It was a transformation of major proportions. Although it began in the late 1800s, the pace quickened in the early 1900s. During the decade of the 1920s, nearly 6 million people migrated off U.S. farms. With the help of a robust and growing national economy, most of the people affected by this transformation were able to adapt and prosper. Some were not, however, and became entrapped in a cycle of poverty. For those who remained in rural areas, physical isolation often added to the problem, restricting access to opportunity in other locations. In some regions, particularly in the South, the problem was aggravated by whole communities becoming poor, thereby limiting the availability of social and community services.

In 1959 over 56 percent of the nation's poor lived in rural (nonmetropolitan) areas.[1] One out of three rural people had an income below the poverty threshold, compared with slightly more than one out of five in urban places. Yet in the early 1960s, when poverty reached the forefront of the national policy agenda, it was defined largely in urban terms.

At the urging of Vice-President Hubert Humphrey, a National Advisory Commission on Rural Poverty was established in late 1966 to give attention to the rural dimension of the problem. In its report a year later, aptly titled *The People Left Behind*, the commission found the problem of rural poverty "... so widespread, and so acute, as to be a national disgrace...."[2] The commission concluded that the problem of rural poverty was not of a single origin but was rooted in many different and often interrelated social, economic, and institutional causes. As a result, in its final report to President Johnson, the commission called for an activist government role in dealing with the problems of rural poverty. Operating during an era of widespread federal intervention on behalf of the poor and minorities, when faith in the Great Society programs of President Johnson was running high, the commission offered over 150 recommendations on topics that ranged from job creation and economic policy to family planning and local government.

Although not all of the commission's recommendations were implemented, many eventually were. Reinforcing the Rural Poverty Commission were many other policy influences, most of them pointing in somewhat the same direction. A report prepared in 1971 by the U.S. Department of Agriculture at the request of the Senate Commission on Agriculture and Forestry examined progress in implementing the commission's recommendations.[3] From this report it is evident that some progress in adopting the recommendations had already begun to occur in the four years immediately after the report was issued.

Rural-Poverty Trends

Now look at some quantitative dimensions of rural poverty and how these dimensions are changing. There are a couple of important points to be made about rural-poverty trends in recent years.

First, although the antipoverty programs of the late 1960s and early 1970s did not eliminate rural poverty, they appear to have helped thin the ranks of the poor. As a matter of fact, they appear to have helped quite a lot. Whereas in 1959 one-third of all rural people (21.8 million) lived below the poverty line, by 1978 the incidence had fallen to 13.5 percent and the total number to less than 10 million.[4] Although the incidence of poverty among rural people remained higher than for urban (13.5 percent versus 10.4 percent), the gains in reducing poverty were far greater among the rural population. There were, of course, important contributing factors other than the antipoverty programs. A healthy, growing economy must get some of the credit. So also, as will be noted, does the increased rate of participation of women in the labor force. And, of course, some rural poor simply moved to the city and became urban poor. Nevertheless, the most important single factor seems to have been the array of federal programs set in motion during this period.

In fact, these measures of poverty underestimate the progress we have made in combating poverty. Since our conventional measures of poverty are based on cash income, they make no allowance for such in-kind benefits as food stamps, Medicaid, and Medicare. Given that in-kind programs (valued at $48.5 billion in 1977) represent a major part of public aid to the poor, to ignore their benefits is to overestimate the number of people whose standard of living is below the poverty level. To illustrate the magnitude of this distortion, an adjustment of 1974 poverty data for this effect reduced the incidence of rural poverty from 14.2 percent to 10.5 percent.[5] Given some of the program reforms that were achieved after 1974, this adjustment would probably have been even greater in the late 1970s.

A second point to be made regarding these trends is that most of the progress made in reducing poverty occurred in the later 1960s and early 1970s. Since then the incidence of poverty has changed comparatively little. In fact, in 1980 the share of the entire population with incomes below the poverty threshold ($8,414 for an urban family of four) rose from 11.7 percent to 13 percent. Thus, although existing social programs provide important income support to those families at or near the poverty level, they are no longer making significant inroads into reducing the number of poor. That phase is now over.

Who Are the Rural Poor?

Despite the progress of the past two decades, there are still over 11 million rural people with incomes below the poverty threshold. Although rural areas have made proportionately greater progress than urban areas in reducing the incidence of poverty, they still account for a disproportionately large share (38 percent) of the nation's poor.[6] The majority of the rural poor (73 percent) are white. Still, the incidence of poverty is much greater for blacks (41 percent) and Hispanics (26 percent) than it is for whites (13 percent). One can find small pockets of rural poverty spread throughout almost every part of the nation. The 1970 Census of Population identified over 16,000 minor civil divisions in rural areas in which 20 percent or more of the population was poor.[7] Despite the occurrence of rural poverty in all parts of the nation, the highest concentration is in the South, where about 60 percent of the rural poor lived in 1970. It should be instructive to see what the 1980 census has to say about the people living in these areas a decade later.

There are some particular characteristics of the rural poor that deserve special note:

1. A significant share of all the rural poor have low incomes despite their participation in the labor force. The majority of the heads of rural poor households work at least part time, and 20 percent work full time. Many rural poor families—about one out of five—rely solely on earnings from jobs for support, receiving no public assistance at all. The problem for them, therefore, would seem to be one of low-skilled labor and low-wage jobs.

2. Many individuals in rural poverty are older, especially in comparison with the urban poor. Of members of rural poor households in 1978, 22 percent were at least 55 years old.[8] The comparable share of urban poor households was 18 percent. Within rural areas the elderly account for a disproportionately large share of the poor. In 1975 they made up 16 percent of the rural poor but only 12 percent of the rural population.[9] This is a function of several

factors. One is the economic transformation described earlier, which has resulted in younger persons migrating out of rural areas in search of better employment opportunities. Another contributing factor is the lower level of income security available to the rural elderly. There is evidence, for example, that the rural aged in 1977 received a smaller share of Social Security benefits than their numbers would warrant.[10] This is due in some measure to the restrictions on eligibility and coverage of Social Security that once worked to the serious disadvantage of many rural workers.

3. A majority of all rural poor households are two parent. In 1978, 61 percent were husband-wife households.[11] This contrasts sharply with the urban poor, among whom 62 percent were single-parent households in 1978.

4. Although many rural poor remain entirely independent of public assistance, others—especially the elderly—are heavily dependent on it. About one-third have no other source of income at all. In fact, if one looks beyond poverty assistance to individual transfer payments for all purposes and to all income groups, it becomes evident that this source of income has become very important to the entire rural population—so much so that between 1968 and 1975 net transfer payments were the largest single source of personal-income growth in nonmetropolitan areas.[12] These transfer payments include Social Security retirement and disability, veterans disability, pensions and insurance, Medicare and Medicaid, military retirement, and unemployment insurance, in addition to public assistance to the poor. In fiscal 1976, Social Security payments accounted for 65 percent of the total.

Poverty and the Distribution of Income

In assessing recent trends in poverty, it is instructive to examine the overall distribution of income among U.S. households as an aid to understanding how and why it has changed. Census Bureau measures reveal that the distribution of per-capita houshold income became somewhat more equal between 1948 and 1977. Whereas in the earlier year the income share of the highest-quintile group was over 11 times that of the lowest quintile, by 1977 it was less than 7 times. By historical standards this represents a significant if not dramatic change.

What is responsible for this shift toward greater equality? One factor that is clearly *not* responsible for the change is the distribution of income from wage and salary earnings, which became decidedly less equal over this same 1948-1977 period. Lester Thurow argues that two factors are largely responsible.[13] One is the rapid increase in income-transfer payments to the poor—programs of the type mentioned earlier. As a share of gross national product (GNP), government transfer payments jumped from 4.1 percent in 1956 to 10.8 percent in 1980. Thurow estimates that the lowest quintile would have had less than half the share of income they realized in the post–World War II period had it not been for these transfer payments.[14] In other words, without these programs the lowest quintile would have lost ground rather than gained. In fact, as noted earlier, the distribution probably equalized more than the numbers suggest, since much of the low-income assistance (such as food stamps, health care, and housing assistance) has been in kind and therefore not captured in measures of income.

The second factor responsible for the equalizing trend in income distribution, according to Thurow, is the increased rate of participation of women in the labor force. As a result, many families have become "two-income families." This has had its greatest effect among the middle-income segment of the population, thereby resulting in an increased share of total income for middle-income people vis-à-vis the highest income class. Between 1950 and 1980 the participation rate of women aged 16 and over rose from 31 to 51 percent.[15]

This has had a phenomenal effect on the size and makeup of the labor force. As Thurow has observed, however, its effect on equalizing the distribution of income is probably about over. If anything, it will now start to have an opposite effect on income distribution, as women in high-income families begin to enter the labor force and as the barriers to higher-earning, male-dominated occupations are broken. This will result in the growth of two-income families among those families already at the high end of the scale.

Future Public Policy

What does the future hold for the use of public policy to combat rural poverty? Does the recent closing of the Community Services Administration, the federal agency charged with administrating antipoverty programs, mean a halt in the war on poverty? Has the body politic turned conservative in its willingness to assume the fiscal responsibility for aiding the poor? Or are we entering a momentary pause while priorities are sorted and more effective measures sought to deal with the problem?

In part, current policy actions are a response to the immediate political context, which is likely to be transitory. Yet the current retreat from federal responsibility is almost certainly not going to be followed by a return to old programs and policies, mostly because some of the forces that have given rise to current conservative policy are deep-seated and long term. Perhaps the most fundamental influence is the slow-down in the rate of productivity growth in the U.S. economy. Annual real growth exceeded 4 percent in the 1950s and 1960s, thanks to impressive gains in productivity. In the 1970s this growth rate slowed significantly, and it has slowed further in the 1980s. The economic consequences of a sluggish, inflation-ridden economy have left many U.S. taxpayers unwilling to support further aid to the poor, especially when they are told by political leaders that the resulting budget deficits are the principal cause of inflation. They are particularly unwilling to see additional public funds go to the poor. This can be seen in public-attitude surveys. Whereas over half of Americans polled in 1980 felt that the government spent too little in such fields as health, education, defense, and protection of the environment, only 14 percent felt that welfare received too little support. In the absence of a strong and growing economy, it will become increasingly more difficult to mobilize political support on behalf of government assistance to the poor.

Beyond this, there is a notable lack of urgency surrounding the poverty issue today. The policy environment of the mid-1960s was one of analytic contrasts and political confrontation. Urban riots, evidence of widespread malnutrition, and racial injustice brought to the public conscience a view of American well-being that contrasted sharply with popular ideals and with a majority of the citizens' sense of fairness. The present setting is much more passive, for a number of reasons. Most important, there has been progress in dealing with many of the problems. Greatly expanded food-assistance programs have essentially eliminated serious food-shortage problems. Housing conditions have improved dramatically, particularly in rural areas. Medicaid has improved access to needed health care. Thus, although disparities in standards of living remain, they are no longer as stark as they once appeared. This is particularly true as it applies to the basic necessities of food, housing, and health care.

What does this suggest about future policy? First, it underscores the importance of coming to grips with the nation's overall economic problems. Until inflation is brought under control and the rate of productivity growth increased, political leaders will encounter diminished public support for aid to the poor. Second, it points to the need for an objective and creative reexamination of the role of government in dealing with the problems of rural poverty. Some antipoverty programs have been outstanding successes; others have failed miserably. Now is the time to sort out the implications of the experience of the past fifteen or twenty years. Finally, it suggests that political representation of the interests of the rural poor will be even more difficult to achieve in the future than it has been in the past. As successes have occurred in reducing the number of poor, the size of their political power base has also been reduced. The removal from poverty of those who could be helped most easily and at lowest cost has left a hard core that is hard to reach. Finally, as tangible evidence of the most extreme deprivation has been eliminated, the opportunity to mobilize general public support has lessened. This opportunity will also be more important, however; for the threat to domestic tranquility bred by a sense of frustration and abandonment could well be greater.

Notes

1. Elizabeth Vinson and Kate M. Jesberg, *The Rural Stake in Public Assistance* (Washington, D.C.: National Rural Center, 1978), p. 37.

2. National Advisory Commission on Rural Poverty, *The People Left Behind* (Washington, D.C.: U.S. Government Printing Office, 1967).

3. Economic Research Service, *The People Left Behind—Four Years Later*, Senate Committee on Agriculture and Forestry Print, 92d Congress, 1st Session (Washington, D.C.: U.S. Government Printing Office, 1971).

4. Irma T. Elo, "Rural Poverty" (Washington, D.C.: National Rural Center, March 1981), p. 1.

5. Stephen F. Seninger and Timothy M. Smeeding, "Poverty: A Human Capital Perspective," Institute for Research on Poverty, University of Wisconsin, updated, p. 54.

6. John M. Cornman, "Rural Poverty and Economic Development" (Washington, D.C.: National Rural Center, 15 September 1981), p. 1.

7. Calvin L. Beale, Economic Research Service, U.S. Department of Agriculture, Washington, D.C., personal interview, February, 1981.

8. Cornman, "Rural Poverty," p. 2.

9. Bob Hoppe, "Despite Progress, Rural Poverty Demands Attention," *Rural Development Perspectives* (Washington, D.C.: U.S. Department of Agriculture, Economics, Statistics, and Cooperative Service, March 1980), p. 7.

10. F. Hines and J.N. Reid, "Using Federal Outlay Data to Measure Program Equity—Opportunities and Limitations," Working paper 7711 (Washington, D.C.: U.S. Department of Agriculture, Economic Research Service, 1977).

11. Elo, "Rural Poverty," p. 2.

12. Kenneth L. Deavers and David L. Brown, *Social and Economic Trends in Rural America* (Washington, D.C.: White House Rural Development Background Paper, October 1979), p. 32.

13. Lester C. Thurow, *The Zero-Sum Society* (New York: Penguin Books, 1981), pp. 159–162.

14. Ibid.

15. President's Commission for a National Agenda for the Eighties, *A National Agenda for the Eighties* (Washington, D.C.: U.S. Government Printing Office, 1980).

Part III
The Problems of Rural
Local Governments

7

The Impact of Rural In-Migration on Local Government

Paul Michael Green

Will County, Illinois, is situated in the southern part of the Chicago standard metropolitan statistical area. In the last decade Will has undergone an enormous population increase (30 percent).[1] The twenty-six municipalities in this large, 845-square-mile county have taken on the brunt of the new residents; but approximately one-third of the newcomers have settled in the unincorporated areas of the county.

This chapter will attempt to analyze how this surge in population has impacted on Will County's existing government structure. It will examine how a once predominantly rural county has coped with a sudden increase of new people, new ideas, and new problems. Specifically, it will examine the areas of public safety, roads, and education and see how population growth has affected budgetary and policy issues in Will County.

In recent years, new residents' demands for public services have increased far faster than government's ability to provide them. Not only has government been unable to respond to some constituents' needs because of limited resources, but often county and township agencies and local school boards are simply not prepared either physically or mentally to deal with new suburban issues or with the suburbanites themselves.

Will County Profile

Population

In 1970 four out of every ten Americans lived in the suburbs, double the 1940 percentage.[2] The 1980 census reveals continued suburban growth; but the demographic trends also reveal one significant new feature in this population shift—the colonization of "exurbia." Former rural areas on the edges of metropolitan suburban growth are now undergoing development, and this fact has placed enormous pressure on their local and county governments.

Will County neatly fits this condition. In the last fifty years the county's population has nearly tripled, with most of the growth taking place in the last twenty years (see table 8-1). Within the county the population boom has been geographically uneven. Joliet, the county seat and the county's largest city, has seen its portion of the county's population dwindle from 39 percent in 1930 to 24 percent in 1980. This percentage decrease occurred even though Joliet's population has doubled in the last fifty years (see table 8-2).

Table 7-1
Will County Population

1930	110,732
1940	114,210
1950	134,336
1960	191,617
1970	247,825
1980	323,458

A good deal of the new growth has taken place in municipalities that did not even exist a few decades ago, such as Bolingbrook and Park Forest South. However, it is in the unincorporated areas of rural townships that the significant population jumps have taken place (see table 8-3).[3] Formerly rural areas like Homer, Troy, Frankfort, and New Lenox townships are now rapidly undergoing suburbanization.

Where did these new people come from? According to Will County planner Harry Heuman, "most of the people are from the Chicago area. They are historically and culturally tied to Chicago. They were educated in or near the city. Their parents and grandparents are from Chicago. And there still is a strong tie."[4] However, these urban-oriented newcomers have not settled in Will County's established older cities like Joliet or Lockport. Instead, they have migrated to the new communities or to unincorporated areas in rural townships.

All demographic-survey data predict continued future growth for Will County. By the year 2000 the county's present 323,000 population should increase to over 450,000. Heuman suggests that "the county cannot avoid an increased population because it is one of the few areas in the Chicago metropolitan area that still has plenty of open space for housing."[5] Thus already hard-pressed rural-oriented local governments in Will County face a future of accelerating demands for services from an ever increasing urban-oriented new population.

Politics

Historically, political battle lines in Will County have been drawn between urban, ethnic, and Catholic Joliet and Lockport on the Democratic side, and the rural, Protestant areas on the Republican side. The GOP rural countryside has usually outvoted the Democratic cities in national, state, and county elections; and most of the county's twenty-four township governments have usually rested in Republican hands.

In recent years, however, suburbanization has complicated party competition in Will County. Suburbanization has created a group of independent,

Table 7-2
Population Growth: Will County Cities and Towns, 1930–1980

City or Town	1930	1940	1950	1960	1970	Preliminary Figures, 1980
Beecher	772	742	956	1,367	1,770	2,018
Bolingbrook	—	—	—	—	6,483	35,936
Braidwood	1,161	1,354	1,485	1,944	2,328	3,421
Crest Hill	—	—	—	5,887	8,322	3,421
Crete	1,429	1,772	2,298	3,463	4,709	5,400
Elwood	257	248	420	746	794	816
Frankfort	590	568	685	1,135	2,325	4,348
Joliet	43,993	42,365	51,601	66,483	74,900	78,165[a]
Lockport	3,383	3,475	4,955	7,560	9,985	8,883
Manhattan	628	601	728	1,117	1,530	1,936
Monee	383	427	554	646	940	1,007
New Lenox	—	—	1,235	1,750	2,855	5,771
Mokena	562	657	903	1,332	1,643	4,598
Naperville	—	—	—	—	—	810
Park Forest (part)	—	—	—	—	2,667	3,299
Park Forest South (part)	—	—	—	—	1,748	6,318
Peotone	1,154	1,146	1,395	1,788	2,345	2,709
Plainfield	1,428	1,485	1,764	2,183	2,928	4,431
Rockdale	1,701	1,532	1,393	1,272	2,085	1,898
Romeoville	133	69	82	3,470	9,945	9,152
Shorewood	—	—	—	499	1,749	4,166
Steger (part)	1,689 pt.	1,768 pt.	2,284 pt.	4,292 pt.	9,285 pt.	5,859 pt.
Symerton	77	82	119	123	155	120
Wilmington	1,741	1,921	3,354	4,210	4,335	4,415

[a]Although Joliet City (pt.) in Troy Township picked up 3,635 over 1970, the greater part of Joilet City in Joliet Township declined from 75,022 to 70,482.

Table 7–3
Population Growth: Will County Townships

Township	1930	1940	1950	1960	1970	Preliminary Figures, 1980
Channahon	747	845	1,193	2,125	2,712	4,416
Crete	4,153	4,210	6,380	11,737	15,270	20,426
Custer	442	548	611	651	949	1,098
DuPage	836	864	1,055	4,725	20,037	49,953
Florence	646	652	615	629	671	929
Frankfort	1,867	2,309	3,311	5,784	9,633	20,339
Green Garden	674	641	642	678	791	1,420
Homer	824	955	1,459	4,078	6,686	13,414
Jackson	1,064	958	1,173	1,461	1,755	2,471
Joliet	71,629	71,466	87,696	94,116	96,001	89,129
Lockport	11,006	12,712	17,468	26,882	33,354	34,222
Manhattan	1,285	1,214	1,239	1,823	2,374	3,373
Monee	1,014	1,136	1,737	5,131	7,240	11,047
New Lenox	1,491	2,104	3,356	6,232	10,049	16,736
Peotone	1,791	1,732	1,982	2,392	2,914	3,317
Plainfield	2,315	2,550	3,519	6,655	11,028	14,578
Reed	1,456	1,590	1,803	2,192	2,646	3,932
Troy	858	945	1,065	2,679	11,568	17,934
Washington	1,758	1,663	1,871	2,347	2,940	3,503
Will	643	658	592	774	750	1,138
Wilmington	2,249	2,514	4,306	5,132	5,296	5,521
Wilton	685	609	558	630	709	687
Total	110,732	114,210	134,336	191,617	247,825	323,458

undecided, and ticket-splitting voters. These new voters are neither urban nor rural; they reflect no traditional voting habits in the county. Rather, these large new suburban precincts act as a third force in county politics. They lean heavily Republican in national and state elections, but in local races they often divide their support between both parties.

This recent suburban invasion has shaken party leaders in both established parties and has given rise to strange coalitions between long-time adversaries. City Democrats and rural Republicans have combined their forces to fight suburban politicians' demands for more centralized planning, stricter zoning, professional administrators to run county government, increased services, and tax-collection reform. In county, township, and municipal elections, suburbanites have not followed any party line but have supported individual candidates regardless of party affiliation.

In short, suburbanization in Will County has created the classic political confrontation between the old-timers, who wish to retain the old-fashioned friends-and-neighbors approach to government, and the suburban professionals, who demand resumes, educational qualifications, and economic-interest statements from their elected officials. This battle has so blurred political-party loyalty that not since 1974 has party identification of a Will County board member (twenty-seven members—nine districts, three elected from each district) been an indicator of an individual's voting habits. According to one long-time Will County political observer, "it is a joke when a county board member calls for a party caucus during a board meeting . . . no one knows who will get up and leave or who will keep their seat."

Employment

Jobs are available in Will County. Total employment in the county has risen continuously during the previous decade. Over two-thirds of the county's employed residents work in Will County, with most of the remaining jobholders commuting to Cook County. Although Will is not in the same category as the heavily industrialized northwestern Cook County-DuPage County employment corridor, it boasts of having thousands of manufacturing and trade jobs.

Joliet is the center of economic activity for the county. In 1972 approximately half of all the county's manufacturing and retail emeployment was based in Joilet Township. (The city of Joliet makes up most of Joliet township, but recently some unincorporated areas of the township have undergone strong commercial development.) However, economic forecasts predict that by the year 2000 Joliet's portion of total county employment will drop below one-third. Suburban industrial parks and new shopping centers will pick up the slack, causing Joliet to lose its economic power position vis-à-vis the rest of the county.

Suburbanization has also had a dramatic effect on farmland and farm employment in Will County. In 1965, 2,053 farms operated in the county, with farmers planting over 388,000 acres of land. Ten years later the number of working farms had dropped to 1,265, a 38.4-percent decrease, with a total acreage of over 316,000 acres (an 18.6-percent decrease). A corollary story is told in the livestock-raised-for-income category. In this same ten-year period, cattle, hogs, and sheep inventory dropped by almost 50 percent. Farmland and farmers were being swallowed up by suburban growth; and groups like the Farm Bureau and water- and soil-conservation societies seemed powerless to stem the tide.

Taxes and Will County Governments

Most of Will County's local governments are financed by a property tax. Assessors are elected to assess real property in each of the twenty-four townships. A supervisor of assessments is appointed by the county board to oversee, but not control, the assessment process. The county treasurer and county clerks' offices have the responsibility to prepare and collect the taxes. An individual can protest his or her property assessment to a board of review—a three-person board that has the power to raise or lower assessed evaluations.

The majority of property taxes in Illinois—60 percent—go to support the public schools; municipalities receive another 20 percent, and the rest of the tax is divided among the county, township, and special districts. The property tax is arrived at by totaling the amount of money needed to support the taxing bodies that service the individual property. Each taxing body has a rate. The total tax rate for property is determined by adding all the rates for individual taxing bodies delivering services to that property. Then the final tax bill is formulated by multiplying the tax rate by the property's assessed valuation (fair market price). Thus a $7.00 tax rate on a property assessed at $10,000 would produce a tax bill of $700 a year.

This simple formula is often complicated by the state or county imposing an equalizer to make tax bills more equitable. This occurs when one area's assessed valuation appears too low or too high compared with valuations of similar property in a different county in the state or in a different township within the same county. Thus in theory the equalizer is a weapon used to maintain consistency of assessing; in reality, however, it is a limited threat that is often factored into an assessor's under- or overevaluating of property in his township.

The assessing process in Will County resembles a "cattle stampede in a field of molasses." Individuals charge off in different directions at the same time, but in the end no one moves very far or very fast. The collection of taxes in the county has become a national joke. Tax bills that should be sent off in August usually arrive between Christmas and New York's Day. Property owners literally beg the county treasurer and county clerk to mail them their tax bill so that they can pay it in time to deduct it on that year's income-tax return.

The tax-collection confusion produces government by crisis in Will County. Local taxing bodies are never sure when they will receive their tax dollars. Budgeting has become an expensive match game in which trustees attempt to outguess the collection process and estimate how far one year's receipts can be stretched into the next year's budget. The outcome of this chaos has been an enormous increase in the use of tax-anticipation warrants to supplement budgets where officials have been unable to meet current dollar demands with previously budgeted money. To illustrate, the tax dollars coming from the second half of 1979 tax bills did not *start* reaching local governments in Will County until mid-February, 1981.

Why does Will County have such a horrendous tax-collection problem? In large part the answer lies in the county's inability to respond to suburbanization. Unlike those in neighboring blue-collar counties, most Will County government units were unprepared for growth. Thus, although suburbanization and its accompanying problems were issues in surrounding areas, in Will County they have become major obstacles that often lead to open confrontations between the old-timers and the new suburbanites.

All Will County property owners belong to one of the county's 293 tax codes. (*Tax code* is the term given to the total tax rate levied against an individual property owner.) An analysis of all Will County tax codes reveals wide disparities between rates paid by various landowners. Without exception in incorporated areas, the highest rates are in the growing suburban villages, the lowest rates in the stagnant older towns. In unincorporated areas the same pattern emerges, with rural areas undergoing suburbanization paying higher rates than stable rural areas. The exceptions to this rule are the highly industrialized cities of Joilet and Lockport, where the city fathers and school-board trustees have raised the rates to make up for a declining tax base.

The tax-rate differential exists in Will County because of two factors. First, suburbanites' demand for services reflected somewhat in their willingness to pay for them. Second, growing suburban villages are being forced to create individual mini city services without having an established, existing service structure to draw on. Thus, despite the current incredible economic inflation, villages are starting from scratch to build modern public-safety and public-works departments, as well as other facilities. Moreover, as will be seen later in this chapter, suburbanites' demands for educational quality have also raised their rates.

The tax-collection chaos and the wide tax-rate differentials are symptoms of the larger problem—suburbanization's impact on formerly rural governments. Local officials hard pressed to deal with the political and cultural conflicts brought about by suburban growth are further hindered in carrying out their duties by an inefficient and out-of-date collection process.

A Case Study Examination of Suburbanization's Impact on Will County Government

Police Services

The main law-enforcement agency in Will County is the county sheriff. The Will County sheriff and his deputies, like county sheriffs in each of the country's 3,044 other counties, perform three main functions. First, they serve as the county's main police force. Second, they act as keepers of the county jail. Third, they act as officers of the county court system, often operating as subpoena servers.

In Illinois the sheriff's office provides the largest—and often the only—police force in the unincorporated areas. Suburban residents living in Will County's unincorporated areas find themselves in a peculiar dilemma vis-à-vis police protection. Because they are not part of a municipality, they benefit in terms of taxes by not having to pay for a village police department. On the other hand, they—like their incorporated suburbanite counterparts—demand high-quality police protection.

Recent data suggest that crime in the United States has increased dramatically in suburban and rural areas. Will County is no exception to this crime trend. In a series of interviews with Will County sheriff's deputies and command personnel, they noted the impact of suburbanization on public safety in Will County.

In the last year, the county's crime rate has increased by almost 10 percent. Burglary, especially daylight burglary, is by far the number-one index crime in Will County. Rising crime rates have mandated an increase in the costs of crime prevention and apprehension of criminals. The total budget of the sheriff's department has doubled in the last five years, and the costs of hardware have increased as well. For example, in 1980 the sheriff's department spent $650,000 on a new radio system. In 1975 this figure would have represented over one-quarter of the entire budget.

According to Lieutenant Robert Sulivoy of the Will County Sheriff's police, part of the problem of increased county policing costs is that "former urban people arrive with expectations of urban service. Most of them think that putting more cars on the streets will take care of crime."[6] Sulivoy and his colleagues believe that most Will County newcomers are moving in from Chicago and do not understand the limits of their new county's police powers. "Taxpayers," says one sheriff's deputy, "expect constant service and instant time response. Altogether, the county his only 137 sworn personnel to police 845 miles and to perform their jail and court duties."

It is generally agreed that it would cost about $1 million to add thirty police officers in Will County. In order to reduce response time significantly, taxpayers would have to kick in over $3 million in new taxes so that the sheriff could hire a hundred more men to meet the suburbanites' demand for service.

The population explosion has also placed new demands on sheriff's deputies. The department is involved in activities it simply did not do ten or fifteen years ago. The service function has increased in direct proportion to the number of new suburbanites arriving in the county. Today deputies spend a good deal of their time answering information calls about road conditions, basement floodings, or keys locked in cars. According to one deputy, "There is so much area to cover . . . yet most of the department's time and resources go to public service, rather than to coverage of criminal activity."

What about the sheriff's department capability of fighting crime in the burgeoning unincorporated areas? Recently, unincorporated subdivisions like Prestwick in Frankfort Township have contracted on their own for private security protection. In response to this and similar actions in other parts of the county, Will County sheriff John Shelley has advocated a special police task force. "This force," claims Shelley, "could be deployed to any area of the county experiencing an upsurge in crime."

In urban terms, Will County will soon have a tactical police unit similar to those in big-city police departments. When the sheriff gets his tactical unit, it will have to compete with another new crime-fighting unit under the loose control of the county state's attorney. This unit, known as Selective Investigation and Prosecution (SIP) has just been approved by the county board. What makes this law-enforcement organization unique is that, though county sanctioned, it will be privately funded. According to Will County state's attorney Edward Petka, "I'm not going to ask the people of this county to foot a bill that could be upwards of $250,000." Thus, in the name of budgetary restraint, the Will County board has approved a public body to act as a private police force, combining in it both investigatory and prosecutorial power.

In sum, public-safety concerns have become paramount in Will County. The county sheriff lacks the manpower and equipment lines in his budget to cover properly a huge county that is filling in quickly with new residents. Citizen complaints have forced officials to formulate some new law-enforcement policies to provide these needed services. Thus the county has entered some questionable policing areas in its attempt to satisfy newcomers' concerns without raising taxes—which would, of course, be political suicide with the county's old-timers.

Roads

The maintenance and construction of roads in Illinois is a highly decentralized operation. The state highway department has jurisdiction of major interstates and has full maintenance and construction control over state roads. Each county also has a county highway department that is responsible for secondary roads in each county. Illinois is a township state; therefore, almost every county has individual township road commissioners who have various mileages of roads under their jurisdiction. Finally, most municipalities have dedicated village or city streets within their corporate limits; to meet these road responsibilities, they have public-works or street departments to handle construction and maintenance problems. Thus an individual driver in Illinois could travel a very short distance and yet ride over roads that were under the control of several different local governments.

Three interstates (I-55, I-57, and I-80) cut through major sections of Will County. Various state roads crisscross the county in several directions, giving Will residents easy access to Chicago and the rest of the state. However, it is at the county and township level that the impact of suburbanization has wreaked the greatest havoc with road systems. The budgetary problems at each of these government levels is largely due to the increased demand caused by increased population. Moreover, local highway people are in near total agreement that the tax dollars generated by new residents do not match their demands for road services.

Will county has sixty separate county roads measuring a little more than 295 miles. County roads come under the jurisdiction of the Will County Department of Highways. Superintendent Roy S. Cousins commands the county highway department with a staff of sixty-two and a current budget of $8,271,406. Interestingly, the county highway department's overall budget in the last decade has doubled, although the employee total has risen only 24 percent.

According to Superintendent Cousins, "In recent years development has changed the road system in Will County from a rural to a suburban orientation."[7] Cousins challenged the notion that development usually follows roads; rather, he argues, it is a two-way street, where roads often follow development. He points out a north-versus-south, urban-versus-rural split in Will County as an example of the budgetary restraints and difficult policy choices affecting his department.

The northern part of the county, bordering on Cook and DuPage counties, is developing faster than the more steadfast rural southern part. Most road improvement centers around the Bolingbrook area in the northwestern part of the county. However, because of skyrocketing inflation and increased road use due to population growth, the county highway department has been barely able to keep up maintenance on these roads. According to Cousins, "It is virtually impossible to build any new county roads. Our efforts are geared to maintenance of existing roads and, when feasible, upgrading roads already in the system, e.g., making two-lane roads four-laners."

The exigencies facing Will County road officials have done little to deter newcomer demands for road upkeep and construction. Although Cousins's manpower has grown little in the last ten years, the calls for services have increased dramatically. Suburbanites demand quick, professional action to deal with road problems. Unlike bygone years, when friends and neighbors worked on these road crews, most county road employees are now strangers to their constituents.

As with policy services, the problems in roads brought about by suburbanization have led to some unique policy decisions. In the area of snow removal, county roads in northwestern Will County are now cleared by the village of Bolingbrook. The county found it cheaper and more efficient to contract snow-removal services with the village than to try to clear its own roads itself. The two garages housing county snow-removal equipment were simply too far away from the northwestern part of the county to provide fast enough service.

Suburbanization has forced the county highway department to redirect its maintenance manpower. In Cousin's view, "The needs of the growth areas have become so great that we are in danger of neglecting the non-growth areas in the southern part of the county." Cousins would like more employees and a bigger budget to satisfy all county residents' problems, but he realizes that he is unlikely to receive either in the foreseeable future.

If increased resources are not available Cousins would like to see a "functional classification" used to delineate road responsibility in Illinois. Under the functional system, whoever uses the roads the most would have maintenance accountability. Individual government jurisdiction would depend solely on the main purpose of each road in Illinois. State, county, township, and municipal highway departments would share maintenance and construction costs on the basis of how people utilize each road. The drawback to this system is that a prime road-funding source would have to be abolished. The motor-fuel-tax paid to county road districts is based on auto registrations in each county. On the surface, this system would appear to favor large and growing counties. However, many of these counties have township roads that under the motor-fuel-tax formula are funded by the mile. Thus overall, geographically large counties with large township-road mileage such as Will might receive the short end in any reformulation of the motor-fuel-tax.

Will County's twenty-four townships maintain over 1,177 miles of roads. Each township has a highway commissioner who sets a road levy that is paid via the property tax. Much of the new suburban growth has placed a heavy burden on township roads and township resources. Will County zoning law permits development of five-acre lots for residential housing. Thus many rural gravel and dirt roads are now dotted with imposing Spanish Colonial and English Tudor homes having former farmland as front yards.

These new home owners pressure beleaguered township road officials for service, maintenance, and often road upgrading. Like their county counterparts, the township road commissioners are having difficulty maintaining the quality of existing roads, let alone involving themselves in new road construction. As one road commissioner put it, "The taxes paid by the new suburban, rural homeowners no way matches the increased costs in servicing his needs. Maintaining farmer access is one thing but residential maintenance is a different story."

Education

The quality of public education has long been a paramount community issue. Few other areas create the tension and turmoil of school policy, school curriculum, or school financing.

From the development of free public education in the United States in the mid-nineteenth century until well into the twentieth century, urban schools were considered better financed, administered, and stronger in curricula. Floyd Reeves, in his landmark 1945 study on rural education in the United States, said of this comparison: "The quality of education provided rural children is a matter of national interest. . . . Because of the low status of agriculture during the 1920's, most rural communities entered the 1930's with an educational program far below that of most cities in both scope and quality."[8]

Reeves's analysis came out at a time when U.S. life-style and residential choices were about to undergo a dramatic change. The 1920 U.S. census revealed that the United States was at last an urban nation; a majority of its people were city and town dwellers. By 1945, however, the suburban movement was underway; with this demographic shift, urban education began to lose its dominant public-school position.

Suburban schools took the lead in public education. They were now considered better financed, more ably administered, and having stronger curricula than their big-city counterparts. It seemed that all suburban schools, whether filled with upper-middle- or working-class students, produced better student results. Their success caused sociologist Ed Wynne to condemn them for a homogenized learning atmosphere and "for emphasizing material wealth, comfort and physical health."[9] Moreover, he argued, suburban schools were too large; they were too technical in their administration, and their faculty was too specialized.

Recent population growth in counties like Will has brought the educational issue into public view. A full educational circle has taken place, with rural areas are now on the receiving end of urban flight. However, rural schools and rural school boards must find a way to accommodate suburbanites' demands for suburban schools without alienating old-time rural taxpayers. A recent article by Gene Schmidt in the *Illinois School Board Journal*, entitled "Let's Attack Problems of Rural Schools," sums up the crisis facing education in student-expanding school districts. Schmidt, a school superintendent, writes, "The rural school official must be aware of the changing make-up of the community and take steps to absorb the shifts in population."[10]

There are twenty-nine school districts in Will County. Geographically, they range from the rural-oriented 207-U and 201-U in the eastern and southern parts of the county to the smaller districts in and around the Joilet and Bolingbrook area in the northwestern part of Will. Another pocket of compact school districts lies just east of Joliet township in the New Lenox–Frankfort region.

Current school populations and future enrollment figures mirror the new demographics of Will County. Districts projected to have the highest growth are Bolingbrook-Romeoville (365-U), Homer (33-C), and nearly all the New Lenox and Frankfort districts. These areas are undergoing enormous suburbanization and, although some of them have existing government structures, Homer Township—directly adjacent to Cook County—was formerly almost entirely farmland.

Not surprisingly, those school districts with the largest drop-off in enrollments rest in the Joliet-Lockport area. Affecting their school-age populations are not only declining total city numbers, but also a move to private schools by remaining residents. Both Joliet and Lockport have expanding minority populations (black and Hispanic); many white residents are sending their children to Catholic schools. For example, Joliet's Catholic high school had to close off enrollments to non-Catholics who were flooding their admission office with applications.

The two major education issues brought about by surburbanization in Will County are the financing of education and the drection of curriculum—college or vocational. According to Matthew J. Racich, superintendent of Educational Service Region, Will County: "The growth rate of 365-U Bolingbrook-Romeoville was so fast that the district reached its maximum level of bonded indebtedness. The result was the implementation of a 45-15 plan to physically accommodate the students in existing structures."[11]

The 45-15 plan divided the total student enrollment of 365-U into four groups. The school year ran year round, and each student group was in school for forty-five days and then given fifteen days off. New school facilities were desperately needed since 365-U was the fastest growing school district in the nation, but the residents were unable to put a referendum package together.[12] Finally, the district applied to the state's Capitol Development Board, which set up a matching grant to fund new construction. The money was to be paid back over many years with very little interest and with minimal impact on local taxpayers. In this instance state government bailed out public officials who were unable to placate or compromise the rural and suburbanite educational interests.

Disputes over budgets carry over into controversies on curriculum. At the high-school level, most suburbanites want a curriculum oriented toward university-bound students that stresses wide-ranging fields of study geared toward college entrance. At the elementary level, these newcomers advocate gifted programs, innovative teaching methods, and modern learning facilities. All these education views have one thing in common—"money"—and although Reaganomics has wide appeal in suburban Will County, new suburban home owners have not foreclosed on the belief that their new life-style will produce better education for their children.

On the other hand, rural residents have long been suspicious of educational funding. Their property-tax bills reveal that the school district takes approximately 60–70 percent of their tax dollars—and many farmers and old-time small-town residents simply do not like it. Referendum fights for increased school taxes, pushed mainly by suburbanites, have failed as the better-organized older residents and their families, who are more often registered to vote, outorganize and outpoll the newcomers. In fact, according to Superintendent Racich, "It has been a very long time since any educational referendum has passed in Will County."[13]

There is a vast imbalance in the learning conditions in Will County schools. Growing areas do not have the space to house new students; yet inflation and resistance from area old-timers prevent the building of new schools. Many districts have resorted to mobile classrooms and nontraditional schedules to maintain educational equity among their students. School administrators, facing a disruptive and confusing tax-collection and -distribution system, have been put on the defensive by having to explain away tax-anticipation warrants and budget deficits. All in all, suburbanization has shaken up education in Will County; as with public safety and roads, suburban demands are straining public officials' capacity to deal with the problems.

Summary

It is generally agreed that four main factors contributed to the upsurge in suburban growth following World War II. First, the automobile became an integral part of many American lives, and this new mobility liberated individuals from a close work-home relationship. Second, the United States underwent a construction boom in road building to accommodate the new auto traffic. Aiding this "pavement production" was the introduction of new technology that quickened the pace and lessened the cost of road building. Third, the great U.S. cities lost their appeal for many of their current residents. Big cities could not meet rising demands for less crime, better education, and a cleaner living environment. Fourth, relatively cheap mortgage money for new-home construction was made available to many Americans through institutions like the Federal Housing Authority.

In the thirty-seven years since the end of World War II, suburbanization has reached far beyond the fringe areas encircling the city. Some of the reasons for suburban flight have changed; but overall, people moving to these new areas have one thing in common—a perception of a better life. What is significantly different is that the new suburbanites now face a stalwart, often unflinching foe—remaining rural residents. These latter individuals hold local power through their control of local government and, in a period of economic cutback, have increased their resistance to new ideas, new expenditures, and new people.

In Will County, police, road, and education officials have been forced to walk a delicate line between the combatants. Although both groups are philosophically conservative, it is the suburbanites who want to redirect existing funds into a more professional government. Suburban cries for modernization and depersonalized efficiency in services have met opposition from a united front of rural and urban old-timers. Because of this confrontation, Will County public officials today suffer from a political malaise. Unsure of which side will emerge triumphant in the county, they mainly try to keep their budgets at subsistence level while fending off nowcomers' demands for new services.

The culmination of this malaise was the sudden appointment of eight professional administrators to direct county services at the conclusion of this research. County officials reacted as they did to political pressures in order, as one put it, not to be caught with their pants down administratively. The burdens of attending to routine service questions as well as the politics of their positions eventually overwhelmed them and led them to see professionalism of county government as a way out of the political woods.

Notes

1. Northeastern Illinois Planning Commission, *Regional Data Report* (Chicago, 1978), p. 11-1.

2. Linda Greenhouse, "Growth Crying Out for Guidance," in Louis H. Massoti and Jeffrey Hadden, eds., *Suburbs in Transition* (New York: New York Times Books, 1974), p. 290.

3. *Joliet Herald News*, 1 March 1981.

4. Ibid.

5. Interview, Paul Green and Will County regional planner Harry Heuman, 12 February 1981. Other quotes from interview sources.

6. Interview, Ms. Mary Jane Blustein and Lt. Robert Sulivoy, 5 February 1981.

7. Interview, Paul Green and superintendent, Will County Department of Highways, Roy S. Cousins, 16 February 1981.

8. Lloyd W. Reeves, *Education For Rural America* (Chicago: University of Chicago Press, 1945), p. 13.

9. Edward A. Wynne, *Growing Up Suburban* (Austin: University of Texas Press, 1977), p. 17.

10. Gene L. Schmidt, "Let's Attack Problems of Rural Schools," *Illinois School Board Journal* (May–June 1979):13.

11. Memo from superintendent of Educational Service Region, Will County, Matthew J. Racich, to Paul Green, 23 January 1981.

12. Interview, Paul Green and Matthew Racich, 12 February 1981.

13. Ibid.

8 Population Growth and Administrative Variations in Small Cities

Alvin D. Sokolow

By now the reverse migration first noted with surprise by demographers in the mid-1970s is an established fact. The 1980 census has confirmed that nonmetropolitan areas of the United States grew more rapidly than metropolitan areas in the past decade, as a result of net migration from urban to rural areas—a reversal of many decades of movement in the opposite direction. The reasons for the change are well known; they include greater affluence among retirees, earlier retirements, increasing dissatisfaction with suburban living, and the willingness of more families to sacrifice income for life-style gains.[1] What is not as clear is the impact of new population growth on the receiving communities—on the processes and forms of institutional change in small and especially rural places.

As representative, priority-setting, and service-delivery institutions, local governments are at the center of these impacts. New and sudden growth generates unprecedented strains on the public sector of a previously stable community. Small-town officials, limited as they are in resources and political experience, are presumably hard pressed to cope with the demands and changing public preferences of increased populations. However, they can improve their ability to cope by changing the ways they make policy and administer programs. If the stereotypical view of rural local government is to be believed, there is much to change. In the traditional picture, policymaking and administration are conducted on an informal, commonsense, friends-and-neighbors basis. Expertise and professionalism are discounted or distrusted, and distinctions between policy and administration are blurred as elected governing boards both legislate and tend to the details of routine management.[2]

By creating new pressures and demands and introducing new political forces, rapid population growth provides both reason and opportunity for revising traditional government practices in small towns. But does it happen this way? Do local governments consciously seek to improve their administrative

An earlier version of this paper, "Administrative Styles in Small Communities: Does Population Growth Make a Difference?", was presented at the annual meeting of the Midwest Political Science Association, Cincinnati, Ohio, April 15-18, 1981. Joan Hogan was the author's principal colleague in the conduct of the research. Carried out by the Institute of Governmental Affairs at the University of California, Davis, in collaboration with the California Office of Planning and Research, the project was supported by grants from Kellogg Public Service Research Program and Title V of the 1972 Rural Development Act.

competence and expertise—"capacity" in the jargon of public administration—when faced with such community changes, if so, what kinds of administrative revisions are attempted and under what conditions?[3]

A partial answer to these questions is reached by drawing on a study of seven small-city governments in northern California.[4] The cities had populations of between 1,600 and 4,800 in 1980. All are located in nonmetropolitan inland regions—three in the Sierra foothills and four in the Sacramento Valley. Only one community lost population in the 1970–1980 period; increase in the other eight ranged from 4 to 32 percent. The data are based largely on lengthy, semi-structured interviews conducted in 1980 with mayors, other council members, administrators, and citizen leaders. Between four and seven persons were interviewed in each city, for a total of thirty-seven in the seven-city sample. We also systematically observed council meetings, clipped local newspapers, and collected other materials over a two-year period.

The Key Variables: Expertise and Centralization

Two common methods for improving the administrative capacity of a local government are to acquire more expertise and to simplify lines of authority by centralizing internal power and responsiblity. Both types of changes ordinarily occur in the most comprehensive type of administrative change undertaken by a small city, the establishment of a chief-administrative-officer (CAO) position.[5] Certainly the creation of a central executive office, filled by an appointed administrator with professional training and experience, is a fundamental step for a municipal organization. Not only does the city manager or other CAO usually bring improved expertise to a number of areas, but the creation of the position is also likely to change the shape and internal dynamics of the entire municipal operation. As administrative responsibilities become centralized in the hands of the new executive, both the role of the council and the power of other administrators are changed.

But adding expertise and increasing centralization can occur independently of each other. For example, a small city can obtain expertise for such specific functions as budgeting, personnel, management, and planning without employing a CAO or otherwise centralizing administrative power. Alternative sources of added expertise include consultants, other governments, such outside agencies as regional planning commissions, existing municipal officers such as clerks or department heads, and even individual members of the council. Furthermore, it is possible to increase or decrease administrative centralization without changing the mix of expertise available since legislative bodies can delegate more or less autonomy and power to individual officers. In this sense a CAO can have a relatively weak or strong position.

Expertise and centralization thus are conceptually distinct variables. As key indicators of a city's administrative character, both are included in this examination of municipal responses to population growth. Initially, existing organizational variations among the seven cities are described. These variations are summarized by ranking the seven cities according to the degree of administrative centralization and relating this ranking to the location of various responsibilities. Finally, the effects of relative population growth on recent changes in the administrative arrangements of the cities are considered.

Organizational Variations

Operating under the general laws of one state, all seven cities had certain common organizational features. In each a five-member council was elected at large in nonpartisan elections for staggered four-year terms. Council members were part-time citizen officeholders, minimally compensated either per meeting or monthly; they selected one of their own to serve as the city's mayor for two years.[6] Each city elected a full-time clerk, and all but one also elected a treasurer. Other city officials and citizen boards were appointed by the council.

In other formal respects, however, each municipality was distinctive—especially in the allocation of administrative responsibilities at the time of the field research and in the degree of centralization that can be inferred from such arrangements. Most significantly, two of the cities had CAOs—a full-fledged manager in one case and a city administrator with slightly lesser powers in the other. For the other five cities in the sample, there were variations in where central powers were lodged and how they were carried out. The cities also differed in terms of council-member roles and relationships to other officials, and in the forms and sources of specialized expertise. Although they were relatively small organizations, the size and scope of municipal activities varied substantially among the seven cities. In 1979–1980 there was a threefold range in budgeted expenditures (from less than $500,000 to $1.6 million) and a sixfold difference in full-time city employees (from eight to forty-eight).

Responsibilities and Powers

As can be assumed from the title, the one city manager in the sample was a powerful executive. His position included virtually all the responsiblities and powers associated with a strong CAO—budget preparation, personnel management, general policy advice and control of information for the city council, and departmental coordination. The city administrator in the sample had similar powers, lacking primarily the important personnel function of hiring and firing department heads.

Such administrative responsibilities in the five non-CAO municipalities were handled in a variety of ways—by the city councils themselves, shared between the councils and other officials, or separately by other officials. Two general patterns can be identified, however, in which the major difference is the degree to which councils relied on city clerks for policy advice and implementation. Strong clerks operated in two cities, relatively weak clerks in the remaining three non-CAO cities. The difference was more in degree than in kind of administrative power, since in the absence of a CAO the natural tendency is for responsibilities to accumulate in the hands of city clerks. They are the principal generalist officials in small cities, as keepers of city records, recorders of council proceedings, preparers of council agendas, originators of reports and most municipal correspondence, and compilers of municipal payrolls and warrants. They supply most of the administrative continuity and focus of non-CAO government, located as they are at the center of organizational linkages between council members, department heads, other employees, members of the general public, and outside agencies.

All the clerks in the non-CAO cities occupied this strategic location to one degree or another. However, the two strong clerks were more active than the others in recommending budgets and policies to their councils, providing a limited amount of departmental coordination, and representing their cities in dealing with state and federal agencies on grants and other items. Budget preparation is an example of how the responsibilities of the clerks varied more in degree than in kind. At the minimum, all the clerks in non-CAO cities (except in one city, where a full-time treasurer handled budgeting) compiled budget details for their councils. This included integrating departmental requests into one document and projecting city revenues. The strong clerks contributed more to the process—by, for example, suggesting expenditure limits to department heads and recommending salary schedules to councils. In recognition of their added responsibilities, councils in the two cities had granted them supplementary stipends and titles—"clerk–finance director" and "clerk-administrator."

Administrative responsibilities in the three non-CAO cities with weak clerks were relatively diffused. For example, budget preparation was assigned to the full-time treasurer in one city.[7] In another city the council had recently given its police chief additional duties by appointing him "director of public services," responsible for supervising the two public-works employees as well as the four-member (including himself) police department.

Council Roles

The presence or absence of a full-time CAO is a key determinant of the range of activities of a small-town governing board. Councils in each of the five non-CAO cities—even those with strong clerks—had ongoing administrative and information-gathering responsibilities. The usual pattern was the assignment of program areas—police, finance, fire, public works, and so forth—to individual council members. In fact, in at least three of the cities they were often identified as commissioners of this function or that, a remnant of the long-abandoned form of municipal government in which voters elected individual commissioners as both directors of particular departments and members of the collective council.[8]

Council-member assignments of this sort differed according to the extent to which they were involved in the direct supervision of employees or other departmental details. It was not uncommon for council members in any of the cities—with or without a CAO—to take a personal interest in certain areas and become involved in some aspects of administrative routine. The consistency and formalization of such intervention varied by city, however. Administrative assignments were most formalized in one weak-clerk city, where a council member explained his duties as "commissioner" of public works:

> There isn't a job description as far as commissioners are concerned. . . . But I am to oversee the director of public works, I am to help with his budgets. I check on his spending and purchase orders. . . . I am supposed to be more or less a liaison between the director and the council. I have asked him to actually attend all the meetings, so that there are two of us that know what we're talking about.—council member, City 21

There were other forms of council-member specialization in the seven sample cities. Some members took a special interest in grantsmanship activities, whereas others paid particular attention to budgeting, self-insurance, or other matters. Committees were frequently formed for special purposes, such as the study of water rates or the employment of a new police chief, although standing committees were not a regular feature of any of the councils. Mayors were generally more active than other council members in administrative details, but not to the extent that they performed as dominant executives.

"Shared responsibilities" best describes the administrative arrangement of the non-CAO cities. Mayors, other council members, clerks, and other city officials all were involved. Although councils in the two CAO cities were less directly involved in administrative routine, the policy-administration division of labor was not followed completely, largely because of the ease with which management details became visible and often controversial issues in these small towns.

Sources of Expertise

Even for small cities, expert information and administration are constant requirements. Beyond the budgeting and other central administrative functions described earlier, the seven cities also required some measure of expertise in such specialized areas as legal advice, engineering, planning, and labor negotiation.

Whether fed into council deliberations as information and advice or implicit in the administration of specific municipal programs, technical expertise was provided by one of two major types of sources: (1) regular personnel—council members, officials, or employees; or (2) outside individuals and organizations such as consultants, part-time contractors, and regional-planning agencies. Each city employed both types of sources.

Outside sources were most commonly used for legal and engineering services. Each city retained a part-time attorney, and all but one used consultant engineers. Sometimes the councils sought additional legal and engineering help from consultants other than their regular contractors, for assistance on special-izied litigation and such major construction projects as wastewater-disposal plants.

The pattern of planning services and related building-regulation activities was more diverse. Two of the cities employed full-time planners, one of whom served also as a grantsman, the other also as the building inspector. Elsewhere, ongoing planning services—including staff work for planning commissions—were provided by outside consultants, including the contract engineering firms for two cities and a regional-planning agency for two other cities. City clerks and, less commonly, city attorneys were also involved in planning activities. Building-inspection activities were carried out by regular employees in three cities (in one this was the responsibility of the fire department) and by outside workers elsewhere, including part-time inspectors with construction experience.

Labor negotiations presented still another set of arrangements. Salary and job-condition negotiations with municipal employees were handled by the two CAOs, by outside specialists in two cities, and by the councils collectively in the remaining three cities.

Ranking Centralization

As a summary of administrative patterns in the seven cities, the information in table 8-1 suggests several relationships between centalization and the location of various municipal responsibilities. The cities are arrayed according to the degree of administrative centralization—measured by the extent to which respon-sibilities were concentrated in the hands of individual officials at the time of our field research. The two CAO cities make up the high end of the scale, the two strong-clerk cities appear in the middle, and the three weak clerk cities are found in the low-centralization category. On the basis of the number and variety of formal responsibilities they held, the two CAOs—a manager and an administra-tor—in the sample far outdistanced officials in the other cities as dominant executive figures. The formal powers of the two strong clerks were not com-parable, although their informal influence in supplying information and advice to city councils was considerable.

Table 8-1
Administrative Centralization and the Location of Responsibilities in Seven Cities

Degree of Centralization	City Ranking	Location of Responsibilities				
		CAO	Clerk	Council	Other City Officials	Outside Sources
High (CAO)	1. Willows (valley)	(Manager) A,B,C,D,F*,G			F*,A,I	J,K
	2. Jackson (foothills)	(City Admin) A,B*,C,D,F,G		B*	I,K	J
Moderate (strong clerk)	3. Colusa (valley)		(Clerk-Fin Dir) A,C,D*	B,D*,F	H,I	G,J,K
	4. Angels (foothills)		(Clerk-Admin) A,C,D*,F*	B,D*,E,F,G		F*,H,I,J,K
Low (weak clerk)	5. Williams (valley)		A*,C,D*	A*,B,D*,F,H*	I	F*,G,H*,J,K
	6. Ione (foothills)		A*,C,D*	A*,B,D*,E,G	D*,I	F,H,J,K
	7. Orland (valley)		D*	A,B*,D,E,G	B*(Treasurer),I	F,H,J,K

Note: Key to responsibilities:

A – Budgeting	E – Department supervision	I – Building inspection
B – Personnel management	F – Grantsmanship	J – Legal advice
C – Policy advice	G – Labor negotiation	K – Engineering
D – Department coordination	H – Planning	

*Indicates shared function.

As would be expected, centralization was closely associated with council-member activities. The councils in the more centralized cities were less involved in administrative tasks, such as coordination, supervision of city departments, and personnel management, than were councils elsewhere. In the relatively decentralized cities, councils shared some of these responsibilities with clerks and others.

A less obvious finding was the greater reliance of decentralized cities on contract consultants and other outside sources for specialized expertise, particularly for assistance in labor negotiation, planning, building inspection, and grantsmanship. These forms of expertise in the two highly centralized cities were provided by the CAOs and other regular staff members, including officials with the combined duties of planning-grantsmanship and engineering-building inspection. As relatively centralized and professional bureaucracies in the sample, the two CAO municipalities internalized expertise that other cities had to obtain from outside, part-time sources.

Population Growth and Organizational Change

Relative population growth in the 1970s was not statistically related to the degree of administrative centralization (as of 1980) of the seven cities as table 8-2 indicates. The two cities with the highest rates of population increase in 1970-1980 ranked as the fourth-most and the least (seventh-most) centralized governments. The relationship to community size was stronger as the largest cities (in 1980) also tended to have the most centralized governments. Of course, this is a static analysis—a look at administrative arrangements at only one point in time—that does not capture well the nature of government change. To examine more adequately the impact of population growth, one must look also at organizational developments over time on a city-by-city basis.

Recent Change

Municipal governments in all seven communities have come a long way in the past decade or two. Those of our respondents who had long tenure in office and good memories told stories of the unstructured character of city government fifteen or twenty years before. They remember when city clerks worked a few hours a week, out of homes or businesses in some cases, and when financial and other procedures were lax and disorganized. A former council member in one city recalled the scene in the early 1960s:

> We had a budget but it was operating out of some guy's lower desk
> drawer. He was the city treasurer, and it was touch and go. We would
> sit in our budget sessions and it was like he would slip a paper out of

Table 8-2
Population Growth, Centralization, and Administrative Change

Cities Ranked by Percentage of Population Increase	1970–1980 Population Change		Ranking of 1980 Population	Ranking of Administrative Centralization	Major Administrative Changes in 1975–1980
	Percentage	*N*			
1. Angels (foothills)	+32.5	+1,178	(4) 2,888	(4) Moderate – strong clerk	None
2. Orland (valley)	+27.3	+1,089	(3) 3,923	(7) Low – weak clerk	None
3. Jackson (foothills)	+20.2	+ 389	(5) 2,313	(2) High – city administrator	City administrator (1978) Engineer inspector (1979)
4. Willows (valley)	+16.7	+ 684	(1) 4,769	(1) High – city manager	Grantsman/planner (1977) Bldg inspec combined with fire dept (1978)
5. Colusa (valley)	+ 6.0	+ 229	(2) 4,071	(3) Moderate – strong clerk	Labor negotiator (1976)
6. Williams (valley)	+ 4.2	+ 66	(7) 1,637	(5) Low – weak clerk	Labor negotiator (1976) Refuse-collection contract (1979)
7. Ione (foothills)	– 7.0	– 167	(6) 2,202	(6) Low – weak clerk	Public-service director/police chief (1979)

Note: Rank-order correlations (*r'*): Centralization and population increase: .10; centralization and population size: 42.

his pocket and say, "Let's see, what have we got . . . no, that's not the one." . . . The council used to be a good ol' boy type of thing. For example, the guy who was elected the same time as I was the man who ran a tire store north of town. At that election he realized that he was elected for four years and not two. He ran for election and he didn't know it was a four-year term!—Ex-councilmember, City 20

City governments have grown larger and more professional since that time. More and better-trained employees were added to city staffs, accounting procedures became formalized, and clerks in all seven cities became full-time officials who keep regular office hours in city halls. All the city councils increased their regular meetings from one to two a month; and, even in the least centralized and professional of the cities, council meetings followed prepared agendas and were recorded on tape machines.

In this context, what have been the major revisions in administrative arrangements in recent years, and to what extent can they be attributed to population increases? According to table 8-2, five of the sample cities undertook major administrative changes—defined as the creation of new positions or the reorganization of municipal services—in the last half of the 1970s. Significantly, no such changes occurred in the two most rapidly growing cities, suggesting that most recent administrative developments in the seven-city sample were not necessarily the result of population increases.

In fact, the reasons for the changes listed in table 8-2 were a mixed lot. Most of the new positions or reorganizations were created by city councils because of internal management and budgetary reasons unrelated to community growth. In one city, a new grantsman-planner position evolved out of a Comprehensive Employment Training Act-funded (CETA) job filled by a recent university graduate. The availability of the position coincided nicely with the city manager's desire to be relieved of the portion of his work load required to staff the planning commission and with the anticipated need to administer major grants for park development and wastewater-plant construction. Even after the CETA funding gave out, the position was continued with support from other grants and general city funds. This city also implemented, in 1978, a unique consolidation of city functions by merging building-inspection services into the fire department. This was done for several reasons—unhappiness with the competence of the previous full-time inspector, a desire to reduce city expenditures in the aftermath of Proposition 13 (California's constitutional amendment limiting property taxes), and the presence of a professional and highly regarded fire chief who had some construction experience and who saw a close connection between fire prevention and building regulation. Two slower-growing valley towns both hired outside consultants in the mid-1970s to handle negotiations with city employees. This was a result of the formalization of employee relations, produced by state collective-bargaining legislation, and the desire of council members to be removed from the unpleasant task of negotiating with employees who were also friends and neighbors in these small cities.

There is at least one solid case of population-related change. The third-fastest-growing city established a city-administrator position in late 1978, in part because council members believed they were overburdened by routine administrative chores. The demands had been building up for some time, but the council acted only when the city clerk—the council's administrative mainstay for many years—announced her resignation and recommended strongly the employment of a city manager. Rather than hiring a full-fledged manager, however, the council opted for the lesser position of administrator in order to retain some direct control over personnel and other matters. After his arrival, the new administrator instituted further changes in the city's organization, including the employment of a full-time city engineer with building-inspection experience to replace the work of part-time outsiders.

Incremental and Contemplated Change

That the effects of relative population growth did not show up directly in organizational changes among our cities can be traced to a basic feature of small-town politics. The natural tendency is to resist formal and major reorganizations, such as the adoption of a city-manager arrangement, that threaten to reduce the administrative powers of elected officials and the governmental access of citizens. Faced with population pressures and internal management problems, small-town governments may initially seek other, less radical ways of coping. Major reorganizations may eventually occur—but only after long consideration and reconsideration. This appears to be the story of the two fastest-growing cities, Angels and Orland, with population increases in the 1970s of 32 and 27 percent, respectively.

For these two cities the absence of major administrative change in the late 1970s was not necessarily an indication of government stability and satisfaction. Both had recognized management problems, due at least in part to rapid community growth. In Orland the council was concerned about its ability to coordinate municipal departments and, specifically, its control over a large (eighteen-person) public-works department headed by a director who was politically at odds with a majority of council members. In Angels the issue was the city's control over land development and construction on a fragile hillside environment. Council members bemoaned their lack of sophistication in dealing with land developers, a result of not having a city staff with technical expertise.

One answer for such problems was to obtain assistance from outside consultants. Angels relied heavily on an engineering firm for development review and inspection services. Another solution employed in both cities was to expand the work of city councils in supervising departmental operations. Council members operated as commissioners for particular areas of municipal government. The Orland council also responded to its public-works issue by appointing an expanded commission composed of council members and citizens to oversee that department.

These steps were not seen as entirely satisfactory or permanent arrangements in either city. The talk often turned to more fundamental and formal changes in city organization, including the creation of new professional positions. Because community growth was outstripping the capacity of their contract engineers to review new development, council members in Angels considered the employment of a full-time building inspector and an engineer who would direct all the city's public-works functions and perhaps act as general administrator. In Orland there was some discussion of the possibility of eventually employing a city manager or administrator—a proposal especially favored by the city's elected clerk and treasurer, who desired increased coordination and stronger direction for city departments. However, voters in the community overwhelmingly turned down a ballot proposition in 1978 to eliminate the elected status of the clerk and treasurer—a proposal seen as a step in the direction of a city manager. The council member who initiated the proposal was later defeated for reelection, a point interviewees later made when explaining their reluctance to accept the idea of a professional executive.[9]

Yet the possibility of moving in this direction was often contemplated in all five non-CAO cities. Some council members saw a manager or administrator plan as inevitable for their cities, and as likely when a certain population size was reached—the 5,000–7,000 range was usually mentioned. The major argument given for making such a change, however, was the increasing burden and frustration of serving on a council without professional assistance. With or without substantial community growth, the job of running municipal government in these small cities had become more complex in the areas of personnel, budget, planning, and environmental review, largely because of expanding state and federal requirements. On the negative side there was the belief that professional executives and their support are too expensive for small-city budgets. Council members also feared losing direct control over city business, and they sensed that citizens at large were not receptive to centralizing power in the hands of one official.

These mixtures of reluctance and inevitability indicate why rapid community growth does not automatically or quickly bring about major reorganizations in city administration. Local political systems are cautious and react slowly to changing community conditions. When major administrative changes are undertaken, they may be implemented hesitantly and for brief periods. For example, two of the non-CAO cities in the sample actually employed city administrators in the early 1960s but quickly abandoned the positions as unsuccessful experiments.[10]

Conclusion

The general message of this seven-city study of administrative arrangements is that small municipal governments deal with rapid growth in a variety of ways.

Faced with problems that require more administrative competence and expertise, some cities employ professional central executives, such as city managers; some expand the responsibilities of incumbent officials; and some of both the same cities and others turn to consultants and other outside sources of aid.

The amount of population increase in a community is not necessarily related to the kind or degree of administrative change, at least in the short run. For example, the two cities in the California sample with the most rapid growth in the 1970s did not create new administrative positions or adopt other reorganizations during the latter half of this period. At the same time, cities with lesser rates of change did undertake reorganizations—including in one case the creation of a CAO position.

It is natural for political leaders in small towns to resist major formal changes in their governments, especially those that promise to increase administrative centralization and expertise at the expense of city-council control and citizen accessibility. Why, however, should some cities move more expeditiously in this direction than others, with no apparent direct relationship to the rate of community growth? The simple answer, of course, is that many other community characteristics are involved—most of them more qualitative and uniquely historical than the rate of population increase. Small cities have diverse administrative arrangements to begin with, regardless of the rate of growth. Thus they can build on existing arrangements in various ways, such as assigning additional responsibilities to incumbents or—in a generally sophisticated public sector such as California's, with its many private and public providers of expertise—obtaining expert information and even administration from part-time outsiders. A city need not appoint a CAO for greater professionalization; but when it does, the immediate motivation can be as circumstantial as the resignation of an invaluable clerk or a sharp upturn in a city council's sense of burden and frustration.

Notes

1. Alan Kirschenbaum, "Patterns of Migration from Metropolitan to Nonmetropolitan Areas: Changing Ecological Factors Affecting Family Mobility," *Rural Sociology* 36(1971):315-325; Peter A. Morrison and Judith P. Wheeler, "Rural Renaissance in America? The Renewal of Population Growth in Remote Areas," *Population Bulletin* 31(1976); Curtis C. Roseman, *Changing Migration Patterns within the United States* (Washington, D.C.: Association of American Geographers, 1977); Andrew J. Sofranko and James D. Williams, *Rebirth of Rural America: Rural Migration in the Midwest* (Ames, Iowa: North Central Regional Center for Rural Development, 1980).

2. William M. Dobriner, "The Natural History of a Reluctant Suburb," *Yale Review* 49(1960):398-412; Art Gallaher, Jr., *Plainville Fifteen Years Later* (New York: Columbia University Press, 1961); Roscoe Martin, *Grass Roots Politics* (University, Alabama: University of Alabama Press, 1957); Granville Hicks, *Small Town* (New York: Macmillan, 1946); Alvin D. Sokolow,

Governmental Response to Urbanization: Three Townships on the Rural-Urban Gradient (Washington: U.S. Department of Agriculture, Economic Research Service, 1968); Arthur J. Vidich and Joseph Bensman, *Small Town in Mass Society: Class, Power, and Religion in a Small Community* (Princeton, N.J.: Princeton University Press, 1958).

3. For definitions and uses of the concept of *capacity*, see Leigh E. Groesenick, "Grass Roots Capacity Building and the Intergovernmental System," *National Conference on Nonmetropolitan Community Services Research* (Washington, D.C.: Committee on Agriculture, Nutrition and Forestry, U.S. Senate, 1977); Robert Hawkins, *What is Capacity Building: A Study of Capacity Building in California* (Davis: Cooperative Extension Service, University of California, 1980); Anthony Brown, "Technical Assistance to Rural Communities: Stopgap or Capacity Building?" *Public Administration Review* 40(1980): 18-23; Beth Walter Honadle, *A Capacity-Building Framework* (Washington, D.C.: U.S. Department of Agriculture, State and Local Government Program Area, 1980).

4. The seven cities were part of a larger study of twenty-six cities of under 10,000 population located in both metropolitan and nonmetropolitan areas of California. Primarily concerned with local responses to federal and state programs, the study also dealt with small-city policy and administrative styles and the impacts on municipal government of community growth and change.

5. The most popular version of the CAO arrangement is the city-manager plan. David A. Booth, *Council-Manager Government in Small Cities* (Washington, D.C.: The International City Manager Association, 1968), pp. 106-108; Ronald O. Loveridge, *City Managers in Legislative Politics* (Indianapolis, Ind.: Bobbs-Merrill, 1971); Richard J. Stillman, "The City Manager: Professional Helping Hand, or Political Hired Hand?" *Public Administration Review* 37(1977):659-670.

6. Mayors preside over council meetings and often are the spokespersons for their cities in dealing with regional, state, and federal governments. Most of their formal powers are shared with other council members, although some mayors are more effective than others in leading their councils. In terms of formal organization, the five non-CAO cities fit the standard textbook category of weak mayor-council government.

7. In the other cities, elected treasurers were part-time officials whose minimal responsibilities included the supervision of municipal deposits and investments. They had no part in budget preparation.

8. As a formal option for general-law (noncharter) cities in California, the commission plan was eliminated by legislation in 1947. However, a modified commission arrangement is recognized as the actual practice in many small cities.

9. Some months after the completion of our field research, in early 1981, Orland hired its first full-time professional executive, a "city administrative officer." Although deliberately avoiding the label and power connotations of either "city manager" or "city administrator," the council assigned numerous

responsiblities to the position—including budgeting, personnel management (other than hiring and firing), planning, and implementation of state and federal legislation. The occasion for creating the position was the impending resignation of the city clerk and the perceived work overload on the city treasurer.

10. The one municipality in the sample with a city administrator (hired in 1978) backed off somewhat in 1981 from its innovation when the first occupant of the position resigned to take the manager's position in a larger city. To fill the vacancy, the council initially advertised for an "office manager" with professional management (M.B.A. or M.P.A.) training. When that approach failed to obtain the type of executive desired, the council assigned administrative responsibilities on a temporary basis to the part-time city attorney and the former city clerk, who was rehired for a short period.

9

Rural Regionalism: Renaissance or Epitaph?

Lewis G. Bender

In 1975, campaigning presidential hopeful Ronald Reagan voiced his position on the expanding role of multicounty, substate regional organizations in the affairs of general-purpose local governments. In Mr. Reagan's view, the regionalism movement represented a conspiratorial attempt by "bureaucrats" and "planners" to wrest control from local elected public officials and concentrate authority in larger, nonrepresentative regional governments.

Mr. Reagan's views are illustrative of the position assumed by many politicians and public officials regarding the development and growth of substate regional organizations. Opponents of regionalism often speak of losing local-government autonomy and endangering representative government when they discuss the expansion of substate regionalism.

Proponents of regionalism, however, speak of governmental fragmentation, duplication of services, lack of coordination, inefficiency, and lack of economy of scale as factors that render the current mosaic of local governments ineffective in dealing with crucial social problems. Supporters of substate regional organizations argue that regionalism is an attempt to strengthen general-purpose local governments, not to wrest control from them. These proponents contend that the substate approach is the only viable way to keep local control over problems that transcend local (city and county) boundaries. The regionalists borrow from their opponents' line of reasoning by holding up the specter of Washington controlling and orchestrating local programs because of the inability of local governments to handle the situation effectively. Eugene T. Gualco, former president of the National Association of Regional Councils and a local-government official, summarizes the proregional position: a salvation rather than a threat, an aid to limited local resources in dealing with complex problems, an extension of the local unit under local control, and an opportunity to make the new federalism—with its emphasis on local decision making—work.[1]

Few proponents of regionalism argue in support of regional councils evolving into areawide governmemts. Rather, they insist that substate regional organizations are there to assist local governments, not replace them.

Advocates of regionalism often cite the problems facing the rural United States and the inability of rural local governments to deal with those problems effectively as evidence of the need for continuing and expanding the assistance provided by substate regional organizations. They point to the diseconomies of scale, lack of expertise, and limited resources of many rural local governments as factors that exacerbate any attempts to resolve the larger issues of rural

115

poverty, crime, unemployment, and inadequate and substandard housing. Regionalists argue that if rural local governments are to deal with these problems effectively, they must be provided with the expertise, resources, and coordinative activities of substate regional commissions.

However, recent federal budget cuts in programs supporting regional-commission activities may render meaningless any discussion of the role of these organizations. The new questions to be debated may well be: Can substate regionalism survive? Will the resulting cuts in staff and program resources eliminate regional commissions as viable entities for dealing with local concerns? Should the epitaph for the regional reform movement be written? Or will the loss of federal funding mark a new era of increased financial and political support for regional-commission activities from local-government entities?

This chapter examines the viability of the regionalism alternative in rural areas. The first section reviews the current status and program offerings of nonmetropolitan regional commissions. Particular attention is given to the types of programs offered by regional commissions and the kinds of services they provide to local governments. The impacts of the Reagan administration's budget cuts on regional-council activities will also be outlined. The second section examines the attitudes of nonmetropolitan public officials from two states—Georgia and Michigan—regarding the present and future operations of substate regional commissions. The goal is to determine whether rural public officials are willing to grant regional planning and development commissions more authority than their urban counterparts. It is highly unlikely that regional commissions could significantly increase or sustain their power and authority without at least tacit approval from local elected and appointed public officials. Therefore, it is important to ascertain how public officials feel about the growth and development of regional commissions. Throughout the chapter comparisons are made between rural and urban regional commissions.

Substate Regionalism in Nonmetropolitan Areas

A famous slogan of the 1960s challenged: "If you're not part of the solution, you're part of the problem." The same challenge might be appropriately leveled at many local governments in rural areas. Have they been a positive force in dealing with such problems as rural unemployment, substandard housing, and poverty—or have they been a hindrance? The Advisory Commission on Intergovernmental Relations (ACIR) has concluded that local governments are "one of the major problems" in rural areas.[2] The ACIR studies use 1972 Census Bureau figures to show that 72 percent of the local governments in this country were outside of standard metropolitan statistical areas (SMSAs). Thus 72 percent of the nation's local governments serve only 30 percent of the nation's population.[3] Too many governments are serving too few people.

Diseconomies of scale are created in which the per-capita costs of delivering basic services become unreasonably high. The net effect has been to reduce the number and quality of services offered by rural local governments.

The multitude of local governments also serves to disperse the available individuals with talent and expertise, rather than concentrating these individuals into larger and potentially more effective government organizations. Lack of expertise often means that rural governments are unable to take advantage of the federal and state programs and monies that are available to them. The politics and expertise of effective grantsmanship are beyond the capability of many local governments, which are often administered on a part-time basis. Thus the problems of declining economies and financial bases are often compounded by the inability of rural local governments to take advantage of outside sources of income.

Despite the comparatively large number of local governments in rural areas, the biggest problem for nonmetropolitan substate regional commissions is not coordination of services but, rather, *initiation* of services. Although local governments are comparatively numerous in rural areas, they are also much smaller than urban-area governments. As stated previously, most rural local governments lack the personnel and financial resources to tackle the myriad problems confronting nonmetropolitan areas. Thus rural regional commissions must contend with the problem of finding and pulling together the necessary resources to initiate desperately needed services and programs. The ACIR notes this problem in regard to federal areawide programs:

> But, whereas the regional thrust of the [federal] programs in metropolitan areas is to coordinate diverse and often overlapping efforts, the regional thrust in nonmetropolitan areas is more directed toward pulling enough resources together in one place at one time to get anything at all going. In other words, economies of scale, often realized by individual local governments in metropolitan areas, and even the simple ability to launch a program, are often realized only at the regional level in nonmetropolitan areas.[4]

Current Regional Programs

Even with these differences, however, the types of programs offered by nonmetropolitan and metropolitan commissions are remarkably similar. In a 1972 survey of rural and urban regional commissions, the ACIR found that programs in land-use planning, water and sewer development, open-space preservation, and solid-waste management were in the top rankings for both metropolitan and nonmetropolitan commissions.[5] The 1972 survey also revealed that nonmetropolitan commissions were more inclined to emphasize programs in economic development than were urban councils.

A more recent survey, conducted in 1973 by the National Association of Regional Councils (NARC), concluded that rural councils emphasize human resources and conservation programming in addition to economic development. In contrast, urban councils have tended to focus on transportation and environmental concerns.[6] Nonetheless, both studies tend to confirm Vincent Marando's findings that regional councils attempt to avoid programs with high social-conflict potential (life-style) and concentrate in areas with low social-conflict potential (systems maintenance).[7] This tendency can be explained in large part by the voluntary nature of regional-commission membership. In most regional commissions, member local governments are free to withdraw if they feel membership is not in their best interests. Thus commissions tend to avoid high-social-conflict issues for fear of alienating member local governments.

As indicated in table 9-1, regional commissions are engaged in a wide variety of programs and services beyond those already mentioned. Typically, regional commissions have been most active in program areas that have low conflict potential and/or are not traditionally handled or controlled by local units of government.[8] Indeed, local-government officials often welcome regional-commission involvement in programs such as air- and water-pollution control, rural development, and rural transportation because local officials perceive these programs as additional burdens that they would prefer to avoid. However, attempts by regional commissions to develop programs in areas previously controlled by member local governments are often viewed as unnecessary intrusions into local-government affairs.

Regional Services

The most basic differences between rural and urban regional commissions are not the program areas they deal in but, rather, the kinds of services they provide to local governments and public officials. Because of the lack of expertise in rural areas, the staffs of regional commissions must devote a major portion of their time to technical-assistance activities. Indeed, in many areas the regional commissions are the only agencies with the necessary expertise to deal with some local problems. It is not uncommon for rural-commission staffs to be engaged in all phases of program development. Staff members conceive of the program idea, sell it to local-government officials, develop the funding sources, and assist in its implementation. Regional-commission staffs often write the actual programmatic policies that are adopted by local city councils and county boards.

Rural commissions are more likely to be involved with service activities such as grantsmanship assistance, program development, and professional circuit-rider programs (table 9-1) because there is more need of—and less competition for—these services than in urban areas. By contrast, urban local governments usually require coordinative and managerial assistance from regional commissions. Nonmetropolitan commissions are more involved in the political and

Table 9-1
The Variety of Regional Council Activities

Federally Required Activities	Other Activities (Often Federally Assisted)
Project review and comment (544)	Housing (222)
Comprehensive planning (517)	Energy conservation (104)
Criminal justice (242)	Energy impact (95)
Economic development (204)	Coastal-zone management (58)
Aging (198)	Rural-development, Sec. 111 (128)
Urban transportation (145)	Noise control
Water quality (229)	Historic preservation (50)
Solid waste (140)	Farmland preservation (40)
Air quality (112)	Recreation and open space (92)
Local development, Appalachian (66)	
Health systems (72)	Employment and training (138)
Community action (161)	Tourism
	Mental health
Services to local governments	Alcoholism and drug abuse
	Nutrition
Grantsmanship assistance (417)	Child development/day care
Professional circuit riders:	Social services, Title XX (68)
Planners (112)	Youth programs
Finance budget officer (61)	Senior volunteers (27)
City manager (60)	Arts (14)
Legal council (31)	Regional-library coordination
Engineer (26)	
Building-code inspector (8)	Emergency medical (73)
Codify local ordinances (77)	Disaster relief
Cooperative purchasing (30)	Fire protection (13)
Centralized accounting and finance (17)	Coordinate 911 program
Centralized property assessment billing (6)	
	Rural transportation (184)
Independent operations	Airport systems (92)
	Railroads
Coordinate car/van pooling (70)	
Operate a transit system (18)	Census preparation (139)
Operate solid-waste facilities (6)	Surplus-property disposition (46)

Source: As reported in Bruce McDowell, "Substate Regionalism Matures Gradually," *Intergovernmental Perspective* Washington, D.C.: (Advisory Commission on Intergovernmental Relations, Fall 1980).

Note: Number of regional councils involved is noted in parentheses ( ) when available.

[a]Represents only those councils with heavy involvement.

entrepreneurial tasks of initiating, organizing, and promoting regional programs. Thus rural commissions tend to be more involved in the "broad" spectrum of decision making" than their urban counterparts.[9]

In recent years much has been written about the need to develop the administrative and resource capacities of rural local governments.[10] Despite differences over the means of increasing rural-government capacities, scholars tend to agree that *sustainability* is a crucial factor for success. That is, if local-government officials are to develop new skills, sustained contact must be developed with individuals and agencies possessing those desired skills. Sustainability refers not only to skill development, but also to the marshaling of necessary economic resources at the local level. George Honadle uses the metaphor of fishing to make this point.

> Although much remains to be learned both about what capacity is and how to build it, it is nevertheless certain that to a bureaucrat or to a peasant it is not enough to learn the art of fishing. Rather, resources must be focused on those barriers to keeping the fish.[11]

Rural regional commissions not only provide a source of training for local officials in the "art of fishing," but also help provide the means of "keeping the fish." Interestingly, most of the capacity-building literature has ignored substate regional organizations as important entities for expanding skills and resources in rural areas. Yet is is equally clear that these organizations are providing services (technical assistance and expanded resource bases) that fall under the heading of capacity building.

Indications are that rural commissions have enjoyed a relatively high degree of success in providing technical assistance to member local governments. The ACIR measured the success rates of metropolitan and nonmetropolitan commissions in providing technical assistance and solving local-government problems and found that nonmetropolitan commissions were usually more successful (tables 9-2 and 9-3). With respect to providing technical assistance, metropolitan commissions ranked in the upper two "successful" categories only 26.5 percent of the time (table 9-2) compared with the nonmetropolitan rate of 39.2 percent successes. The bottom two categories are equally revealing.

Table 9-2
Success of Regional Councils in Providing Technical Assistance to Member Governments

		Metropolitan Councils		Nonmetropolitan Councils	
Degree of Success		Number	Percentage	Number	Percentage
Not successful	1	39	28.7	13	10.8
	2	30	22.1	19	15.8
	3	31	22.8	41	34.2
	4	26	19.1	24	20.0
Very successful	5	10	7.4	23	19.2
N =		136	100	120	100

Source: ACIR/NARC Survey, as reported in ACIR, *Regional Decision Making: New Strategies for Substate Districts*, vol. 1 (Washington, D.C.: U.S. Government Printing Office, October 1973), p. 271.

Table 9-3
Success of Regional Councils in Solving Particular Local-Government Problems

Degree of Success		Metropolitan Councils		Nonmetropolitan Councils	
		Number	Percentage	Number	Percentage
Not successful	1	7	4.9	4	3.2
	2	14	9.9	12	9.5
	3	36	25.4	16	12.7
	4	48	33.8	47	37.3
Very successful	5	37	26.1	47	37.3
$N =$		142	100	126	100

Source: ACIR/NARC Survey, as reported in ACIR, *Regional Decision Making: New Strategies for Substate Districts*, vol. 1 (Washington, D.C.: U.S. Government Printing Office, October 1973), p. 271.

Metropolitan commissions were "not successful" at providing technical assistance 50.8 percent of the time. In contrast, nonmetropolitan commissions were "not successful" only 26.6 percent of the time.

The same trend is evident with respect to the successes of metropolitan and nonmetropolitan regional commissions in solving particular local-government problems (table 9-3). Again combining the top two categories, nonmetropolitan commissions enjoyed a success rate of 74.6 percent compared with the metropolitan rate of 59.9 percent. The "not successful" rate, however, was very close at 12.7 and 14.8 percent, respectively.

These figures indicate that the missions of metropolitan and nonmetropolitan regional commissions are quite different. Nonmetropolitan commissions fill an expertise void and are called on to initiate programs and assist in their development and implementation, whereas metropolitan commissions must compete with other local experts to get ideas accepted and programs implemented.

Federal Budget Cuts: Impacts on Regionalism

Despite the apparent successes of regional councils in providing services to member local governments, the future of substate regionalism is uncertain. Recent federal cuts in domestic programs that support regional-council activities "along with the announced intention to consolidate categorical programs into block grants and to delegate federal programs to the states" could result in the virtual extinction of many regional councils.[12] At present, federal dollars account for approximately 76 percent of the average regional council's budget. State funding averages only 10 percent for the regional councils, and local funds provide about 12 percent of the average regional-council budget.[13]

Metropolitan councils depend more heavily on local funds to augment federal dollars, whereas nonmetropolitan councils are somewhat more dependent on state funding sources.[14] Still, with the imminent loss of Economic Development Administration (EDA) funding (December 1981) and the projected loss of HUD 701 planning funds (September 1982), federal funding support for regional councils will be practically nonexistent.

Clearly, if many regional councils are to be spared the fate of not functioning "in any capacity except as a Wednesday afternoon tea party for local government officials,"[15] the contributions of state and local governments must be significantly increased. Future state and local contributions to regional councils depend on a number of factors, such as the vitality of their respective budgets and the overall economic health of the nation. These factors notwithstanding, it is reasonable to assert that the future of regional councils also depends on how they are perceived by elected and appointed public officials. If they are perceived as unnecessary federal appendages that were imposed on local governments from Washington, their future survival is in great peril. However, their future prospects will be greatly enhanced if local public officials view them as needed allies in dealing with local problems.

Public Officials' Attitudes

Before the current budget-cutting wave in Washington, urban and rural local public officials in Michigan and Georgia were surveyed regarding their views about the past and present operations of regional commissions.[16] The questions were designed to determine whether public officials perceived regional commissions as organizations that were serving the best interests of their respective areas.

Public officials were also asked a series of questions regarding their views about expanding the authority of regional commissions. It was expected that rural officials would view regional commissions in a more positive manner than their urban counterparts.

Attitudes Regarding Current Programs

Urban and rural respondents were initially asked if they felt that the interests of local governments were in conflict with the interests of area planning and development commissions (APDCs–Georgia) or regional-planning organizations (RPOs–Michigan). The vast majority of urban and rural officials in the combined surveys (table 9-4) felt that conflict occurred infrequently (sometimes, rarely, or never). This is not particularly surprising given that most regional commissions attempt to avoid alienating member governments. Contrary to expectations, however, rural officials perceived more conflict with regional

Table 9-4
Public Officials' Perceptions of Conflict between Regional Commissions and Local Governments

Question: I find that the interests of local cities/counties (townships) and the APDCs (RPOs) are in conflict.

Responses	Michigan, Officials, Urban		Rural		Georgia, Officials, Urban		Rural		Combined Urban		Rural	
	Number	Percentage	Number	Percentage	Number	Percentage	Number	Percentage	Number	Percentage	Number	Percentage
All the time	0	0.0	5	4.2	0	0.0	0	0.0	0	0.0	5	2.4
Many times	7	20.6	25	20.8	2	3.4	5	5.7	9	9.7	30	14.4
Sometimes	23	67.6	78	65.0	30	50.8	32	36.4	53	57.0	110	52.9
Rarely	4	11.8	12	10.0	21	35.6	38	43.2	25	26.9	50	24.0
Never	0	0.0	0	0.0	6	10.2	13	14.8	6	6.5	13	6.2
Totals	34	100.0	120	100.0	59	100.0	88	100.0	93	100.0	208	100.0

Source: Originally reported in Lewis G. Bender, "The Viability of Expanding Substate Regional Control: Urban and Nonmetropolitan Considerations," *Southern Atlantic Urban Studies Journal* (College of Charleston, Charleston, S.C.) 5 (August 1981):116–134.

commissions than did urban officials. Almost 17 percent of the combined rural officials perceived conflict "many times" or "all of the time." This compared with only 9.7 percent of the responding urban officials.

A closer examination of the data revealed that Michigan rural officials perceived much more conflict than did Georgia rural officials. Only 10 percent of the Michigan officials felt that conflict occurred "rarely" or "never," compared with 58 percent of the Georgia officials.

Michigan and Georgia rural officials also disagreed about the issue of the amount of power possessed by regional councils. When asked whether regional councils currently have "too much power," "the right amount of power," or "two little power," over 43 percent of the responding rural-Michigan officials felt that regional councils held too much power. This contrasts with a negative response rate of only 14.1 percent for rural-Georgia officials. It should be noted, however, that the majority of rural-Michigan officials (56.5 percent) felt that regional councils had either the right amount of power or not enough power. Nonetheless, throughout the survey, Michigan officials tended to be much more negative about the current and possible future operations of regional councils than were their Georgia counterparts.

This difference can be attributed in part to the perceptions of Michigan and Georgia officials regarding the role(s) regional councils play in their respective states. When asked if regional councils primarily serve federal, state, or local interests, only 40 percent of the rural and 47 percent of the urban officials in Michigan felt that regional councils primarily serve local interests. By contrast, over 75 percent of the rural-Georgia officials and over 80 percent of the urban officials felt that local interests were served by regional councils.

Historical factors might partially explain the differences in perceptions of regional councils in Georgia and Michigan. Georgia regional councils were started in the early 1950s (Coosa Valley APDC, Rome) by a coalition consisting of local public officials, the Georgia Power Company, and representatives from the University of Georgia. The idea was to develop regional organizations that would encourage desperately needed economic development in rural areas. In Michigan, however, most regional councils [excluding the Southeast Michigan Council of Government (SEMCOG) in Detroit] were developed in the late 1960s as a result of federal programs and the initiatives of the governor. Thus many local Michigan officials perceive regional councils as creatures of the federal of state government, whereas Georgia officials view them as creations of local government. In addition, regional councils in Georgia have had more time to break down local barriers than have their counterparts in Michigan.

There are indications that rural officials in Michigan are seeking regional-council assistance with greater frequency now than in past years (table 9-5). For example, over 45 percent of the surveyed rural-Michigan officials felt that local governments were more likely "to turn to the regional council for help now than they did three years ago." Only 28.8 percent felt this was "less likely"

Table 9-5
Views about the Dependence of Local Governments on Regional Commissions

Question: In terms of attempting to solve local problems, would you say that local governments are more or less likely to turn to the APDC (or RPO) for help now than they did three years ago?

| | Michigan, Officials, | | | | Georgia, Officials, | | | | Combined | | | |
| | Urban | | Rural | | Urban | | Rural | | Urban | | Rural | |
Responses	Number	Percent-age	Number	Percent-age	Number	Percent-age	Number	Percent-age	Number	Percent-age	Number	Percent-age
More	17	51.5	55	45.5	42	71.2	81	87.1	59	64.1	136	66.7
Same	12	36.4	24	21.6	12	20.3	7	7.5	24	26.1	31	15.2
Less likely	4	12.1	32	28.8	5	8.5	5	5.4	9	9.8	37	18.1
Totals	33	100.0	111	100.0	59	100.0	93	100.0	92	100.0	204	100.0

to occur. However, Georgia officials remained more supportive of regional councils than Michigan officials. Over 87 percent of the rural-Georgia officials felt that local governments were more dependent on regional councils.

Attitudes Regarding Increases in Regional-Council Authority

In general, the majority of Michigan and Georgia officials were supportive of the present powers of regional councils. Most public officials support the advisory and assistance-oriented activities of substate commissions. However, this support did not extend to the notion of *expanding* the authority of regional councils. As indicated in table 9-6, the majority of Georgia and Michigan rural officials did not support the idea of expanding the authority of regional councils in rural areas. More rural Georgia officials supported this idea (48.8 percent) than were opposed to it (35.2 percent). But the number of "neutral" responses (16.5 percent) indicates that this is still an open question in the state of Georgia. As expected, more Michigan rural officials opposed expanding regional authority in rural areas than supported the idea.

Public officials were even less supportive of granting *specific* programmatic control to regional commissions. For example, respondents in this survey were asked to select which programs (from a list of eleven) they felt should be controlled by substate regional councils in their respective states. The programs that received the highest rankings from rural-Georgia officials were: preservation of open spaces (31 percent), air-pollution control (26.4 percent), and recreational development (22.8 percent). Georgia officials were least supportive of regional-council control of programs in: education (1.1 percent), welfare (2.3 percent), and law enforcement (7.6 percent). Overall, Michigan officials were even less supportive of programmatic control than were Georgia officials. Air-pollution control received the highest ranking from rural-Michigan officials (18 percent), followed by preservation of open spaces (15.9 percent) and water-pollution control (14.7 percent). All the other programs received less than 10 percent support from rural Michigan officials (table 9-7).

Clearly, the idea of expanding regional authority and power is opposed by the vast majority of rural public officials. This finding is supported by other surveys of public officials. In 1974 the National Association of Counties surveyed elected public officials throughout the nation regarding the service functions of regional organizations. In that survey, 87 percent of the respondents agreed that regional-council activities should be restricted to an advisory and assistance role.[17] In a similar survey of public officials in three New England cities, Nelson Wikstrom found that public officials were uniformly opposed to granting regional councils "added powers."[18] The consensus of research in this area is that regional councils cannot look to local public officials for support in expanding their programmatic authority or responsibility.

Table 9-6
Expanding the Authority of APDCs and RPOs in Rural Communities

Question: If rural communities (under 10,000 population) are to have any chance of solving their problems, they must give more authority to substate regional organizations (such as APDCs and RPOs).

| | Michigan, Officials, | | | | Georgia, Officials, | | | | Combined | | | |
| | Urban | | Rural | | Urban | | Rural | | Urban | | Rural | |
Responses	*Number*	*Percent-age*	*Number*	*Percent-age*	*Number*	*Percent-age*	*Number*	*Percent-age*	*Number*	*Percent-age*	*Number*	*Percent-age*
Strongly agree	4	11.8	7	5.4	4	6.9	8	8.8	8	8.7	15	6.8
Agree	14	41.2	33	25.6	31	53.4	36	39.6	45	48.9	69	31.4
Neutral	4	11.8	27	20.9	2	3.4	15	16.5	6	6.5	42	19.1
Disagree	10	29.4	38	29.4	13	22.4	25	27.5	23	25.0	63	28.6
Strongly disagree	2	5.9	24	18.6	8	13.8	7	7.7	10	10.9	31	14.1
Totals	34	100.0	129	100.0	58	100.0	91	100.0	92	100.0	220	100.0

Note: Originally reported in Lewis G. Bender, "The Viability of Expanding Substate Regional Control: Urban and Nonmetropolitan Considerations," *Southern Atlantic Urban Studies Journal* (College of Charleston, Charleston, S.C.) 5 (August 1981):116–134.

Table 9-7
Rank Ordering of Public Officials' Responses Regarding Which Program Areas APDCs or RPOs Should Control

Program Area	Combined Rank	Michigan Officials				Georgia Officials			
		Urban		Rural		Urban		Rural	
		Rank	Percentage[a]	Rank	Percentage	Rank	Percentage	Rank	Percentage
Air pollution	1	1	7.0	1	18.0	1	35.3	2	26.4
Preserve open spaces	2	2	5.3	2	15.9	2	30.2	1	31.0
Water pollution	3	3	4.2	3	14.7	3	25.5	4	17.6
Housing	4	7	1.4	4	9.8	4	11.5	5	17.2
Recreational development	5	5	2.0	6	6.6	8	7.1	3	22.8
Sewage treatment	6	5	2.0	5	6.7	6	10.9	6	15.1
Public-health service	7	4	2.7	7	4.7	4	11.5	8	13.2
Zoning	8	8	1.2	10	0.6	7	10.7	7	13.5
Law enforcement	9	10	0.6	10	0.6	10	5.5	9	7.6
Welfare	10	9	3.1	8	0.8	9	5.8	10	2.3
Education	11	11	0.0	9	0.8	11	0.0	11	1.1

[a]Indicates percentage of residents in each category (for example, Michigan–Urban) supporting APDC or RPO control over a program area.

Conclusion: The Prospects for Rural Regionalism

Crystal-ball gazing is always a shaky business. Nonetheless, there are strong indications that the survival of many rural regional councils is in grave peril. The central question is whether states or local governments will attempt to fill the funding void left by the withdrawal of federal dollars. In areas where regional-council activities are viewed as valuable inputs to local-government activities, the future holds some hope. However, in localities where regional activities are viewed with suspicion, the future may be dim.

This study suggests that rural regional commissions have greater support among local public officials for continuing current program activities and services than do their urban counterparts. This could be due in part to the greater need rural governments have for regional-commission expertise and resources. However, this study also suggests that rural regionalism may have a better chance of survival in those states like Georgia where regional commissions have a longer history of service to local governments. In states like Michigan, where the history of regionalism is comparatively short, the prospects are much less promising.

In their classic study of Springdale, New York, Vidich and Bensman point out the propensity of rural-community residents to view "outsiders" with suspicion and distrust.[19] They also note that it may take years, even generations, before outsiders are accepted into the fold of village and small-town life. Most of the nation's rural regional commissions, as in Michigan, were created in the later 1960s as part of Lyndon Johnson's Great Society programs. There is considerable doubt whether these commissions have had enough time to break down the traditional suspicions of rural small-town society. Nonetheless, even if rural commissions have gained the support of rural officials, it remains in question whether local governments will have the resources to support regional activities in a meaningful way.

As indicated previously, rural commissions receive a slightly greater percentage of their funds from state coffers than do metropolitan commissions. Despite the numerous "ifs," this factor could provide a ray of hope for rural regionalism. If the states become the new depository of federal dollars under Reagan's federalism, it could result in increased state funding support for rural regional commissions. However, it is also evident that regional commissions could be placed in the uncomfortable position of competing with member local governments for scarce state funding support. This would constitute a no-win situation for most regional commissions.

Speculation aside, it is clear that without significant increases in funding support from state and/or local governments, surviving regional-commission activities will be dramatically reduced. The irony is that effective regional programming may well die during the time when areawide consolidation of resources is most needed to tackle increasingly complex social and financial problems in rural areas.

Notes

1. Eugene T. Gualco, "Maintains Local Control," *Outlook* (Washington D.C.: National Association of Counties), 24 June 1974, 6-9.

2. Advisory Commission on Intergovernmental Relations (ACIR), *The Challenge of Local Governmental Reorganization*, vol. 3 (Washington, D.C.: U.S. Government Printing Office, February 1974), p. 112.

3. Ibid.

4. Advisory Commission on Intergovernmental Relations, *Regional Decision Making: New Strategies for Substate Districts*, vol. 1 (Washington D.C.: U.S. Government Printing Office, October 1973), p. 260.

5. Ibid., p. 270.

6. Bruce D. McDowell, "Substate Regionalism Matures Gradually," *Intergovernmental Perspective*, vol. 6 (Advisory Commission on Intergovernmental Relations, Fall 1980), pp. 20-26.

7. Vincent Marando, "Metropolitan Research and Councils of Governments," *Midwest Review of Political Science* (January 1971):2-15.

8. Lewis G. Bender, "Georgia Area Planning and Development Commissions: Prospects for the Future," in Charles B. Tyer, ed., *Substate Regionalism in the United States: Perspectives and Issues* (Columbia: University of South Carolina, 1978), p. 41.

9. ACIR, *Regional Decision Making*, p. 270.

10. J.W. Eaton, ed., *Institution Building and Development* (Beverly Hills, Calif.: Sage Publications, 1972); B.W. Honadle, *Capacity Building for Local Governments: An Annotated Bibliography*, Rural Development Research Report no. 28 (Washington D.C.: U.S. Department of Agriculture, Economics and Statistics Service, 1981); George Honadle, "The Art of Fishing Is Not Enough: An Examination of Capacity Building for Rural Development" (Paper presented at the American Society for Public Administration National Conference, April 1981).

11. Honadle, "Art of Fishing."

12. Victor Jones, "Regional Councils and Regional Governments" (Paper presented at the American Society for Public Administration National Conference, April 1981), p. 30.

13. McDowell, "Substate Regionalism," p. 22.

14. J. Norman Reid, *A Statistical Profile of Substate Regional Organizations*, ESS Report no. 8 (Washington, D.C.: U.S. Department of Agriculture, Economics and Statistics Service, May 1981), p. 8.

15. Jones, "Regional Councils," p. 8.

16. The respondents in these surveys are self-described urban and rural residents. In Georgia, selected categories of public officials (mayors, city managers, council members, and so forth) were surveyed in three counties of each of four selected APDCs. The counties were randomly selected from stratified rankings provided by each APDC-county contact within the last year. Georgia respondents were surveyed in the summer and fall of 1976. In Michigan the same study format was used. However, officials were surveyed in two counties in each of two RPOs. Survey instruments were mailed in the spring of 1980. The return response rate was 25.4 percent (168 of 660). Because of space limitations, only a few of the supporting tables are presented.

17. Terry Schuten, *County News*, 16 December 1974, p. 2.

18. Nelson Wikstrom, *Councils of Governments: A Study of Political Incrementalism* (Chicago: Nelson Hall, 1977), pp. 30–33.

19. Arthur J. Vidich and Joseph Bensman, *Small Town in Mass Society: Class, Power and Religion in a Rural Community* (Princeton, N.J.: Princeton University Press, 1958).

**Part IV
Specific Policy Problems**

10 State Land-Use Policies and Rural America

Jan E. Dillard

Industrial expansion, urban growth, and population dispersion are forcing citizens and decision makers to reevaluate policies regarding state development and the future of rural areas. As states face these increasing pressures, government leaders must reassess the importance of rural lands and communities and determine the measures they are willing to take to protect them. Policymakers and citizens alike have begun to realize that land-use policies, or the lack of such policies, will have important implications for the future of rural America.

Land-use policies have traditionally been an area in which only local government had legitimate power. The inability of local governments to handle development problems adequately, however, has resulted in an increased awareness of the need for a broader perspective and greater control in determining land uses. State government has thus become a more legitimate source of decision-making authority in this policy context.

The purpose of this comparative state-policy study is to examine the factors associated with state intervention in land-use decision making. The research investigates a relatively new area of state-policy activity, namely, state land-use policies, in the tradition of comparative state-policy studies. The factors that lead states to intervene actively in land-use decisions will be identified.

The Nature of Land-Use Policies

In the United States, land use has traditionally been an area in which only a minimum of government intervention has been thought necessary or desirable.[1] As industrialization and urbanization increased, controls over land use—such as zoning, building codes, and subdivision regulations—were devised but limited only to that which directly protected the health, safety, and welfare of the community. Regulation of land use has been a local-community concern, and only local government has been considered an appropriate regulator of land development. The only state-government involvement considered legitimate was the adoption of enabling legislation for the local controls.

The failure of local governments to guide planned development resulted in the haphazard scattering of growth and the loss of natural resources. The lack of comprehensive planning and the failure to coordinate government programs often led to serious development problems. The shortcomings of these past policies encouraged many to reevaluate the appropriate role of state government in guiding the use of land.

135

Land-Use Research and Comparative State-Policy Studies

Because land-use policies have historically been the concern of local governments, the assertion of authority in land use by state governments has been called by Bosselman and Callies the "quiet revolution" in land-use controls.[2] Since Hawaii adopted a statewide land-use law in 1961, conceptions of the appropriate role of state government in land-use decisions have changed rapidly. Many states, including Vermont, Florida, and California as well as Hawaii, have passed innovative laws allowing the state government a direct role in guiding land use. These laws have covered such areas as the classification of all state land, mandatory local comprehensive planning, tax incentives for agricultural lands, and the regulation of activities in environmentally sensitive areas.

Numerous research efforts have been undertaken to clarify the implications of the changing state role in land use.[3] Since Bosselman and Callies called attention to the role of the state in guiding land use, various research surveys have attempted to document the acceptance of the state policies, whereas other studies have tried to explain the factors that led to their adoption.[4] Research seeking to identify the determinants of land-use policies has relied primarily on the case-study approach, however. These case studies usually examine selected states and the process associated with the adoption of certain land-use policies.[5] Very little systematic research has been conducted across all fifty U.S. states regarding the factors associated with the adoption of state land policies.[6]

Comparative state-policy studies, on the other hand, have applied a systematic and comprehensive analysis to the investigation of state-policy determinants.[7] Of key interest to policy researchers is the identification of variables that explain why certain policies are adopted by state governments. The comparative state-policy studies incorporate an analysis of all fifty states and have focused on the debate over whether social and economic factors explain more of the variation in policy acceptance than political factors do. The research of Dawson and Robinson became a landmark in state-policy study by questioning the explanatory value of political forces on policy outputs.[8] Their findings have resulted in a growing body of literature that seeks to demonstrate the relative importance of socioeconomic and political variables in determining state outputs.[9] The debate has resulted in an inconclusive discussion of the independent importance of political forces in the state-policy adoption process.

Research Design

This chapter seeks to determine why some state governments have become directly involved in determining how the land of the state is used. What factors account for the differences in the extent of this state intervention? Do socioeconomic factors account for more of the variation in policy acceptance than political factors do? To analyze the reassertion of state authority in land-use decision making, fourteen state land-use policies were examined (see appendix 10A). The acceptance of these policies is based on data collected by the American Institute of Planners and is compiled from secondary sources prepared by the states in conjunction with the 701 Housing and Urban Development (HUD) program.[10] The policies documented are those in operation by the time of the 1975 Overall Program Design (OPD) stipulated by HUD.

The policies chosen represent the broad context of state land involvement but by no means include all such policies. The policies were selected on the basis of three criteria: (1) each is applicable to all fifty states; (2) each has been adopted by at least three states; and (3) each has been the subject of previous land-use research. To determine the factors associated with a state's acceptance of this new role, a composite score of the fourteen land policies was derived for each of the fifty states. The score is a simple additive index of the total number of laws adopted by a given state. Each of the fifty states is thus identified by a specific composite score. These scores represent each state's acceptance of the state's role in land-use decision making (table 10-1). States with higher scores have accepted state government as a more legitimate source of authority in land-use decision making.

The independent variables used in analyzing the adoption of these policies include those factors consistently recognized as influential in policy determination and considered theoretically relevant to explaining state land-use involvement. In the tradition of the comparative state-policy studies, the variables are classified into two basic categories: socioeconomic factors and political-system factors. Previous studies have found these forces to have varying importance in determining policy outputs, and this analysis seeks to explain their relative impact on state land-use intervention.

The analytical techniques employed in this investigation include simple and partial correlation as well as multiple regression analysis. These techniques make it possible to relate individual variables to policy outputs, to quantify the relative strengths of the association, and to determine the extent to which we can explain the variation in these policy adoptions by a given set of factors.

Social and Economic Forces

Previous research in both land-use studies and comparative state-policy studies has emphasized the importance of social and economic forces such as urbanization, industrialization, and income in determining the outputs of state government.[11] As urbanization and industrialization increase, state and local governments face land-use decisions related to the loss of prime farmland, degradation of the natural environment, and destruction of open spaces and amenities previously enjoyed by the public.[12]

Table 10-1
Composite Scores of State Land-Use Involvement

State	Composite Score	State	Composite Score
Alabama	3	Montana	7
Alaska	5	Nebraska	4
Arizona	3	Nevada	7
Arkansas	5	New Hampshire	5
California	9	New Jersey	10
Colorado	11	New Mexico	4
Connecticut	10	New York	5
Delaware	9	North Carolina	5
Florida	11	North Dakota	4
Georgia	5	Ohio	4
Hawaii	7	Oklahoma	3
Idaho	7	Oregon	11
Illinois	6	Pennsylvania	6
Indiana	7	Rhode Island	8
Iowa	3	South Carolina	6
Kansas	5	South Dakota	10
Kentucky	8	Tennessee	6
Louisiana	6	Texas	8
Maine	6	Utah	11
Maryland	12	Vermont	11
Massachusetts	10	Virginia	8
Michigan	5	Washington	11
Minnesota	10	West Virginia	4
Mississippi	4	Wisconsin	7
Missouri	5	Wyoming	5

Note: The composite score is a simple additive index of the total number of laws adopted by each state.

Support for the importance of socioeconomic forces in state land use is found in much of the land-use research.[13] Various land-use studies have asserted that the drive behind the state legislature to assert power in land-use decisions often may evolve from such social and economic issues as rapid increases in population, the extensive growth of urban areas, and the related loss of agricultural lands. The state assertion may also be the result of a perception of threatened environmental resources such as the rapid loss of natural coastal areas, the drainage of wetland areas, and the destruction of visual environmental amenities.

Evidence supporting the importance of socioeconomic factors is rather extensive. For example, Robert Healy notes that along previously undeveloped parts of the California coast, ranches, artichoke fields, and the like have been converted to new urban areas complete with shopping centers, office buildings, and industrial facilities.[14] Luther Carter points out that in Florida the increasing number of high-rise condominiums, planned-unit developments, and residential clusters has led to rapid increases in the population.[15] Nelson Rosenbaum has emphasized the differences in relative growth pressures as a prime factor in the difference between eastern- and western-state acceptance of state growth-management practices.[16] Additional evidence for the importance of socioeconomic factors is provided by Godschalk and the Council of State Governments, who point to the impact of tourists and second-home development in Vermont's acceptance of comprehensive land-use policies.[17]

The comparative state-policy studies likewise present support for social and economic variables as key determinants of state policies. A major aspect of the debate in the comparative state-policy research has been establishing evidence that socioeconomic variables are more highly associated with state-government outputs than political factors are. Dye's collection of social and economic variables accounted for 59 percent of the variance in a collection of various state policies.[18] Sharkansky and Hofferbert explained 68 percent of the variance in state-highway–natural-resource policies with socioeconomic factors.[19] Cnudde and McCrone found in their analysis of welfare policies that socioeconomic factors were considerably important for old-age-assistance policies and per-pupil education expenditures.[20]

From the findings of the comparative state-policy research and the land-use literature, it is expected that the acceptance of state involvement and the extent of that involvement may well be determined by certain social and economic forces within the state. Population growth, urban development, level of income, and growing industrialization are expected to exert pressures on both the citizenry and the governmental institutions that lead to changing conceptions of state involvement in land-use decisions. Therefore, the following hypotheses are proposed:

1. States with higher levels of income, education, urbanization, and industrialization will more likely exhibit state involvement in land-use policies.
2. States with greater population-growth rates will be more likely to adopt state land-use policies.

Those states with the higher composite scores should be the states with greater population growth, more growth in urban areas, higher levels of industrialization, and greater affluence. As such factors increase, state government is expected to assume a greater responsibility for managing the resulting by-products of such socioeconomic forces.

Findings

The data revealed only partial support for the expectations. Three socioeconomic variables were found to be significant determinants of state composite scores: population growth, urban population, and industrial growth (table 10–2).

Table 10–2
Socioeconomic Variables Associated with State Land-Use Involvement

Variable	r	Beta	R^2	F
Population growth	0.4755	1.2771	0.2261	22.383
Urban population	0.2405	−0.5047	0.2474	6.285
Industrial growth	0.0928	−0.7785	0.3199	12.091

Note: The full equation of these three variables yields an R^2 of 0.3199 with an F value of 8.936 at the .05 level of significance.

As expected, population growth was a most important socioeconomic force behind the state composite scores. Strongly correlated with total involvement, population growth accounted for more than one standard unit change in the composite score (β = 1.2771). It seems quite likely that the pressures of population growth will encourage state policymakers to reassert the state into land-use decisions. When entered into a separate equation, population growth alone explains 23 percent of the variation in the composite scores.

However, high urbanization and growing industrialization seem to discourage state intervention in land-use decisions. In fact, our investigation reveals that a state's total involvement in land use declines as the level of urban population increases (β = −0.5047) and as industrial growth increases (β = −0.7785). A state with a large urban population and much industrial growth is not likely to be one to assert state government into land-use decision making.

There are several possible explanations for these findings. One is that the states that are asserting state government into land use may be those that have traditionally been rural states. These states have not yet experienced great increases in urban growth, and industry has not yet arrived in full force. Yet these states are experiencing population growth, which may be great relative to past population levels. The rural character of these states is being threatened, and state government is a mechanism for controlling future use of state lands.

Another explanation may be that the collinearity among the independent variables disguises the true contribution of each factor. Population growth has a rather high correlation with urbanization (r = 0.5595) and industrial growth (r = 0.6688). Factors other than social and economic forces may also intervene. Such factors could influence both the independent variables and the explanation of the dependent variables. Therefore, attention is directed to investigating other factors that may affect a state's involvement in land use.

Political Factors

In the continuing debate over the determinants of state policy, certain researchers still emphasize the importance of political variables in determining the adoption of state policies.[21] The extent of total state involvement in land use may be in part the result of various political forces acting within the state.

Land-use studies have pointed to the importance of certain political variables—specifically, the power and independence of local governments within the state. Healy and Godschalk point out that in areas where local government does not have sufficient resources to assert control over growth, the state government is more likely to intervene in land-use decisions.[22] Those states in which local governments have established regulations sufficient to regulate development will be less likely to experience a great deal of intervention by the state government. Such intervention will be opposed by local government. Stronger local governments will object to state regulations as a usurpation of local power. Where local government is stronger, representation of this strength should be evident in the state legislature, and this representation should oppose the adoption of state-level land-use laws. Thus, those states with greater state involvement in land use should be those with less local-government independence. The strength of local government is believed to be a viable factor in determining state land involvement; therefore, the following hypothesis is examined:

3. As the strength of local government declines in relation to total government responsibility, the state government will be more likely to adopt state land-use laws.

The earlier comparative state-policy studies found such forces as interparty competition and electoral participation to be important in determining state-policy adoption. Interparty competition and electoral participation represent the political system's ability to allow full expression of competing ideas. Consequently, the following relationships are predicted:

4. States with greater interparty competition and higher electoral participation will be more likely to adopt state land-use policies.

Legislative professionalism affects the organization and effectiveness of the state lawmaking body. The degree of professionalism should have an influence on the ability of the state legislature to challenge established policies. Thus the following hypothesis is advanced:

5. The more professionalized state legislatures will be more likely to adopt state land-use policies.

Past acceptance of new ideas indicates the willingness of a state to evaluate policy changes. State land-use laws require the state government to assert its authority in a relatively new policy area, one previously reserved for local government. It is expected that the more innovative states will adopt land policies. Consequently, the following hypothesis is proposed:

6. States that have been innovative in the past will more likely adopt state
    land-use policies.

Also important to the assertion of state government in land use is previous
state involvement in such policies. Sharkansky and Cowart contend that state
governments are more likely to adopt policies that do not represent a sharp
departure from existing policies.[23] Participation in state environmental programs
should indicate a state's willingness to address concerns related to natural-
resource protection. As a result. The following hypothesis is investigated,

7. States with proportionately higher state expenditures for environmental
    programs will be more likely to adopt state land-use policies.

These environmental expenditures represent incremental extensions of existing policy, and land-use adoption should be positively associated with such
extensions.

Findings

The findings of this study revealed that the political factors important to state-
policy adoption include the state's previous innovativeness, policy incrementalism, and the strength of local governments within the state (table 10-3). No
support exists, however, for the independent significance of the more traditional
electoral variables. The variables that do contribute to an understanding of the
composite scores seem to be founded on previous policy adoption and the
strength of local government.

Related to a state's previous policy acceptance, an important factor seems
to be state innovativeness. A state's propensity for new ideas does carry over to
the area of state land policies. The innovativeness of a state appears to be a
prime contributor to the determination of state land involvement ($\beta = 0.6052$).

Table 10-3
Political Variables Associated with State Land-Use Involvement

Variable	r	Beta	R^2	F
Policy incrementalism	0.2769	0.4535	0.0767	10.008
Innovation score	0.3306	0.6052	0.2163	13.830
Local-government strength	−0.0007	−0.4109	0.3260	6.188

Note: The full equation of these three variables yields an R^2 of 0.3260 with an F value of
6.1271 at the .05 level of significance.

The findings of this study also provide support for the contention of earlier studies that policies are more likely to be accepted when they are incremental extensions of existing policies. The extent to which state government is already committed to protecting natural resources is highly associated with a state's involvement in land-use decisions. As policy incrementalism increased, so did the state composite score ($\beta = 0.4535$).

The strength of local government is also important to a state's acceptance of land-use involvement. It seems that when local government is stronger, land-use regulation at the state level decreases. As predicted, the evidence revealed that the greater the local strength, the less likely a state will be to intervene in land use ($\beta = -0.4109$). States with greater intervention are those in which there is no great opposing force from local areas.

The research offered no support for the independent importance of electoral-system variables. Such factors as interparty competition, electoral participation, and legislative professionalism were found not to be significant factors. State land-use policies do not seem to be the product of partisan, electoral variables as much as they are related to previous policies, innovativeness, and local independence.

These findings should be noted with some caution. The multicollinearity among the political variables may influence the results of this research. Although the study attempted to reduce any high degree of interdependence among the independent variables by eliminating those pairs of political variables that had correlations above .7000, multicollinearity may be affecting the findings. A state's innovativeness is rather highly related to interparty competition, local-government expenditures, and legislative professionalism. The importance of this one variable may be inflated, and the contribution of other variables may be less significant because of the interdependence. Future research efforts not only must seek to clarify the appropriate measures of the political forces but also must attempt to reduce the interdependence among the variables being used in the research effort.

Conclusions

The overall acceptance of land-use laws by state governments has occurred at quite different rates. This chapter has investigated the variables associated with greater overall acceptance of such laws. To fulfill this objective, the investigation has examined the composite state scores for fourteen land-use laws and attempted to single out their most important determinants. The purpose of this study has been to identify those variables that contribute the greatest explanation to the state variations in this relatively new area of state policy.

This examination of the determinants of state involvement reveals that both socioeconomic factors and political factors provide significant contributions to explaining total state involvement in land-use decisions. When tested separately, population growth, urbanization, and industrialization are significant socioeconomic contributors, whereas policy incrementalism, state innovativeness, and local-government autonomy provide important political explanations for total state involvement in land use. The equation was also examined in which the three socioeconomic variables and the three political variables previously found to be important were entered together. The results of this investigation, as summarized in table 10–4, reveal that three variables alone explain 43 percent of the variation in the state composite scores. These variables include population growth, industrial growth, and local-government expenditures.

The prime contributor of state land use appears to be population growth. This one growth variable accounts for the greatest amount of change in the state composite scores (β = 1.0185) and alone explains 23 percent of the variance. These findings suggest that the areas most likely to assert state government into land-use decisions are those experiencing increases in the state's population. This population growth, however, is not concentrated in the urban, industrial areas. The areas asserting state government into land use are those experiencing an influx of people, but whose growth is not in the industrial centers.

State intervention is also associated with a lack of local autonomy. The reassertion of the state in land use seems to occur where there is no strong local force to oppose the reassertion, whether that force is industrialization or local government. Consequently, strong centers of local growth do not exist to oppose the assertion of state government in the traditionally local policy area of land-use decisions. State government has become the viable mechanism for controlling growth-related impacts.

Again, note the problem of multicollinearity. The two socioeconomic variables and one political variable that are found to be important in the final equation are interrelated with some of the other independent variables. Many variables that fell out of the equation at the .05 level of significance may be related to the final three significant variables. These interrelationships could affect the strength of the explanations accounted for by the three variables.

Table 10–4
Determinants of State Land-Use Involvement

Variable	r	Beta	R^2	F
Population growth	0.4755	1.0185	0.2261	28.485
Industrial growth	0.0905	−0.5518	0.3166	10.272
Local-government strength	−0.0007	−0.3993	0.4334	7.828

Note: The full equation of these three variables yields an R^2 of 0.4334 with an F value of 11.477 at the .05 level of significance.

Nevertheless, almost one-half of the variation in total state involvement is explained by identifying these variables (R^2 = 0.43349). Of these factors, the most significant contribution is provided by the state's population growth. States experiencing increasing population growth may turn to the state government to guide future uses of the state's lands. Yet such a move occurs when the population growth is not associated wtih the development of urban, industrial centers and when local governments are not strong enough to oppose the state intervention.

Government policies regarding the use of land may very well determine the future of the U.S. farming system, the preservation of agricultural areas, and the character of rural communities. The adoption of new policies or the absence of any government direction will directly affect how lands are to be used. Increasing industrial growth, expanding urban and suburban areas, and growing populations will require both citizens and their government leaders to reevaluate the priorities of state growth and the future of rural areas. The protection of U.S. farming resources and the preservation of rural communities will greatly depend on the land-use policies we now establish.

Notes

1. U.S. Senate, *Land Use Policy and Planning Assistance Act,* Report no. 93-107 (Washington, D.C.: U.S. Government Printing Office, 1973), p. 72.

2. Fred Bosselman and David Callies, *The Quiet Revolution in Land Use Control* (Washington, D.C.: U.S. Government Printing Office, 1971).

3. For an overview of these efforts see: Elaine Moss, ed., *Land Use Controls in the United States: Handbook on the Legal Rights of Citizens* (New York: Dial Press/James Wade, 1977); Nelson Rosenbaum, *Land Use and the State Legislature: The Politics of State Innovation* (Washington, D.C.: Urban Institute, 1976); Robert Healy, *Land Use and the States* (Baltimore, Md.: Johns Hopkins University Press for Resources for the Future, 1976); William K. Reilly, ed., *The Use of Land: A Citizen's Policy Guide to Urban Growth* (New York: Thomas Y. Crowell, 1973).

4. For a sample of this literature see: James Coffin and Michael Arnold, eds., *A Summary of State Land Use Controls* (Washington, D.C.: Plus Publications, 1974); Council of State Governments, *The Land Use Puzzle* (Lexington, Ky.: Council of State Governments, 1974); Leslie C. Hyde, *State Land-Use Laws in the Northeast: A Compendium and Classification of Selected Statutes* (Ithaca, N.Y.: Northeast Regional Center for Rural Development, 1975); U.S. Senate, Committee on Interior and Insular Affairs, *State Land Use Programs: Summaries of Land Use Regulations in Eight States,* and *A 50-State Survey of State Land Use Controls,* 93rd Congress, 2nd Session (Washington, D.C.: U.S. Government Printing Office, 1974.

5. Such case studies include: Luther J. Carter, *The Florida Experience: Land and Water Policy for a Growth State* (Baltimore, Md.: Johns Hopkins University Press for Resources for the Future, 1974); Elizabeth Haskell and Victoria S. Price, *State Environmental Management: Case Studies of Nine States* (New York: Praeger, 1973); Charles E. Little, *The New Oregon Trail* (Washington, D.C.: Conservation Foundation, 1976); Phyllis Meyers, *Slow Start in Paradise* (Washington, D.C.: Conservation Foundation, 1976); Phyllis Meyers, *So Goes Vermont* (Washington, D.C.: Conservation Foundation, 1976).

6. One attempt at a more comprehensive analysis is offered by Nelson Rosenbaum, *Land Use and the Legislatures: The Politics of State Innovation* (Washington, D.C.: Urban Institute, 1976).

7. For an overview of the comparative state-policy studies and recent directions in the research area, see: Thomas R. Dye and Virginia H. Gray, eds., "Symposium on Determinants of Public Policy: Cities, States, and Nations," *Policy Studies Journal* (1979):652-803.

8. Richard E. Dawson and James A. Robinson, "Inter-Party Competition, Economic Variables and Welfare Policies in the American States," *Journal of Politics* 25(1963):265-289; Thomas R. Dye, *Politics, Economics and the Public: Policy Outcomes in the American States* (Chicago: Rand McNally, 1966); Richard I. Hofferbert, "The Relation between Public Policy and Some Structural and Environmental Variables in the American States," *American Political Science Review* 60(1966):73-82; Michael S. Lewis-Beck, "The Relative Importance of Socioeconomic and Political Variables for Public Policy," *American Political Science Review* 71(1977):559-566.

9. Ira Sharkansky and Richard I. Hofferbert, "Dimensions of State Politics, Economics, and Public Policy," *American Political Science Review* 63 (1969):867-899; Brian R. Fry and Richard F. Winters, "The Politics of Redistribution," *American Political Science Review* 64(1970):508-522; Andrew T. Cowart, "Anti-Poverty Expenditures of the American States: A Comparative Analysis," *Midwest Journal of Political Science* 13(1969):219-236; Ira Sharkansky, *Spending in the American States* (Chicago: Rand McNally, 1968).

10. American Institute of Planners, *Survey of State Land Use Planning Activity* (Washington, D.C.: U.S. Government Printing Office, 1976).

11. Dawson and Robinson, "Inter-Party Competition"; Dye, *Politics*; Hofferbert, "Public Policy and Some Variables"; Lewis-Beck, "Socioeconomic and Political Variables"; Bosselman and Callies, *Quiet Revolution*; Healy, *Land Use*; Reilly, *Use of Land*; and Rosenbaum, *Land Use*.

12. A. Allan Schmid, *Converting Land from Rural to Urban Uses* (Baltimore, Md.: Johns Hopkins University Press for Resources for the Future, 1968); Healy, *Land Use*.

13. Carter, *Florida Experience*; Healy, *Land Use*; and Bosselman and Callies, *Quiet Revolution*.

14. Healy, *Land Use*.

15. Ibid.; for other information on Florida's policies see Carter, *Florida Experience*.

16. Rosenbaum, *Land Use*.

17. David R. Godschalk, "State Growth Management: A Carrying Capacity Policy" in Randall W. Scott, ed., *Management and Control of Growth*, vol. III (Washington, D.C.: Urban Institute, 1975); Council of State Governments, "State Housing Actions: Programs and Alternatives," in Randall W. Scott, ed., *Management and Control of Growth*, vol. III (Washington, D.C.: Urban Institute, 1975).

18. Dye, *Politics*.

19. Sharkansky and Hofferbert, "Dimensions of State Politics."

20. Charles F. Cnudde and Donald J. McCrone, "Party Competition and Welfare Policies in the American States," *American Political Science Review* 63(1969):1118–1124.

21. Sharkansky, *Spending*; Cowart, "Anti-Poverty Expenditures"; Edward T. Jennings, "Competition, Constituencies and Welfare Policies in the American States," *American Political Science Review* 73(1979):414–429.

22. Healy, *Land Use*; Godschalk, "State Growth Management."

23. Sharkansky, *Spending*; Cowart, "Anti-Poverty Expenditures."

Appendix 10A:
Dependent Variables
Analyzed

State land-use planning program: Denotes the existence of a statewide program operated for the explicit purpose of influencing decisions as to how land is used.

State economic-development program: Denotes the existence of a comprehensive economic-development program, including a state mechanism for identifying agency activities designed to accomplish economic-development objectives.

State capital-development program: Denotes a formal state mechanism for coordinating capital development in the state with state growth policies.

State critical-areas-designation program: Denotes the existence of a program for designating geographic areas of critical state concern and that such designation indicates some state involvement.

State environmental-impact-statement process: Denotes that the state has established a program for reviewing the environmental impact of state actions.

Differential tax assessment: Denotes that the state provides for differential tax assessment for certain types of land use.

Regulation of developments of greater than local impact: Denotes action in designating certain types of development to be of greater than local impact and the establishment of state review of such projects.

Umbrella agency: Denotes the existence of a single agency responsible for preparing at least three different functional plans.

Review of functional plans: Denotes the existence of a requirement (legislative or executive) that all functional plans be reviewed through some central mechanism.

Areawide planning organization: Denotes that the state has authorized the existence of areawide planning organizations.

Local review of state plans: Denotes the existence within the state of a formal process by which local governments or areawide planning organizations have an opportunity to provide input into state functional plans.

149

Required process for local planning: Denotes that the state has prescribed specific procedures or contents for local or areawide planning organizations.

Futures commission: Denotes the existence of a specific commission charged with the responsibility of developing a state growth policy.

Executive-branch policy-adoption plan/review process: Denotes the existence of an established unit within the executive branch with the responsibility and capacity for examining the future of the state and evaluating the long-term impact of proposals and programs.

11 Housing Vouchers for Rural America

Daniel M. Ebels and
Harriet Newburger

In the fall of 1981 the President's Commission on Housing concluded that the housing needs of low-income Americans could best be met through a system of vouchers, or direct-transfer payments, earmarked for housing. Receipt of a voucher would be conditioned on a household's dwelling unit meeting prescribed standards of physical adequacy.[1] The commission's recommendation is the strongest reflection to date of a shift in emphasis by policymakers from supply-oriented housing programs to demand-oriented programs as the best means to provide low-income families with decent, affordable housing. Most previous housing programs have directly attempted to increase the stock of physically adequate housing available to low-income households. To do so, these programs have in effect attached housing subsidies to particular housing units. Housing vouchers, on the other hand, aim directly to increase the ability of low-income households to purchase adequate housing; subsidies are attached to households rather than to dwelling units. The commission's call for a large-scale demand-oriented program has been foreshadowed by the continuing Experimental Housing Allowance Program (EHAP), which began in 1972 and was sponsored by HUD to test the impact of housing vouchers and by HUD's Section 8 existing-housing program, which began in 1974 and has many features in common with a housing-voucher program.

In making its recommendation, the Housing Commission implicitly accepts two rationales for government provision of housing assistance to low-income households that also appear to underlie supply-side programs. First, housing is treated as a merit good, in the sense that society believes that all households should consume some minimum level of housing services. Second, policy reflects a belief that decent housing should be affordable, in the sense that its purchase does not unduly constrain the purchase of other necessities.

Proponents of housing vouchers have argued for their relative effectiveness in meeting these goals on both efficiency and equity grounds. From an efficiency standpoint, they point out that the overall quality of the housing stock has improved dramatically over the past few decades; they argue that the principal housing problem of the low-income household is not its ability to find physically adequate housing, but to find such housing at a price it can afford.[2] Therefore, demand-side subsidies are well suited to the nature of today's low-income housing needs, and the increased ability of the low-income group to pay for housing services should stimulate a correction of the relatively minor maintenance problems that today are the key source of inadequacy in the low-income housing stock.

Housing vouchers are also felt to be more efficient because the subsidy to allow a low-income household to find physically adequate housing in the private sector would be much lower than the subsidy required to provide and maintain a subsidized unit for that household. Moreover, administration of a system of housing vouchers would be far simpler than administration of the current vast array of housing programs. For the low-income household, housing vouchers would also be more efficient since they would provide greater flexibility than supply-side programs do in choosing the type and amount of housing to consume.

From an equity standpoint, it is argued that because of the lower subsidy needed per household, housing vouchers could serve a larger percentage of low-income households than the relatively small percentage who currently live in subsidized housing units. Moreover, a housing-voucher system could be better targeted to the neediest families; costs associated with the construction and maintenance of new subsidized units today mean that often the rents are too high for the poorest families. Finally, housing vouchers are suited to meet the needs of both owners and renters, whereas supply-side programs are largely focused on renters.

But although these are strong arguments for the effectiveness of housing vouchers relative to supply-side housing programs, they must also be viewed as being somewhat abstract in the absence of an actual large-scale housing-voucher program. In practice, relative effectiveness will depend on the actual structure of a housing-voucher program and so on the available capacity to carry out different types of housing programs. The level of funding for housing programs also assumes particular importance in determining relative effectiveness at a time of general contraction in the fiscal resources available for social programs. Finally, it should be noted that arguments for the superiority of housing vouchers are based on national data on the nature and extent of housing need and on a perception of an average national experience with supply-side housing programs. To the extent that the aggregate national picture of the country does not hold for particular subparts, arguments about the relative effectiveness of housing vouchers may have to be adjusted.

For rural America this final point assumes particular importance. Rural U.S. communities have a wide range of experience with existing housing programs; they also have a disproportionate share of the nation's low-income households and of its substandard housing. The impact of a switch from existing housing programs to housing vouchers is, therefore, potentially high here. Yet too often the national experience with government housing programs and the urban experience with these programs have been equated; in turn, the potential impacts of a switch to housing vouchers have not, for the most part, been evaluated from a rural point of view. Carrying out a preliminary evaluation of this type is the goal of this chapter.

The Nature and Extent of Rural Housing Need

Housing need has traditionally been measured along two dimensions— inadequacy of physical structure and inadequacy caused by overcrowding. Recently a third measure of housing need—the inability to afford physically adequate housing for some specified percentage of income (usually 25 percent—has also been considered. Along the first of these dimensions, structural inadequacy, rural housing need is more severe than that of the United States as a whole. For example, table 11–1 shows that although housing conditions have improved dramatically throughout the country since 1960 in terms of the drop in percentage of houses lacking complete plumbing, rural households were more likely to live in housing that was inadequate according to this measure; in 1970, 16.9 percent of rural housing lacked some plumbing; the corresponding figure in urban areas was 3.4 percent.

Data for 1976 from the Annual Housing Survey, undertaken for HUD by the Census Bureau, provide more detailed information on structural inadequacies

Table 11–1
Housing Characteristics

	All Housing			Black Housing		
	Total	*Urban*	*Rural*	*Total*	*Urban*	*Rural*
United States (1970)						
Total population (millions)	203.2	149.3	53.9	22.6	18.4	4.2
Percentage units without complete plumbing	6.9	3.4	16.9	16.8	8.5	62.3
Percentage occupied units with more than one person per room	8.2	7.6	10.1	19.9	18.1	30.1
Percentage owner occupied	62.9	58.4	76.2	41.6	38.8	56.6
South (1970)						
Total population (millions)	62.8	40.5	22.2	12.0	8.1	3.9
Percentage units without complete plumbing	11.9	4.8	25.1	29.1	14.4	65.1
Percentage occupied units with more than one person per room	10.3	9.1	12.6	24.3	21.6	31.0
Percentage owner occupied	64.7	60.1	73.5	46.9	43.2	56.1
United States (1950)						
Percentage units without complete plumbing	35.4	20.0	62.8			

Sources: U.S. Bureau of Census, *1970 Census of Housing,* vol. I, part 1, tables 2, 7; *1950 Census of Housing,* vol. I, part 1, table 7.

in the U.S. housing stock (see table 11–2). Although these data suggest that rural housing continues to improve, they also indicate that those structural problems that remain tend to be qualitatively different from problems in the urban housing stock. Whereas maintenance problems were the major cause for classifying urban dwellings as physically unsound, rural dwellings were more likely to be categorized this way because of lack of complete plumbing or complete kitchens, or lack of sewage systems. Moreover, rural dwelling units were more likely to have multiple flaws. In short, the nature of structural rural housing problems is such that they are likely to cost more to correct than urban housing problems.

Rural housing need is also greater than urban need when measured along the other two dimensions described earlier. Rural dwelling units are more likely to have more than one occupant per room than are urban dwelling units (10.1 percent and 7.6 percent respectively in 1970). Moreover, on the basis of Annual Housing Survey Data, it is estimated that 80 percent of U.S. households could find adequate housing for 25 percent or less of their incomes, whereas in rural areas only 74 percent of households would be able to do so.[3] This latter finding is not surprising, given rural America's disproportionate share of households living below the poverty level.

Finally, a few points about the distribution of housing need among subgroups of the rural population are important as background to understanding the ability of housing vouchers to meet this need. First, although table 11–1 indicates that rural residents are more likely to own their homes than are urban residents, owner-occupied homes are more likely to be substandard in rural areas than in urban areas. For example, the share of owner-occupied substandard housing is 45 percent of total substandard units, compared with a 25 percent share in metropolitan areas.[4] Second, Annual Housing Survey Data indicate that in 1977, 12 percent of elderly rural households lived in physically deficient housing units.[5] Although this percentage is about the same as for nonelderly

Table 11–2
Units with Flaw as Percentage of Total Units

	National	All Rural Units	Rural White Units	Rural Black Units
Plumbing	2.6	5.6	4.0	31.1
Kitchen	1.8	3.3	2.0	24.1
Maintenance	4.1	4.0	3.2	15.6
Sewage disposal	1.3	4.2	2.9	26.0
Percentage of flawed units with more than one major flaw	26.4	43.7	35.8	74.7

Source: *How Well Are We Housed? 5: Rural* (Washington, D.C.: Department of Housing and Urban Development n.d.), tables 4, 5, 8, 9.

rural households, it is of particular concern because the ability of the elderly to move or to upgrade their homes may vary from that of the population as a whole. Moreover, the elderly are far more likely than the rest of the rural population to have housing needs related to housing affordability. The third point about the distribution of housing need within rural areas is that although rural areas in general have a disproportionately high level of housing need compared to urban areas, rural housing need is particularly concentrated in the South and, within the South, particularly concentrated among black households (see tables 11-1 and 11-2). The incidence of substandard housing conditions among blacks is due in part to a high incidence of poverty; however, it is also likely that discrimination in rural housing markets has limited black access to physically adequate housing. Recent studies by Stegman and Sumka and by Marantz, Case, and Leonard have documented extreme racial segmentation in nonmetropolitan housing markets.[6] The extent to which black households have access to physically adequate housing will be important in determining how effectively a housing-voucher system can serve rural housing needs.

The Rural Experience with Subsidized Housing Programs

Of the three major subsidized housing programs operating in rural areas, two are directed by HUD and the third is directed by the Farmer's Home Administration (FmHA). Under the first of these, public housing—which is the oldest of subsidized housing programs and which began in 1937—HUD subsidizes both the production and operation of housing projects; tenants pay a fixed percentage of their income in rent. Program development and administration are in the hands of Local Housing Authorities (LHAs) whose existence is authorized by state legislative action; they are largely independent of local government. As of 1979, 266,846 units were occupied in nonmetropolitan areas.[7] (Whenever possible, statistics for "truly rural" communities—that is, those with populations under 2,500—will be provided. Rural communities are located in both metropolitan and nonmetropolitan areas, although the majority of the rural population lives outside of metropolitan areas. When rural figures are not available, nonmetropolitan figures are used.)

HUD's second program, Section 8, authorized by the Housing and Community Development Act of 1974, actually has three components. Under the first two components, New Construction and Substantial Rehabilitation, developers provide rental housing using financing from private or other public sources, and HUD guarantees that it will provide rent supplements for a fixed period of time for tenants living in a percentage of the project's units. Rent supplements, which are thus attached to particular dwelling units, are based on the difference between a percentage of the tenant's income and a HUD-determined "fair market rent" for the unit. The third component of Section 8,

Existing Housing, is a completely demand-oriented subsidy. Households accepted into the program (with acceptance determined on the basis of income and the number of program slots available) receive a rent supplement (equal to the difference between a fixed percentage of their income and their rent, or the fair market rent for their area, whichever is less) if they live in or move to units meeting specified physical standards. Section 8 existing housing is administered by LHAs, whereas the other two components are administered by HUD area offices. In response to the program, a large number of new LHAs have been established at county, regional, or state levels. Through 1979, 189,276 units of Section 8 housing had been built or were in process in nonmetropolitan areas under the new-construction and substantial-rehabilitation program;[8] and 111,289 households were being served in 1979 under the existing-housing component.[9]

Finally, the FmHA Section 515 program loans money to public and private profit and nonprofit groups to purchase, rehabilitate, or construct housing for elderly and low- and moderate-income households. Depending on the nature of the sponsor, loans may be made at below-market interest rates. Through 1979, 191,578 units of housing had been provided.[10] Section 515 may be used in tandem with Section 8 subsidies from HUD.

HUD, FmHA, and other agencies also run a number of additional smaller-scale programs that make housing aid available to both low-income home owners and renters. Congress has stipulated that 20–25 percent of available monies for Section 8, public housing, and a number of other HUD programs are to be allocated to nonmetropolitan areas; it has been estimated that the nonmetropolitan share has been closer to 20 than 25 percent.[11] Within nonmetropolitan areas, funds are allocated to counties using a formula designed to reflect level of housing need. Within counties, allocations among programs are based on overall local demand; developers or LHAs with housing proposals compete for funding. FmHA funds have generally been allocated on a first-come, first-serve basis.

These brief profiles of the three major housing programs serving rural America suggest that a number of features of the housing-delivery system may limit its ability to address rural housing need. These features include the following:

*Fragmentation of Responsibility for Rural Housing Programs
among Government Agencies*

A 1978 report by a HUD-sponsored task force on rural and nonmetropolitan areas described a lack of coordination between HUD and FmHA in targeting housing aid to the most distressed areas.[12] Field offices for FmHA and for HUD cover different geographical areas; moreover, HUD and FmHA use different record-keeping procedures and identify communities by different codes. Both these problems inhibit coordination, and the latter problem is particularly vexing because it is extremely difficult to trace the level of aid that any particular community has received.

*Features of Systems Allocating Money between Rural
and Urban Areas*

The allocation system poses problems at two levels. First, the HUD allocation to nonmetropolitan areas, where most rural communities are located, is disproportionately low when considered in relation to the share of U.S. housing need that occurs in nonmetropolitan areas. A recent study on HUD housing allocations notes that it is unclear whether FmHA programs compensate for this disparity.[13]

Second, truly rural communities (those with populations below 2,500) in both metropolitan and nonmetropolitan areas must compete with much larger communities for housing aid. (For example, nonmetropolitan cities may have populations as high as 50,000, whereas FmHA programs serve communities with populations as high as 10,000.) A recent study sponsored by HUD indicated that among cities with populations under 50,000, the larger communities are more likely to receive assisted housing allocations,[14] even though, within this group, truly rural communities have a disproportionate share of housing need.[15] Although this may occur in part because of a greater preference on the part of these larger cities for assisted housing, it is also probable that the larger cities are more likely to have the program knowledge necessary to attract developers for assisted housing projects. (In recent years this situation has been exacerbated, as HUD has tended to distribute nonmetropolitan housing aid to those communities participating in the small-cities component of the Community Development Block Grant program, in which larger small cities are disproportionately represented.)

Structure of Individual Housing Programs

The structure of individual assisted housing programs limits their ability to meet rural housing need in a variety of ways. First, most assisted housing programs serve renters, although, noted earlier, a much larger share of substandard housing is owner occupied in rural areas than is the case in urban areas. Second, subsidies on such assisted housing programs as Section 8 are not deep enough to help the poorest households. Although a similar situation exists with respect to housing programs in urban areas, it may be a more severe problem in rural America, with its large share of households in the lowest income categories. Third, programs such as Section 8 new construction and FmHA Section 515 rely on private developers and/or nonprofit sponsors. Developers or organizations with the capacity to undertake such projects may not be available in some rural areas. In addition, some developers may not find it economically attractive to undertake construction projects on the small scale appropriate for many rural communities. Finally, programs like Section 8 new construction require developers to locate financing for their projects. Since credit tends to be less available in rural than in urban areas, developers may find it relatively more difficult to undertake such projects.

But although there are major shortcomings in the means by which low-income housing assistance is delivered to rural areas, there are a number of ways in which assisted housing programs in rural America have been extremely successful, as the following illustrations indicate.

Overall Contribution to Housing Stock

Public housing, the oldest of the nation's subsidized housing programs, forms a larger percentage of the total housing stock in nonmetropolitan than metropolitan areas. Stegman and Sumka point out, for example, that in 1973 outside of SMSAs, 6 percent of the total housing stock was made up of public housing units, whereas the respective figures for central cities and SMSAs as a whole were 4 percent and 2 percent. More important, public housing units represented 15 percent of the stock of rental units in nonmetropolitan areas but only 7 percent and 5 percent of the rental stock in central cities and SMSAs, respectively. Long-standing differences in the quality of the nonmetropolitan and metropolitan housing stocks further underline the overall contribution of subsidized housing to nonmetropolitan areas: In nonmetropolitan areas, housing programs have been a more important factor in the general upgrading of the housing stock. In recent years new public housing and Section 8 new construction have been a larger share of the subsidized-housing mix relative to Section 8 existing housing in nonmetropolitan areas than in SMSAs, suggesting that supply-side housing subsidies continue to play an important role in the development of physically adequate housing stock.

It might be argued that in the absence of subsidized housing, the private sector would have taken a larger role in building the nonmetropolitan housing stock. However, such an argument is weakened when one considers that credit is generally less available in nonmetropolitan areas than in SMSAs; in turn, the importance of the government role is strengthened. In addition, the households served by subsidized housing programs are those whom one might expect to be least likely to be served by the private sector. The nature of this population is the topic of the section.

Population Served by Subsidized Housing Programs

Over the past decade a disproportionate share of public housing has gone to nonmetropolitan areas. For example, Stegman and Sumka note that between 1968 and 1973, 35 percent of all public housing units constructed in the United States were built in nonmetropolitan areas.[17] After the inception of the Section 8 program in 1974, public housing continued to be relatively more popular in nonmetropolitan areas than in SMSAs. The relative popularity of public housing is important because of its clientele. Because it is more deeply subsidized than other programs, it serves a lower-income population.

Within this lower-income population, public housing has played a particularly important role for black households in the South. For example, Stegman and Sumka found that in four small North Carolina cities, black households were disproportionately represented in public housing units.[18] Because of extreme segmentation of housing markets by race in the South, subsidized-housing programs have played a key role in making physically adequate housing available to the black population.

Relative Cost Efficiency in Development and Operation of Housing Projects

Development costs per unit of subsidized housing tend to be lower in nonmetropolitan areas than in SMSAs; in turn, the cost to the federal government in amortizing the debt associated with unit construction is lower. For example, Stegman and Sumka estimate that in the four small cities they examined, monthly amortization costs for public housing units were 56 percent lower than the national average.[19]

Operating costs have also been lower for public housing in nonmetropolitan areas. In their study cities, Stegman and Sumka trace key differences in costs to wage differences, differences in the level of payments made by LHAs to local governments in lieu of taxes, and differences in losses due to nonpayment of rents. Indeed, in these four cities, revenues from tenants exceeded operating expenses, and federal operating subsidies were not made.[20]

To the extent that fair market rents are lower in nonmetropolitan areas than in SMSAs, the cost of providing rent supplements under the various components of Section 8 can also be expected to be lower.

Development of Capacity to Administer Assisted Housing Programs

In response to the public housing program, numerous local housing authorities were set up in small communities; in 1970 there were 2,971 such authorities in communities with populations below 2,500, or 49 percent of the total number of LHAs. These LHAs were available to administer the various Section 8 programs that began in 1974;[21] in addition, in response to Section 8, a large number of new LHAs have been established at county, regional, or state levels. The existence of this broad network of agencies suggests that administrative capacity is already in place for the operation of a housing-voucher system in rural America; this point is strengthened by the participation of these agencies in the Section 8 existing-housing program, which operates in much the same manner as would a housing-voucher program, albeit at a much smaller scale. Moreover, the increased development of multijurisdictional LHAs covering both incorporated and unincorporated nonmetropolitan areas in response to Section 8 has increased the percentage of the rural population that can potentially be served by assisted housing programs and may also increase the administrative efficiency with which housing vouchers can be delivered to the rural population.

It should be noted, however, that the existence of a network of LHAs that are largely autonomous from local governments is not necessarily an unmixed blessing. Partly in response to this system, local governments have tended to view the provision of low-income housing as a federal role. Thus, for example, a 1979 HUD study, *Developmental Needs of Small Cities* showed that although 65 percent of the local officials from communities with populations below 2,500 who participated in the study felt that the condition of low-income housing was a serious problem, only 13 percent ranked it as a key development priority. The study noted two reasons for these results: (1) the existence of more critical infrastructure problems, and (2) the view of the officials that housing problems are not a local responsibility.[22] This view may limit the ability of small communities to develop overall strategies to meet their community development needs.

In summary, then, existing subsidized housing programs demonstrate both strengths and weaknesses in meeting the housing needs of rural America. The nature of both the shortcomings and the successes will be important in comparing the relative effectiveness of the existing programs with a system of housing vouchers.

Results from the Experimental Housing Allowance Program

The Experimental Housing Allowance Program (EHAP) was designed to address a variety of issues relevant to the implementation of a large-scale housing-voucher program. The study, sponsored by HUD, began in 1972; although some parts of the study will continue through 1984, most results are now available. Under the various components of EHAP, which included a supply experiment, a demand experiment, and an administrative experiment, over 15,000 low-income households have received housing allowances, the levels of which were based on household income and local rent levels.[23] Generally, to receive an allowance, a household was required to live in a dwelling unit that met certain physical and occupancy standards, to upgrade its unit to meet standards, or to move to such a unit; however, for some households in the demand experiment, such requirements were not imposed. Only renter households participated in the demand and administrative experiments, whereas both renters and owners participated in the supply experiment.[24]

EHAP provides information on the average relative costs of using a supply-side program to provide a low-income household with a unit of standard housing and providing a household with a demand-side subsidy on the condition that it live in standard housing. For example, in 1980 the monthly subsidy to a unit of public housing (including both production and rent subsidies) was estimated to be almost $500 per month.[25] On the other hand, the projected administrative cost to provide a housing allowance to a family is estimated at $256 per year on the basis of EHAP (where administrative costs cover program outreach, household enrollment, housing inspection, and so forth).[26] The average monthly subsidy to the household is estimated to be about $65, with payment equal to the difference between the local cost of adequate modest housing and 25 percent of household income.[27] Although the monthly voucher payment to families eligible for public housing might be considerably higher because public housing serves a lower-income clientele than other subsidized housing programs, the cost savings associated with housing vouchers would nonetheless be substantial.

Moreover, a number of EHAP findings have particular relevance in evaluating how well a housing-voucher system can meet rural housing need. In particular, EHAP provides information on the types of households most likely to enroll in a voucher program, on the types most likely to qualify for payments, and on how program structure affects whether a household ultimately qualifies. EHAP suggests that less than half of the population that is eligible on the basis of income is likely to apply. The working poor and the elderly tend to be under-represented among program applicants, whereas welfare recipients are more likely to apply (in part because such households were referred from other agencies). Those households with a greater history of mobility (and presumably a greater willingness to move if housing does not meet program standards) were also more likely to apply. Among those who applied, the poorest households, as well as large households, minorities, households headed by couples, and welfare recipients, were less likely to receive payments when such receipt was linked to dwelling-unit condition, because their initial dwelling units were more likely to fail to meet housing standards. Moreover, less than half of those households whose dwelling units initially failed inspection eventually qualified for payments. On the other hand, households with a greater history of mobility were more likely eventually to qualify for payments. The size of the subsidy a household potentially could receive affected both its willingness to apply to the program and its willingness to move or upgrade if necessary to meet program standards.[28] Another feature of program structure that affected household qualification was the level of service provided by agencies administering the program to those households that had to move in order to meet program standards: such services were particularly important to black households in tight housing markets.[29]

Other EHAP findings that are particularly relevant in evaluating the impact of housing vouchers on rural America deal with the cost of repairs that were made on those units that were upgraded in order to meet program standards and the overall response of the housing market to a large-scale housing allowance. For those households in which upgrading took place, the average cost was low (an average of $60) both because needed repairs were minor and because the household and/or landlord contributed necessary labor.[30] (Related to the low cost of repairs is the more general finding that households are unlikely to change housing-consumption patterns, beyond changes that may be necessary to qualify for the program. Instead, households are more likely to use housing allowances to reduce housing expenditures relative to expenditures on other goods.)[31] With respect to the overall impact on the housing market, program impacts were negligible: neither rent levels nor supply of new housing seemed to be affected.[32]

The results cited earlier concerning program participation and program impact on the housing stock may be affected by the knowledge of program participants and suppliers of housing that EHAP was a relatively short-lived experiment (three years in the case of the demand and administrative experiments, and ten years for the supply experiment). To the extent that results are valid for a long-term program, however, they indicate that a housing-voucher program may on average be cheaper to implement for a given number of households than a supply-side program. However, they also indicate that the structure of the housing-voucher program may limit its ability to help those of the rural poor whose housing need is most severe; this is a characteristic housing vouchers would share with many supply-side programs.

Relative Effectiveness of Housing Vouchers for Rural America

Early in this chapter it was noted that a dual rationale appears to underlie government provision of housing assistance to low-income households through either supply- or demand-side subsidies. First, policy reflects a view that all households should achieve at least some minimum consumption of housing services; second, there is a belief that decent housing should be affordable to all households in the sense that purchase of housing does not unduly constrain purchase of other necessities. When these goals are considered in conjunction with the nature of rural housing problems, the experience of rural America with currently operating housing programs, and the results from EHAP, the evidence is mixed regarding the effectiveness of a housing-voucher system relative to supply-side programs in meeting housing need.

This mixed picture emerges for both efficiency and equity criteria. For example, with respect to efficiency, a housing-voucher system appears to be clearly superior to the current array of housing programs on administrative grounds. Such a program would reduce the fragmentation of responsibility among government agencies for major housing programs. In turn, it would allow the development of a more accurate and complete data base on the level and distribution of rural housing need, which could be used to track progress in meeting this need over time. In terms of the availability of resources to undertake different types of housing programs, the housing-voucher system may also have an edge over supply-side programs. The network of LHAs now in existence represents a strong base on which the administrative capacity to run a housing-voucher system can be built; on the other hand, resources needed to undertake supply-side programs in rural areas, such as credit or developers able to operate on a large enough scale to make projects economically feasible, have often tended to be in short supply. The scale of operation of supply-side programs may also put such programs at an efficiency disadvantage relative to housing vouchers because the critical mass of eligible households necessary to make a housing project economically feasible may not always be present in rural areas; housing vouchers may be better suited to meet the needs of low-density rural communities. Closely related to this scale argument is the argument that housing vouchers provide households with a greater element of choice in determining what type and level of housing services to consume once they have satisfied required standards. The relatively large percentage of low-income households that own their own homes or rent single-family dwellings in rural areas may prefer to upgrade these units rather than move to the multiunit projects typical of supply-side programs. (It should be noted, however, that for some rural households, housing vouchers may limit choices relative to those available under a supply-side program. For example, for black households in racially segmented housing markets, subsidized programs may offer the best hope of obtaining housing of a desired quality.)

The most important efficiency advantage of housing vouchers is related to their cost-effectiveness in making decent housing affordable *for those households that participate.* In a housing-voucher program of the type tested in the EHAP experiments, this goal would be achieved at less cost than if these households were provided with dwelling units under a supply-side program. Cost effectiveness relative to supply-side programs would not be as great as in urban areas because the cost of subsidizing a unit tends to be lower in rural areas. Moreover, administrative costs would probably tend to be higher for rural LHAs covering large geographic areas than in urban areas because of the greater distances to be traveled in conducting outreach services and in inspecting dwelling units. Nonetheless, one could expect substantial savings on a per-household basis under a housing-voucher system.

Clearly, efficiency in providing decent, affordable housing for participating households is key advantage to a voucher system. On another key point, however, housing vouchers may not perform as well. Whether a housing-voucher system can more efficiently lead to a general upgrading of the housing stock and to greater consumption of standard housing across the spectrum of low-income households is open to question, particularly in rural areas. As noted earlier, housing-voucher proponents base such a claim in large part on statistics that indicate that the overall quality of the U.S. housing stock is good and that most substandard classifications are due to relatively minor problems that can be repaired cheaply. For much of the housing stock in rural America, however, these assumptions are incorrect. Much of the substandard rural housing stock has major deficiencies that would require large outlays of money up front; it is not clear that a housing-voucher system would provide such up-front money or that it would stimulate such repairs. Indeed, in those cases where EHAP stimulated repairs, the average cost of $60 was far lower than would be needed to correct the major deficiencies common in substandard rural housing. Moreover, the nature of upgrading required by substandard rural housing would be likely to involve far more complicated negotiations between landlords, housing occupants, lenders, and contractors than tended to occur during EHAP; the complexity of such negotiations might serve as a further barrier to upgrading. Finally, as Stegman and Sumka suggest, the condition of much of the substandard rural stock is such that rehabilitation is not practical. Thus there may be a need for new low-cost housing. Yet the EHAP supply experiment did not stimulate housing construction. In summary, then, for rural areas a housing-voucher system may not be well suited for addressing problems of substandard housing. Supply-side programs, on the other hand, appear to have played a relatively large role in increasing the overall quality of the housing stock outside of SMSAs. Thus, although housing vouchers clearly have a variety of efficiency advantages relative to supply-side programs, this advantage is not clear in relation to one key goal of low-income housing policy.

As noted earlier, a mixed picture also appears when housing vouchers and supply-side programs are compared on equity criteria. If receipt of vouchers were not conditioned by dwelling-unit adequacy, vouchers would be clearly superior on a variety of equity grounds. Rural areas would tend to receive a share of funds commensurate with their share of low-income households; in turn, the share of funds going to rural areas would also be more in line with their disproportionate share of substandard housing than is probably the case under the allocation of current programs. At the household level, vouchers would have an advantage over supply-side programs in terms of their ability to target the neediest households; in addition, because of the lower subsidy per household associated with housing vouchers, resources for low-income housing could be spread more evenly among low-income households. Moreover, unlike supply-side programs, which chiefly target renters, housing-voucher aid would be spread among owners and renters on the basis of need.

When receipt of housing vouchers is conditioned by dwelling-unit quality, however, the equity advantages of housing vouchers relative to supply-side programs generally decline and in some cases may be reversed. EHAP indicates that those who initially live in housing that meets adequacy standards are more likely to receive vouchers; the neediest families and minority families (who more often live in substandard housing) are less likely to qualify. For rural households living in substandard housing, the problem is exacerbated by the high cost of repairs that may be required to upgrade housing for program qualification and in some cases by the general impracticability of rehabilitation. For black households in the South, who make up a large share of rural households living in substandard housing, the situation may be further worsened by segmentation of the housing market along racial lines and a severe shortage of adequate housing in the black market. Such families would thus find it difficult to qualify for housing vouchers by moving to better-quality units. Overall, because the lower quality of the housing stock in rural areas would limit the ability of individual households to participate, it would also tend to reduce the total share of housing funds going to rural areas relative to their housing need. The share might still be higher than it is under the allocation system for supply-side programs. In general, however, it is possible that supply-side programs, and particularly public housing, have been better able to target the neediest rural families than would a housing voucher whose receipt is conditioned by dwelling-unit quality.

However, although the previous discussion suggests that there are key areas in which housing vouchers may not perform as well a supply-side programs, on balance, a housing-voucher system can be relatively more effective in meeting rural housing need. The greater potential of vouchers to correct imbalances in the allocation of housing funds between urban and rural areas, to reduce the fragmentation of responsibility for housing programs among government agencies, to provide choice to households in terms of the type of housing services consumed, and to provide solutions to housing problems on a scale appropriate to rural densities supports this belief. Just as important in reaching this conclusion is a consideration of the current fiscal climate for provision of social services. Although supply-side programs may have an advantage over housing vouchers in expanding the supply of standard housing for the neediest segments of the population, the level of funding for housing-assistance programs during the course of the decade is likely to be too low for supply-side programs to serve this function in a significant manner. This relative advantage of supply-side programs is thus greatly diminished. At the same time, the ability of housing vouchers to spread funds among a larger number of low-income households because of lower per-household subsidies becomes particularly attractive when funding declines. Nonetheless, deficiencies associated with the type of housing-voucher system that has been most widely tested in the United States would be particularly severe in rural areas, and program designs that are better suited to rural housing needs must be considered. Two possible modifications to the EHAP design are considered in the next paragraphs.

The first modification would attempt simultaneously to correct the negative-equity features of a housing-voucher program that conditions subsidy receipt on housing quality and to improve the overall quality of housing inhabited by rural households. It would do so by increasing the probability that the need-iest households can meet qualification standards. Such a program would rely heavily on an increase in the services provided by the administering agencies to potential recipients. In turn, the average cost to provide a subsidy for a house-hold with a given income level would rise in rural areas, although it would still be less than the cost of providing a unit of subsidized housing; moreover, the greater involvement of agency staff with clients could lead to a perception that housing choices were being controlled by this staff. But these negative features might well be outweighed by gains in vertical equity and improvement in hous-ing quality.

Specific features of such a program might include changing the requirement that housing meet quality standards prior to receipt of the housing voucher to allow for a grace period in which payments were received while upgrading took place;during this grace period housing-agency personnel would work with reci-pients, landlords, lenders, and so forth to determine how housing-voucher funds could best be used to support any major upgrading that was necessary. For those households wishing to participate in the program for whom upgrading is not practical, intensive housing-search services could be provided. Such services would be particularly crucial for black households; programs to reduce the level of housing discrimination might also be considered. Finally, the severity of a region's problems with substandard housing might be considered in determining the level at which households are subsidized. Despite such efforts, it is likely, given the quality of the rural housing stock, that new construction of standard units would be required, especially for black households. To the extent that the private market did not provide such housing, some production of subsidized units might be warranted. But such a supply-side program could be operated at a much lower funding level than current programs and, using data collected through the housing-voucher program, could be better targeted at the neediest areas.

A more drastic charge in the housing-voucher system would involve greatly relaxing or removing altogether, the requirement that households must live in or move to standard dwelling units in order to qualify for the program. Such a policy would be implemented nationally and would implicitly recognize three points:

1. In an era of fiscal austerity it may not be possible to treat the problems of housing affordability and housing quality jointly.
2. Of the two problems, the affordability issue can be addressed more cheaply and in a more equitable manner.
3. The affordability problem is serious enough to be the primary focus of a housing policy.

A voucher program of this type would still increase the ability of recipients to raise their housing consumption; it would also given them greater flexibility than exists under an EHAP-type system in deciding whether to use the voucher to reduce the housing-cost burden or to purchase more housing. (Indeed, the voucher would be akin to a direct transfer of income; however, this situation would not differ much from that produced by EHAP, wherein recipients used the bulk of their housing allowances to reduce rent burden rather than to increase housing consumption beyond the level needed to qualify for the program.) Most important, of course, it would ensure that the program could be targeted to those familieies with the lowest incomes, regardless of their ability to locate standard housing or their propensity to move. It would thus be particularly likely to increase the participation of rural blacks and the elderly.

The adoption of a policy that focused on housing affordability should not completely preclude attempts to improve housing quality. Particularly in rural America, serious problems of physical housing inadequacy continue to exist. In some cases these problems can be met through upgrading or through production in the private sector; but, as in the discussion of the previously suggested modification, a limited role for supply-side programs may still remain.

In summary, then, a housing voucher can be relatively effective in meeting rural housing needs when compared with supply-side housing programs, particularly in an era of fiscal constraint. However, policymakers need to consider carefully how design features affect the program's ability to serve this need, and they must be particularly aware of the type of policy goals that housing vouchers can be expected to meet. Finally, when necessary, they must be willing to consider using housing vouchers in conjunction with other types of housing programs.

Housing Vouchers in the Broader Context of Rural Community Development

Up to now the effectiveness of assisted housing-delivery systems for meeting rural housing need has been considered independently of other programs that address local community-development problems. That it has been possible to do so reflects in part the fact that housing programs tend to be administered by agencies that are largely independent of local governments. This autonomy, as noted earlier, has also contributed to an attitude on the part of local officials that housing is not a local responsibility. Because a system that delivers housing assistance through vouchers is relatively invisible compared with one that builds new dwelling units, one would not expect this attitude to be reversed by a voucher system.

Housing problems and community-development problems are closely related, however. The existence of severely substandard housing is not only a problem for its inhabitants, but can also have negative environmental impacts on the community as a whole. Conversely, improvements to local infrastructure may be crucial before the expansion of a locality's adequate housing stock can be carried out. Consequently, housing and other community-development needs can more effectively be addressed in a comprehensive manner. To this end, it seems crucial that policymakers at the federal, state, and local levels begin to consider ways in which a housing-voucher system can be more effectively integraded with other community-development activities at the local level. Such integration is likely to be far easier at the program's outset than after it has been in operation for a number of years; in the long run, the payoff to this effort should be high.

Notes

1. President's Commission on Housing, *Interim Report,* 30 October 1981.

2. John Weicher, "A Decent Home: An Assessment of Progress toward the National Housing Goal and Policies Adopted to Achieve It," in Donald Phares, ed., *A Decent Home and Environment: Housing and Urban America* (Cambridge, Mass.: Ballinger, 1977), pp. 144-145.

3. U.S. Department of Housing and Urban Development, *How Well Are We Housed? Part 5: Rural,* November 1979, p. 16.

4. U.S. Department of Housing and Urban Development, *Report of the Task Force on Rural and Non-Metropolitan Areas,* July 1978, p. 13.

5. U.S. Department of Housing and Urban Development, *Housing Needs of the Rural Elderly and Handicapped,* November 1980, p. 7.

6. Michael Stegman and Howard Sumka, *Nonmetropolitan Urban Housing,* (Cambridge, Mass.: Ballinger, 1977), pp. 13-15; Janet Marantz, Karl E. Case II, and Herman B. Leonard, *Discrimination in Rural Housing: Economic and Social Analysis of Six Selected Markets,* (Lexington: Lexington Books, D.C. Heath and Company, 1976), pp. 143-147.

7. U.S. Department of Housing and Urban Development, *Housing Needs of the Rural Elderly and Handicapped,* November 1980, p. 12.

8. Ibid., p. 15.

9. Ibid., p. 16.

10. Ibid., p. 14.

11. John L. Goodman, Jr., *Regional Housing Assistance Allocations and Regional Housing Needs* (Washington, D.C.: Urban Institute, 1979), p. 38.

12. Department of Housing and Urban Development, *Report of the Task Force on Rural and Non-Metropolitan Areas,* July 1978, p. 7.

13. Goodman, *Regional Housing Assistance Allocations,* p. 39.

14. Kenneth Bleakly and William Sketchly, "The Housing Assistance Plan," Draft report prepared for the Department of Housing and Urban Development, February 1981, p. 110.

15. U.S. Department of Commerce, *1970 Census of Housing,* vol I: *Housing Characteristics for States, Cities, and Counties,* part I: *United States Summary,* table 2.

16. Stegman and Sumka, *Nonmetropolitan Urban Housing,* p. 259.

17. Ibid., p. 259.

18. Ibid., p. 261.

19. Ibid., p. 263.

20. Ibid., p. 264.

21. Stephen Butler, Susan Peck, and Gordon Cavanaugh, "Alternative Low Income Housing Delivery Systems for Rural America," in *Housing in the Seventies: Working Papers,* vol. I (Washington, D.C.: U.S. Department of Housing and Urban Development, 1976), p. 640.

22. U.S. Department of Housing and Urban Development, *Developmental Needs of Small Cities,* March 1979, pp. 41, 73.

23. Francis Cronin, "Participation in the Experimental Housing Allowance Program," in Raymond Struyk and Marc Bendix, Jr., eds., *Housing Vouchers for the Poor: Lessons from a National Experiment* (Washington, D.C.: Urban Institute, 1981), pp. 84–85.

24. U.S. Department of Housing and Urban Development, *Experimental Housing Allowance Program: Conclusions, the 1980 Report* (February 1980), pp. XV–XVII.

25. Katherine Bradbury and Anthony Downs, eds, *Do Housing Allowances Work?* (Washington, D.C.: Brookings, 1981), p. 386.

26. U.S. Department of Housing and Urban Development, *Experimental Housing Allowance Program: Conclusions, the 1980 Report.*

27. Ibid., p. 70.

28. Ibid., pp. 5–13.

29. James Zais, "Administering Housing Allowances" in Raymond Struyk and Marc Bendix, Jr., eds., *Housing Vouchers for the Poor* (Washington, D.C.: Urban Institute, 1981).

30. U.S. Department of Housing and Urban Development, *Experimental Housing Allowance Program: Conclusions, the 1980 Report,* p. 53.

31. Ibid., pp. 20–29.

32. Ibid., pp. 52–54.

12 Problems of Developing Crime Policy for Rural Areas

Fred A. Meyer, Jr., and
Ralph Baker

Since the emergence of the United States from a frontier society, crime has not been identified with rural areas. In fact, sociologists have generally portrayed crime as an urban phenomenon. In rural areas, informal social controls have been seen as sufficient to limit the behavior of the indigenous population. Cities, on the other hand, were the places in which formal means of control were necessary to limit the behavioral propensities of the population. The breakdown in informal social controls in urban areas has been cited for contributing to various manifestations of personal disorganization: "juvenile delinquency, crime, prostitution, alcoholism, drug addiction, suicide, mental diesease and political instability."[1] Thus crime has historically been associated with negative aspects of urbanization. However, there is evidence that crime is increasing rapidly in rural areas. The historical linkage of cities and crime appears to have diverted schorlarly attention away from the phenomenon of rural crime.[2]

The study of rural crime has been complicated by conflicting definitions of *rural*. For the Census Bureau, areas with places of less than 2,500 or open countryside are indicative of rural existence.[3] However, the data that have been gathered by the Law Enforcement Assistance Administration (LEAA) assumed that all areas outside standard metropolitan statistical areas (SMSAs) are rural.[4]

In addition to the foregoing emphasis on ecological criteria, sociologists have suggested a variety of other approaches to defining *rural*. For example, defining the concept in terms of cultural characteristics was suggested by Bealer, Willits, and Kuvlesky in 1965.[5] They suggested that the concept is a multifaceted one with no one definition that is appropriate for all situations.[6] This lack of conceptual clarity makes comparative analysis of rural crime more difficult. In fact, the first comprehensive rural-crime study in the United States, by Phillips for the state of Ohio, was not published until 1975.[7]

If we accept the lack of conceptual clarity, comparisons are made that might explain differences in the occurrence of crime. Demographic characteristics have been compared for SMSAs and areas outside SMSAs.[8] The major differences in rural areas are evidenced in racial and income characteristics. There are more whites in rural areas; 92 percent of the non-SMSA population is white. The income level of rural areas is generally lower: rural areas have fewer families earning $15,000 per year or more. This category accounts for 23 percent of rural families, compared with 30 percent of city families and 39 percent

171

of other SMSA families. Rural areas are quite similar to the metropolitan areas in age, sex, and marital status.

Some significant economic changes have been taking place within rural areas. First, the nature of employment has been changing. The population has been moving away from agricultural and resource-based employment into industrial and professional jobs. From 1960 to 1970, 41.17 percent of the jobs in the agricultural, forestry, and fishery industries were eliminated. At the same time an increase of 150 percent in the professional and related service categories took place. In addition, increases of 20–30 percent occurred in wholesale and retail trade, durable goods, and nondurable goods.[9] The changing nature of rural employment implies the potential for increasingly significant losses as a result of rural crime. There appear to be an increasing number of areas for lucrative property crime.[10]

The studies that have been done of rural areas, then, suggest that the potential exists for significant criminal activity in rural areas. Organized crime has become aware of the potential for activity in this environment.[11]

Incidence and Nature of Rural Crime

Crime is a serious problem in rural America. Historically, however, rural crime rates have been much lower than urban rates.[12] Several hypotheses have been offered to explain these lower crime rates. Some writers have argued that a rural setting provides less opportunity for certain kinds of crime.[13] Others have ascribed at least a portion of the differences to the keeping of less accurate records by rural law-enforcement agencies.[14] A third hypothesis is that fewer persons are apprehended for the commission of rural crimes.[15] These traditional hypothese have recently been placed in perspective by G. Howard Phillips: "Most of these explanations are historical and do not reflect the changes in transportation and communications of modern rural communities nor do they reflect the improvements in methods of rural law enforcement agencies."[16]

Although rural crime rates today are still lower than urban rates, in absolute terms the rate of growth in rural crime has not surpassed that of urban crime (see table 12–1). The rate of increase in the total crime index for the years 1969–1978 is almost 50 percent greater for rural areas than urban areas. Murder and nonnegligent manslaughter, robbery, burglary, larceny, and auto theft have all risen more rapidly in the country. Only rates of occurrence of rape and aggravated assault have quickened more rapidly in the metropolis.

Studies of crime in rural Ohio have provided scholars with a much clearer picture of the nature of rural crime. Vandalism was found to be the leading crime in rural Ohio, constituting 38 percent of all the crimes committed there. Mailboxes were the most frequent targets of vandals; but other acts of vandalism inflicted damage on cars, windows, lawns, shrubs, and other property.[17]

Table 12-1
Changes in the Crime Rate per 100,000 Inhabitants, 1969–1978

	1969		1978		Net Change 1969–1978		Percentage Change 1969–1978	
	Urban[a]	Rural	Urban	Rural	Urban	Rural	Urban	Rural
Total crime index[b]	3,095.8	858.6	5,870.2	1,997.9	+2,774.4	+1,139.3	+89.6	+132.6
Murder and non-negligent manslaughter	8.2	5.6	9.9	7.5	+1.7	+1.9	+20.7	+33.9
Rape	22.2	10.0	36.7	14.0	+14.5	+4.0	+65.3	+40.0
Robbery	206.5	13.0	249.2	20.9	+42.7	+7.9	+20.6	+60.7
Aggravated assault	179.6	85.2	288.1	132.3	+108.5	+47.1	+60.4	+55.2
Burglary	1,188.2	408.4	1,626.7	746.3	+438.5	+337.9	+36.9	+82.7
Larceny	910.2	263.7	3,101.1	953.3	+2,190.9	+689.6	+240.7	+261.5
Auto theft	580.9	72.8	558.6	123.5	-22.3	+50.7	-3.8	+69.6

Source: Federal Bureau of Investigation, *Uniform Crime Reports—1969*, table 1, p. 56, *Uniform Crime Reports—1978*, table 1, p. 38 (Washington, D.C.: U.S. Government Printing Office, 1970 and 1979).

[a]These data are those reported for standard metropolitan statistical areas (SMSAs), each of which is made up of a core city or cities with a combined population of 50,000 or more.

[b]The total crime index is the aggregate of the seven part I offenses that are identified in this table.

Larceny was found to be the second-largest category of crime in rural Ohio. If the frequency of larceny is added to that of other types of theft, such as burglary, fraud, consumer fraud, robbery, and auto theft, the "theft" category would be almost as large as vandalism. In Ohio, gasoline was the item most often stolen in rural areas, with 20 percent of all the thefts involving gasoline. Auto thefts are most likely to be reported and fraud least likely to be reported.

Farmers are of course potential victims of theft, according to a study of rural crime in Iowa.[18] Cattle and farm machinery were the most frequent targets of thieves, and the greatest monetary losses were incurred with the loss of farm machinery. This Iowa research also revealed that only 17.5 percent of the value of the stolen farm property was ever recovered.

Rural Victimization

Rural crime in the United States, with its emphasis on property crimes, victimizes over 8 million persons per year. Focusing on the victims makes the problem of rural crime more apparent in human terms. Victimization studies gives us clues to how crime may be affecting the quality of life of rural residents. Also, if it is known who is being victimized, it may be possible to learn why and how they are being victimized.

A rural Ohio victimization study selected nine counties on a stratified non-random basis.[19] Counties chosen in each of three substate areas were adjacent to each other so that patterns extending across county lines could be explained. The sample population was drawn from the population of ten randomly selected townships in each of the nine counties. The starting point for the continuous sample was an intersection of two roads arbitrarily picked from a map.

The Ohio study related a variety of victimization variables with the frequency of the property crimes of burglary, theft, and vandalism. Many of the variables chosen were linked to the notion of visibility.[20] Circumstances that perhaps contributed to increased time in or around the residence on a day-to-day basis were originally believed to decrease the chances of that residence being victimized. However, in comparing farmers—who are presumed to spend much time at home because of the proximity of their work—with rural nonfarm residents, no significant differences were found among these two occupational groupings. There was a slight tendency for nonfarmers to be burglarized more often than their farmer neighbors but to be vandalized less often. The size of the family and the occupational role of the wife—whether she spent more time at home as a full-time homemaker—were also unrelated to the incidence of burglary, theft, or vandalism. In a study of Pike County, Indiana, households were categorized according to the ages of all household members. One category included households in which all members were 60 years or older, and the other contained households in which at least one member was less than 60 years old. It was theorized that older persons would more likely be retired and spend more time around the home. However, no significant differences were found between older and younger households. Older households were only slightly more likely to be the victims of vandalism and slightly less likely to fall victim to burglary or larceny. Nevertheless, this finding is important because it suggests that the pattern of victimization in rural areas may be different from that in urban areas.[21] In urban locations the victimization rates for property crimes decrease with age. When violent crimes are combined with theft in personal crime-victimization rates, as was done in the Benton County study, the youngest respondents have the highest victimization rate, and the oldest ones have the lowest rates.[22] This suggests that youths are still the most vulnerable group with respect to crimes of violence, even in a rural setting.

Other variables that have been tested in victimization studies include income, sex, church membership, and contact with neighbors. In the past it has been thought that higher-income persons would be more likely to be the target of property crimes.[23] The rural Ohio study only partially confirmed this notion. There were no significant differences in the rates of burglary or theft; but the higher-income group reported almost twice as much vandalism as did the middle- and lower-income groups. The Benton County, Indiana, study also found no significant relationship between family income and the occurrence of burglary or larceny. However, the latter study did reveal a link between the sex of the victim and personal crime victimization. Although making up only 47.2 percent of the sample, males were the victims of 63 percent of the crimes of violence and theft in Benton County. The Ohio study found that church members had their property vandalized more often than was the property owned by non-church members. As a result, vandalism was related to both church membership and income in rural Ohio. It has also been hypothesized that crime is easier to detect and prevent in a neighborhood in which most people know one another. More than 80 percent of the rural residents in Ohio said they knew their neighbors well or moderately well. However, the degree of acquaintance with neighbors did not result in significant differences in rates of burglary, theft, or vandalism.

In addition to the testing of several socioeconomic characteristics of victims and nonvictims with regard to rural crime, other variables have been examined, such as the time of the day crime was perpetrated, the day of the week the crime occurred, the number of acres owned, the type of terrain, the type of road near the residence, the distance from an urban place, the number of farm buildings, and the visibility of buildings to neighbors. As the susceptibility of certain rural population groups becomes better known, the policy implications of rural crime will be more identifiable as well.

Rural-Crime Offenders

The Ohio study provides us with important data about who was committing crimes in rural Ohio. The source of the data was the offender reports kept by the sheriffs in the nine counties studied. This benchmark study indicates that the nine sheriffs found 60 percent of those arrested to be urban residents, suggesting the importance of mobility in modern rural crime. Most of the culprits were white males (87 percent were males, and 93 percent were white). Sixty-three percent of the persons were 24 years old or younger. The marital status of these Ohio offenders was predominantly single; one one-third were married. This profile of the rural offender also concludes that 27 percent were students, 15 percent were unemployed, and 31 percent had known records. When arrested, 54 percent were in a group, and 30 percent were intoxicated.

Since vandalism was the most frequently occurring crime in rural Ohio, an attempt was made to learn more about the vandal.[24] A questionnaire was distributed to high-school sophmores, more than half of whom reported being involved in one or more acts of vandalism. This figure included two-thirds of the males and one-third of the females. Vandalism goes beyond the phenomenon of "boys just being boys." When asked why they committed acts of vandalism, the student respondents suggested a number of reasons. Sixty percent said they did it for fun or as a game, viewing the property damage as incidental to the game. A much smaller group of vandals act to get revenge, to express rage, or in combination with the commission of a more serious offense. One difficulty in curbing rural vandalism may lie in the way offenders view such behavior. Seventy percent of the respondents viewed their acts of vandalism not as crimes but, rather, as pranks. They did not view their behavior as wrong.

In contrast to the vandals is the professional criminal with links to organized crime. There is increasing evidence that organized crime plays a part in rural crime.[25] The complex process of marketing agricultural products has been suggested as one of the factors increasing the possibility of organized-crime activity.[26]

In a rare empirical study of this phenomenon, Barber used open-ended interviews of a small number of professional thieves. His study suggest that organized criminals are active in two main types of theft: livestock, including carcasses, and farm machinery.[27] In addition, some of the professional activity involved burglary. It was suggested that the thieves generally wait until the owners of the targeted property depart from the theft site before they begin.[28] The organized criminal working in the rural environment needs some well-developed mechanical skills because equipment may have to be disconnected or loaded and transported in such a way as not to damage it. The work of the professional criminal is facilitated by the existence of business proprietors who are willing to act as fences. For example, some used-farm-machinery dealers are reputedly willing to sell stolen merchandise.[29]

Public Perceptions of Crime

The attitudes of members of the public toward their personal safety are further indicators of the environment of crime in rural areas. The Ohio victimization study, which sampled rural residents living outside unincorporated areas, included a series of questions on attitudes toward personal safety. Farm respondents were compared with rural nonfarm respondents. Fifty-four percent of the farm respondents and 48 percent of the nonfarm respondents felt it was safe for a woman to be alone in a neighborhood during the day. About one-fifth of both farm and nonfarm respondents felt it would be safe for a woman to walk alone at night. Two-fifths of both farm and nonfarm respondents felt that a woman walking with another adult would be safe at night. Seventy percent of farm respondents and 77 percent of the nonfarm respondents indicated they were very or somewhat concerned about their houses being broken into. Fifty percent of farm and 60 percent of nonfarm respondents indicated they locked their doors most of the time when they left their homes. Seventy-one percent of the farm respondents usually locked their doors at night, whereas 82 percent of the nonfarm respondents locked their doors most of the time. Similar proportions of farm and nonfarm respondents indicated they locked their doors most of the time while at home. Approximately three-fourths of the farm and nonfarm groups kept a gun in the house for protection.[30] The major difference between the farm and nonfarm groups is that "farm respondents were less likely to practice crime prevention."[31] The experience of victimization resulted in "some (but negligible) movement toward greater concern about crime and greater awareness of locking doors."[32]

Citizens' attitudes about crimes are manifested in the crime-prevention practices they engage in. In the Ohio study, it was found that 61 percent of automobiles were not locked and that 92 percent of farm equipment was not locked. Ninety-three percent of barns were left unlocked. Eighty-one percent of garden tools were not locked up. Sixty-seven percent of gas tanks were not locked.[33]

The relation of age to crime attitudes was investigated in a study of Pike County, Indiana.[34] Little difference was found between the groups over 60 years and those under 60 in their perceptions of the increase of crime in the preceding year. About one-fifth of each group felt crime was on the increase. Of those below 60, 91.2 percent felt safe all the time, whereas only 75 percent of those 60 and older experienced this feeling.[35] Of those under 60, 76 percent felt very safe at home during the day, compared with 61.3 percent of those over 60.[36] Those above 60 in Pike County appeared to have a higher fear of crime.

Policy Responses

The increasing rural crime rate has brought with it more research into the nature of rural crime and potential policy responses to the problem. Since the first comprehensive rural-crime study in the United States was not published until 1975, the study of policy responses to rural crime is in the stage of very early speculation. As G. Howard Phillips wrote recently, "Research on crime prevention in rural areas virtually does not exist."[37] Without such research on prevention, policy proposals need to be considered and tested before implementation. Even the research on the nature of rural crime discussed in this chapter indicates some gaps in our knowledge. The existing victimology studies exhibit the need for the isolation of more significant victimization variables. Smith and Donnermeyer suggest the need for "comparative analyses of the volume and type of crime occurring to persons and households from different types of rural areas."[38] There is the need to identify high-risk crime targets more accurately.[39]

On the basis of the existing studies, a variety of policy responses have been suggested. Because of the remoteness of many rural crime scenes, the emphasis in most of the policy suggestions is on the coproduction of responses. Phillips suggests a variety of strategies to reduce rural crime. He suggests trying to educate local residents to take preventive measures such as locking their implements and engraving identification numbers of their possessions.[40] Phillips also suggests programs to educate potential teenage vandals to the seriousness of their acts and possible legal sanctions.[41] To deal with professional criminals, it has been suggested that the public be educated to the problems of buying merchandise from fences and the potential legal sanctions involved.[42] Farmers might form preventive patrols that work closely with the county sheriff. It has been suggested that counties be divided into subdivisions, each having its own patrol association.

Any policy responses to the problem of rural crime must take into consideration the law-enforcement problems associated with a small, rural police department. Such departments have limited financial resources, high turnover rates, lack of training programs aimed at a small department's needs, lack of personnel, and large jurisdiction areas. Suggested policy responses include reinforced patrols in problem areas, increased personnel, state funding of all police training, and the development of research studies to determine small-department training needs. Some analysts argue that only through the consolidation of small police departments with large departments or through a variety of cooperative arrangements among departments can existing law-enforcement agencies cope with rising rural crime rates. However, researcher Elinor Ostrom has challenged the argument that small police departments in a metropolitan area are less competent agencies than large, central-city ones.[43] Obviously, more research is needed in the area of needed policy responses by law-enforcement agencies in the face of increasing rural crime.

Among the other institutions that may need to change in order to meet existing conditions are rural courts. Yet it is difficult to suggest concrete proposals at this stage of rural-crime research. As one study of rural courts expressed with regard to its policy considerations: "As aptly stated by one of the workshop participants, 'determining what rural courts are and the nature of their problems is as difficult as climbing a fence leaning toward you or kissing a girl leaning away.' "[44] This study also stressed the difficulty of making generalizations about rural courts because few courts within states are similar enough to justify even broad generalizations. It is clear, however, that the need for greater fiscal resources and improved physical facilities is growing. The study does believe that court reorganization is not a panacea.

After reviewing the nature of rural crime, we believe the most evident policy response to be increased funding for further research.

Notes

1. Philip M. Hauser, "Urbanization: An Overview," in Jeffrey K. Hadden, Louis H. Masotti, and Calvin Larson, eds., *Metropolis in Crisis,* 2d ed., (Itasca, Ill.: Peacock Publishers, 1971), p. 61.

2. For a discussion of the seriousness of rural crime, see Charles R. Swanson, "Rural and Agricultural Crime," *Journal of Criminal Justice* 9(1981):19–27.

3. U.S. Bureau of the Census, Public Information Office, "1980 Urban Population Proportion Registers Smallest Gain in U.S. History, Census Tabulations Show," *U.S. Department of Commerce News,* 13 August 1981.

4. John J. Gibbs, *Crimes against Persons in Urban, Suburban and Rural Areas* (Washington, D.C.: U.S. Department of Justice, Law Enforcement Assistance Administration, National Criminal Justice Information and Statistics Service, 1979), pp. 17–18.

5. Robert C. Bealer, Fern K. Willits and William P. Kuvlesky, "The Meaning of 'Rurality' in American Society: Some Implications of Alternative Definitions," *Rural Sociology* 30(1965):255–266.

6. Ibid., p. 266.

7. G. Howard Phillips, *Crime in Rural Ohio* (Columbus: Ohio State University Agricultural Research and Development Center, 1975).

8. See Gibbs, *Crimes against Persons,* p. 19.

9. See Ray Marshall, *Rural Workers in Rural Labor Markets* (Salt Lake City, Utah: Olympus, 1974), p. 18.

10. See Swanson's proposition about the significance of property losses in rural areas in "Rural and Agricultural Crime," p. 23.

11. Ibid.

12. Everett M. Rogers, *Social Change in Rural Society* (New York: Appleton-Century-Crofts, 1960); Alvin L. Bertrand, *Basic Sociology: An Introduction to Theory and Method* (New York: Appleton-Century-Crofts, 1967); Walter C. Reckless, *The Crime Problem,* 4th ed. (New York: Appleton-Century-Crofts, 1967); Martin H. Neumeyer, *Juvenile Delinquency in Modern Society* (New York: Van Nostrand, 1961).

13. Rogers, *Social Change,* p. 258.

14. Ibid., p. 1.

15. Ibid., p. 2.

16. Phillips, *Crime in Rural Ohio,* p. 2.

17. Acts of vandalism to public property such as churches, schools, places of business, and cemeteries are not included in the study.

18. Iowa Statistical Analysis Center, *Farm Related Theft in Iowa, 1979,* Des Moines, 1981.

19. Phillips, *Crime in Rural Ohio,* pp. 3-4.

20. Howard Phillips and Todd N. Wurschmidt, "The Ohio Rural Victimization Study" (Paper presented at Rural Sociological Society Meetings, 1979), p. 21.

21. Joseph F. Donnermeyer, G. Howard Phillips, and Mary Jo Steiner, "Age, Fear of Crime and Victimization in Rural Areas" (Paper presented at North Central Sociological Meeting, Cleveland, Ohio, 1981), p. 6.

22. See Brent Lamar Smith, "Criminal Victimization in Rural Areas: An Analysis of Victimization Patterns and Reporting Trends" (Ph.D. diss., Purdue University, 1979).

23. See T.A. Reppetto, *Residential Crime* (Cambridge, Mass.: Ballinger, 1974).

24. G. Howard Phillips, "Dimensions of Rural Crime" (Paper presented at the Academy for Criminal Justice Sciences, 1974), pp. 15-20.

25. See Swanson, "Rural and Agricultural Crime," p. 23; See also Rollin M. Barber, "The Professional Style of Rural Thieves and Their Vocabularies of Motive" (Ph.D. diss., Ohio State University, 1976).

26. Barbar, "Professional Style," p. 8.

27. Ibid., p. 53.

28. Ibid., p. 64.

29. Ibid., p. 59.

30. Joseph F. Donnermeyer and Robin Cox, "Criminal Victimization and Attitudes toward Crime and Crime Prevention among Farm Operations: A Comparative Analysis" (Paper presented at the North Central Sociological Association Meeting, 1981), pp. 11-12.

31. Ibid., p. 12.

32. Ibid., p. 17.

33. Phillips, "Dimensions of Rural Crime," p. 25.

34. Donnermeyer, Phillips, and Steiner, "Age, Fear of Crime and Victimization."

35. Ibid., p. 8.

36. Ibid.

37. G. Howard Phillips, "Director's Notes," *Clues for Rural Crime Prevention* (December 1981).

38. Brent L. Smith and Joseph F. Donnermeyer, "Criminal Victimization in Rural and Urban Areas: Comparative Analysis," Report prepared in part under Grant no. 78-NI-AX-OC32 from the Law Enforcement Assistance Administration, U.S. Department of Justice, and in part from Hatch Project 45068-26-11455, Agriculture Experiment Station, Department of Agricultural Economics, Purdue University.

39. Ibid., p. 223.

40. Phillips, "Dimensions of Rural Crime," pp. 31–32.

41. Ibid., pp. 32–33.

42. Barber, "Professional Style," p. 105.

43. Elinor Ostrom and Dennis Smith, "On the Fate of 'Lilliputs' in Metropolitan Policing," *Public Administration Review* 36(March–April 1976):192–200.

44. E. Keith Scott, Jr., Theodore J. Fetter, and Laura L. Crites, *Rural Courts* (National Center for State Courts, 1977), p. 69.

13 Public Education in Rural America: A Third Wave?

Daryl J. Hobbs

Alvin Toffler, through his recent widely read book, has added the concept of the "third wave" to our vocabulary.[1] From the historical perspective of the present, it is easy to understand the first and second waves and to appreciate the magnitude of change that accompanied them. The third wave, which Toffler says we are now in the midst of, is less easily understood in either form or consequence.

Although no contention will be made here that the changes in rural education in the United States have been as profound or as far reaching in their consequences as the "waves" described by Toffler, the metaphor does seem to have some applicability to the past hundred years of public education in rural America.

The first wave of rural public schooling was, as in Toffler's analysis, closely linked to agriculture. It produced an organizational form of public education—the widely dispersed one-room country schools—that was a highly workable response to the basic educational needs of dispersed rural populations who wanted, and needed, to learn the three Rs while at the same time being flexible enough and close enough to home that plowing, planting, and picking were not neglected. It would be hard to exaggerate the contributions made by this uniquely rural institution to the subsequent commercialization of agricultural and industrialization of the entire economy.

Despite the contributions of the one-room country school, however, there were early and persistent detractors. One of those who had little good to say about the one-room country school was Elwood Cubberly, who in 1912 stated:

> The country school lacks interest and ideas; it suffers from isolation and from lack of that enthusiasm which comes only from numbers; and it realizes but a small percentage of its possible efficiency. Its site is usually unattractive; its building is too often a miserable, unsanitary box; it too often lacks the necessary equipment for proper instruction. . . . the attendance is irregular, and the conduct of the school is poor.[2]

At the same time, however, there were those who were more appreciative of country life and agricultural necessities and who took a different view of the rural school. H.J. Waters, then dean of agriculture at Kansas State College, wrote in the introduction to Kirkpatrick's 1917 book *The Rural School from Within:*

> Rural betterment is not something which may be handed down from above. It must come up out of the ranks of the country people. The one agency which touches the life of all the country people is the rural school. . . . Few people who write about rural schools understand and love rural life. Few have the good sense and the ability to lead and to direct quietly. Few are attuned to the countryman's point of view. Few are patient with his conservatism.[3]

Thus the stage was set early for debates about the value of rural education and, more especially, the type and form of the schools that provided it. Despite these contentions, the one-teacher country school flourished until at least 1930, when there were 149,000 operating in the rural U.S. Even in 1940 there were 114,000 left, but after that their numbers dropped rapidly to the point of virtual extinction today.

The one-room country schools, with the rural high schools as their companions, appear to have been less a casualty of conflicts between professional educators and the rural people who had established and were paying for the schools, then a casualty of the pervasive industrialization of the economy. Just as specialization, centralization, and consolidation became central themes of a rapidly industrializing and urbanizing society, so too these themes became dominant in public education. The model of the school borrowed heavily from those industrial themes and became the standard by which the effectiveness and efficiency of public schools, wherever they might be located, was to be judged. Thus this second wave, which ran its course from about 1930 into the 1970s, effectively transformed rural schools into larger or smaller replicas of urban and suburban schools. It drastically reduced the number of rural schools and transformed the methods of instruction and administration for most. Transportation quickly became a major function of consolidated rural schools as it became necessary to transport many students to central locations.

There is some evidence that rural education, if not education in general, may now be in the midst of a third wave. As with the third wave Toffler describes, however, its form and substance are not yet clear. There are still thousands of small rural schools, but many of these are regarded as being necessarily existent; there are persistent problems of inequities in rural education that "modern" schools have not solved; and there are dozens of experiments in rural education going on, many of which are attempting to build stronger reciprocal relationships between school and community.[4] It is difficult to find advocates of a return to one-room country schools, but it is far easier to find those who contend that the second-wave model of the school is not appropriate for most rural areas either.

This chapter will provide a brief review of the current status of public education in rural America, review some of the major operational problems, discuss the relationship between rural education and rural development, and conclude with a review of some recent rural-education reforms and what they have produced.

Rural Education: A Description

Any description of rural education in the United States suffers from a lack of applicable data. The National Center for Educational Statistics (NCES) the primary source of data on public education in the United States, has not regularly published data on rural schools. The NCES cites a relative lack of demand for such data as a primary reason for this failure.[5] NCES personnel also identify problems in proper identification of a rural school as a further impediment to more detailed treatment.

There has been a general tendency in recent years to report many federal data sets in terms of a metropolitan-nonmetropolitan division. This is somewhat informative and will be used to some extent in this chapter. However, "nonmetropolitan" is much too global a category for meaningful evaluation of the status of rural education today. Entire states, such as Vermont and Wyoming, have no SMSAs. Furthermore, longitudinal evaluations lose comparability since whole counties may change their status from nonmetropolitan to metropolitan from one decennial census to the next. In any event, data on rural schools are sketchy at best.

The matter of defining *rural,* which deters the NCES from reporting on rural schools, is a general problem for rural research. The old census definition of *rural*—that population residing in the open country and in towns of less than 2,500—includes many towns and places that are close to metropolitan areas and whose residents regard themselves as urban or metropolitan. The Economic Research Service of the U.S. Department of Agriculture has made various recent attempts (USDA) to classify counties in terms of degree of rurality. This has been useful in many kinds of research but does not necessarily simplify matters pertaining to education. As a result of consolidation efforts, many schools, especially in the eastern half of the United States, may have been reorganized into a single countywide high-school district with an enrollment of several thousand. Such schools may serve mostly small-town and open-country (rural) students; yet their size and complexity make them similar, if not identical, to suburban and small-city schools. Are schools to be classified as rural if they serve predominately rural student populations, regardless of their size?

The matter of definition of rural schools and rural education is further complicated by the range of organizational forms embodied in the concept of the school district, which typically is the unit that has an elected school board and that reports many educational statistics. In many states the rural school district is synonymous with the operation of a single high school and one or several supporting elementary schools. Through much of the South, however, school districts are organized on a county basis, with a single district operating several high schools. Within the same county there may be schools that serve relatively affluent student bodies and others that serve economically depressed communities or neighborhoods. Any data reported for such districts average out influences that are important factors in assessing educational outcomes and differences in opportunity.

Despite these limitations of data, however, some generalizations can be made that are at least applicable to nonmetropolitan schools. In the United States in 1972 there were approximately 87,500 schools being operated by about 16,500 school districts. More than 70 percent of these districts (11,900) were located in nonmetropolitan areas. These nonmetropolitan districts were operating about 39,500 schools, which represent about 46 percent of the total number of schools. These schools are attended by one-third of all U.S. public elementary and secondary students. Thus, on the average, nonmetropolitan schools have a smaller enrollment—395 students per school—than do metropolitan schools, which average about 635 students per school. Such data tell us very little, however, since they average the 8 students attending a one-room school in rural Nebraska with the 2,500 students attending a public high school in a small city of 48,000.

What existing statistics dramatically reveal, however, is the extent of consolidation and elimination of rural schools and school districts over the past four decades. In 1930 there were 128,000 school districts in the United States; this frame has now declined to 16,500. There were 149,000 one-teacher elementary schools, which have now virtually ceased to exist (there were 755 in 1980). Virtually all the eliminated districts and schools served rural areas.

Despite the emphasis on consolidation, small schools serving rural areas remain. Of the nearly 12,000 nonmetropolitan districts, 54 percent had a total student enrollment of less than 600; 62 percent of the districts operate two or fewer schools, typically an elementary school and a high school. Carlsen and Dunne, in their national study of small schools, estimated that there were approximately 6,000 schools in the rural United States that fell into one of the following categories: K-12 schools, or districts, with fewer than 300 pupils; high schools with fewer than 200 pupils; and elementary schools with fewer than 15 pupils per grade.[6] The location of these schools suggests a major reason for the continuation with small enrollment: 60 percent are located in the Plains states and 22.5 percent in the West. About 6 percent were located in the Northeast, the South, and the North Central states, respectively. Most of the small schools clearly serve sparsely populated areas.

The revival of interest in rural education over the past several years has focused largely on schools experiencing the double jeopardy of being both rural and small. That frame of reference will be employed in much of the remaining discussion in this chapter.

Since educational outcomes are difficult to measure at best, the comparative data that does exist for rural and urban schools tends to focus largely on educational inputs. From the last reported data nonmetropolitan schools spent only about 80 percent as much per student as either central-city or suburban schools.[7] However, the differential in terms of instructional costs is greater, since nonmetropolitan schools were spending nearly twice as much per student for transportation as central-city schools and about 50 percent more per student than suburban schools.

A past important justification for school consolidation was the need to achieve larger enrollments in order to support more current educational services. For reasons of both size and limited financial resources, nonmetropolitan schools lag far behind suburban and central-city schools in providing various educational-support services. For example, only 45 percent of nonmetropolitan schools, compared with 62 percent of suburban and 86 percent of central-city schools, were offering special education.[8] The difference is just as great for guidance counselors: 50 percent of nonmetropolitan, 67 percent of suburban, and 94 percent of central-city schools reported having guidance counselors. Only 7 percent of nonmetropolitan schools, compared with 14 percent of suburban and 42 percent of central-city schools, report haing audiovisual specialists. This same pattern prevails for other services, such as prekindergarten, kindergarten, librarians, phychologists, teacher aides, and libraries. On virtually all measures of the components of what Tyack refers to as "the one best system," nonmetropolitan schools are lacking—a circumstance that has led many to conclude that rural schools and their inability to afford, or justify economically, a wide range of educational inputs represents a problem in the form of inferior education.[9] This rationale is given greater impetus by comparative data on scholastic performance, to be discussed later.

Sources of Funding

The historical trend in funding of public education in the United States has shifted importantly from local sources to the states; more recently, a more significant share has come from federal sources. In 1930, before any major move toward consolidation, localities were providing 83 percent and states 17 percent of educational revenue. The federal share at that time was negligible. By 1950, however, the local share of support had shrunk to 57 percent; state support had risen to 40 percent; and the federal share was 3 percent. The federal share remained at about that level until the mid-1960s, when the passage of the Elementary and Secondary Education Act raised the federal contribution to its current level of about 9 percent. By 1976–1977 the local share had diminished to 49 percent; state support had increased to 42 percent; and federal support remained at 9 percent.

Although these figures reflect national averages, they gloss over wide variations among the states. Support varies from zero in the statewide, centralized system in Hawaii to nearly 90 percent in New Hampshire. Similarly, federal support, allocated primarily on the basis of poverty criteria, varies from 23 percent of the total in Mississippi to less than 4 percent in several states in the Northeast.

Nonmetropolitan schools are generally more heavily supported by state funds than are either central-city or suburban schools. Across the United States, nonmetropolitan schools received an average of 44 percent of their funds from local sources, 45 percent from the state, and about 9 percent from federal sources. Central-city schools, by contrast, received 55 percent from local, 34 percent from state, and 11 percent from federal sources.

Concern has been expressed by various rural-school advocates that, because of small size, isolation, and lack of administrative staff, small rural schools do not fare as well as urban schools in competing for grant funds and other forms of federal supplementary aid. In general, data, such as those reported earlier, show that nonmetropolitan areas receive a proportionate share of federal funds; but there is a suspicion that smaller rural schools have been neglected in this categorization. In a recent, carefully done study in six states, Bass and Berman employed a refined measure of "rural" in an attempt to determine how smaller rural schools fared in allocations of Title IV-B and Title IV-C (competitive grants) funds of the Elementary and Secondary Education Act.[10] They found that smaller rural schools were receiving at least a proportional share of Title IV-B funds, which are allocated by formula, and in most cases were receiving somewhat more than a proportional share. They did find, however, that in several states more isolated rural districts were receiving a significantly smaller share of Title IV-C funds, which are allocated by competitive grants. They conclude that aggregate data analysis of federal funding patterns to education must be interpreted with caution.

Rural-Student Performance

According to data reported by Fratoe, 19.9 percent of nonmetropolitan, 18.6 percent of central-city, and 13.2 percent of suburban students are classified as scholastically retarded.[11] The National Assessment of Educational Progress conducted from 1969 through 1973 clearly shows differences in performance by place of residence, but also reveals some interesting trends. The assessment data are reported by a detailed breakdown of size and type of community. In terms of science achievement, 17-year-olds in 1969–1970 attending schools in high-socioeconomic-status metropolitan areas, had an average score of 49.2 correct. This compares with 46.2 percent correct for 17-year-old students in medium cities, 43.3 percent correct for students in small places, and 40.6 percent for students in extreme rural localities. However, the lowest scores were attained by 17-year-old students in low socioeconomic metropolitan areas. However, between 1969–1970 and 1972–1973, students in all sizes and types of communities declined in science-test scores except those attending school in small places and extreme rural, both of whom improved. As a result, 1972–1973 students from small places ranked second behind students from high-socioeconomic-status metropolitan areas in science-test performance, and extremely rural students ranked ahead of both main big-city students and those from low-socioeconomic-status metropolitan areas.

The NCES, in *Condition of Education, 1976,* reports comparative reading achievement for 17-year-olds for 1971 and 1974 by the same categories of size and type of community reported earlier.[12] The highest scores at both times were achieved by students from high-socioeconomic-status metropolitan areas, but the greatest improvement was reported for extremely rural students—an improvement that placed their scores at the national median for 1974.

Although the foregoing data are suggestive of an educational disadvantage for those attending school in extremely rural places, other characteristics associated with achievement tend to overshadow the differences by place of residence. For both reading and science achievement there is a very strong and direct relationship between the extent of parents' education and achievement-test scores. An equally strong and direct relationship exists between various racial groups and test scores. These data only provide further support for the well-documented studies of Jencks et al., who concluded that success in school and subsequent occupational and career mobility were influenced far more by the socioeconomic status of the parents of students than by any other factor or set of factors.[13]

Jencks's findings have been strongly reinforced by the work of many rural sociologists who have investigated various factors related to educational and occupational aspirations of rural youth. The results of a recent comprehensive study of the relationship between education, aspirations, and work are reported by Cosby and Charner.[14]

Rural areas of the United States are disproportionately poor, and the average educational level of the adult rural population for all races is below the level for metropolitan areas. Without controlling for these factors, valid conclusions cannot be drawn about the pros and cons of small rural schools and how well they do or do not educate their students.

During the peak of emphasis on school consolidation in the 1950s and 1960s, various studies showed that students from small schools did not perform as well on various measures of educational performance as did students from larger schools.[15] However, more recent studies, which controlled for differences in socioeconomic status of students, reached different conclusions. Coleman et al., in their well-known study of educational opportunity, found no association between school size and achievement and even found that the size of the twelfth-grade class of a school was negatively associated with verbal achievement.[16] The presence of each additional two hundred students in the twelfth-grade class was associated with a decline of one-fifth grade level in achievement. In West Virginia, Raymond studied the freshman-year performance of approximately five thousand students entering the University of West Virginia.[17] He found that consolidation and all other school-based factors were unrelated to freshman performance. Raymond concludes that performance differences between students are attributable almost totally to factors that fall largely outside the control of the school system. Sher and Tomkins review a range of studies that report the association between school size and student performance and reach the conclusion that if socioeconomic status of students is controlled, there is little, if any, advantage or disadvantage associated with size of school.[18]

Another recurrent issue pertaining to the advantages and disadvantages of small schools concerns the cost per student. Much consolidation proceeded on the rationale that larger schools were more efficient and/or would enable offering a more comprehensive program at an affordable price. In a recent publication, Fox reviews thirty-one studies of the relationship between the size of schools and the cost of education.[19] Fox concludes that there are size economies for elementary and secondary schools and district administration. Elementary schools tend to exhaust economies at a relative small level—between 300 and 600 students—whereas secondary schools may experience economies into the range of 1,400-1,800 students. However, some of the more recent studies he reviews, such as that by White and Tweeten, find that when density of the student population is considered, appreciable modification of size economies occurs.[20] Fox concludes that savings are likely to be associated with larger schools if broad course offerings are made available, when populations are fairly dense, and/or when major new capital expenditures are to be undertaken.[21] It is of some interest that twenty-five of thirty-one studies reviewed by Fox have been reported since 1968, basically after the fact of much rural consolidation.

Although the sketchiness of data make it difficult to draw firm conclusions about the small rural school, it does seem justifiable to conclude that consolidation of rural schools did not produce the dramatic results promised by some of its more ardent advocates. Conversely, it seems equally valid to suggest that small rural schools may find that, through attrition of the existing population and because of further financial pressures, consolidation may become necessary.

What does emerge from the foregoing review, however, is that perhaps rural educators have focused excessive attention on the school as the problem. It gives one pause to reflect on the conclusion of Jencks et al., who state "that the character of a school output depends largely on a single input, namely the characteristic of the entering children."[22] Despite that conclusion, schools are likely to continue to be one of the most central of public institutions and to provide a wide range of services greatly valued by the society. In the context of rural schools, however, the foregoing data and conclusions suggest that little is likely to be gained by further efforts to transform rural schools into scale models of suburban schools. The problems of education, development, and economic mobility in rural America run deeper than that.

Operational Problems of Small Rural Schools

Although rural schools are not as inferior as some detractors would claim, smaller schools do have their operational problems. The Northwest Regional

Vocational Laboratory in a 1973 rural-school study listed five primary problems associated with small rural schools, in the following order:

1. poor quality of instruction;
2. difficulty in hiring or retaining good teachers;
3. limited course offerings;
4. limited equipment;
5. inadequate career counseling.

A few recent regional and national studies elaborate on some of these problems.

Small rural schools generally pay lower salaries than their urban and suburban counterparts. Simultaneously, there is a recently reported teacher shortage for rural secondary schools in the Midwest.[23] Whether that reported shortage is attributable to lower salaries is not a simple question.

It is clear, however, that there are some established differences between small-rural-school teachers and administrators and their larger-school, larger-place counterparts. Muse and Stonehocker, in their study of small-school staff in five western states, report that rural teachers tend to come from rural environments, having attended small rural high schools themselves and reinforced their rural orientation by often obtaining their college training in a community of 25,000 or fewer.[24] A majority expressed a desire to continue teaching in the school that now employed them. They considered the greatest strengths of the small school the opportunity for more individual attention for students, better school discipline, closer teacher-student relationships, reduced crime in the community, and the quality of teachers. Ironically, in addition to reduced curriculum offerings, they felt one major weakness of small rural schools lay in school-community relationships. This is noteworthy because much recent attention to small rural schools has focused on the actual and potential strength of school-community relationships.[25]

The Muse and Stonehocker study also reports that in-service teacher training, along with a lack of community amenities such as housing, shopping, cultural, and educational opportunities, were perceived to be disadvantages.[26]

Burlingame, in a recent study of Illinois public school superintendents, found the highest rate of superintendent turnover to have occurred among the smallest school districts. Only four of fourteen superintendents serving very small districts had remained in the same district throughout the twelve-year study period from 1964–1965 to 1976–1977.[27] Burlingame reports that superintendents of small schools tend to be horizontally mobile within a limited geographic region. The idea that a small district is a starting point to upward mobility to larger and more prestigious schools is clearly not supported by the Illinois data.

In their study Muse and Stonehocker profile the typical rural school administrator as being a white male between 30 and 50 who has grown up in a rural environment.[28] Fifty-six percent had been in their present administrative position for less than five years, and none had been in their position for more than fifteen years. With respect to future educational plans, only one-third expressed any aspirations for upward mobility; a full 50 percent planned to remain in their present positions.

In another recent major national study of small-school teachers and administrators, Carlsen and Dunne reported the need for multitalented teachers in small schools. In their survey of 478 small-rural-school teachers nationwide, they found 93 percent of high-school teachers teaching in three or more grades. Of the teachers teaching only in grades 7–12, 82 percent were teaching two or more different subject areas. Although reports of teacher turnover were high, nevertheless about 50 percent of the teachers had been in their present positions for five years or more.[29] Their findings with respect to personal characteristics, professional background, and career mobility of teachers and administrators almost exactly parallel those of Muse and Stonehocker.

More than 80 percent of the teachers reported having, and using in their classroom instruction, a library, reference books, teacher-made materials, films, and nontext printed materials. Fewer than 20 percent reported having, and using, radio broadcasts, team teaching, a community-studies program, computer terminals, and interactive television. Carlsen and Dunne call particular attention to the fact that only 50 percent of the teachers reported using "community resources" and the "out-of-doors" as educational resources, although those resources would be universally available.

In their comprehensive report of the Southern regional youth study, Cosby and Charner draw several conclusions and implications about the career aspirations of rural youth.[30] They conclude that career preferences and aspirations expressed in the senior year reflect a strong endorsement of the American success themes of higher-level educational and occupational achievement. For all sex and race groups, the single most preferred choice beyond high school was for college training. Those who did aspire to occupational entry following high school, typically chose occupations in the upper half of occupational-prestige ranking. Cosby and Charner contend that "it seems that rural youth, even the more disadvantaged, are participating social-psychologically in the 'American success dream,' if not in terms of actual behavior or attainments."[31]

Their findings also have implications for counseling of rural youth. They find, for example, that aspirations of young women tend to be confined by the content of various careers (choosing so-called women's occupations). They suggest that counseling programs oriented toward rural women should emphasize expansion of preference content. Conversely, for rural blacks, they found no particular problem with aspirations but, rather, that black youths had great difficulty in moving from aspirations to the next phase of entry, preparation for careers. They recommend programs designated for rural blacks that would place greater emphasis on strategies for transforming preferences into attainment.

Cosby and Charner's findings serve as a further reminder of the influence of out-of-school factors on the school performance and aspirations of rural youth.

Rural Education and Rural Development

If rural development is defined as those activities that contribute to improving the quality of life of rural people, it is clear that rural schools have made a major contribution and continue to contribute to that objective. There are at least three different ways in which this connection might be evaluated: (1) in terms of the educational attainment of the rural population; (2) in terms of the schooling attained by rural youth and *how* and *where* they utilize that schooling; and (3) in terms of the actual and potential contribution the school, as an institution, makes to the economy and quality of life of the community in which it is located.

The educational attainment of the rural population lags notably behind that of the metropolitan population. This has been so for decades and continues despite some attenuation of the differences in recent years, especially for whites. In 1975 urban white males had completed a median of 12.6 years of school, compared with 12.2 and 11.4 for rural nonfarm and rural farm residents, respectively. Rural-urban differences for white females were not as great. For rural minorities, the educational lag is far more serious. For example, black adult males in urban areas had completed a median of 11.6 years of school in 1975, whereas their rural nonfarm counterparts had completed only 8.1 years; and rural farm adult black males had completed only 5.9 years.[32]

These differences are generally held to reflect past differences in educational opportunity and incentive, especially for minorities, and the effect of migration on both urban and rural education-attainment levels. Almost without exception, past rural-to-urban migrants have been drawn most heavily from among the more educated youth of rural areas, leaving a residual older, less educated adult population. Thus educated rural youth migrating to metropolitan areas add to the median for urban areas and subtract from the median for the rural areas they left behind.

The past history of migration, coupled with the traditions of school finance, raise important issues of equity with respect to the costs and benefits of investment in schooling in rural areas. As noted previously, about 9 percent of all public elementary- and secondary-school support today comes from federal funds, an average of about 42 percent from state sources, and the remaining 49 percent from local-district sources. Thus the community or district, which makes much of the educational investment, stands to lose much of the direct benefit from it as the educational recipient leaves for typically brighter labor-market opportunities. Similarly, throughout the twentieth century rural communities and their taxes have contributed significantly to metropolitan industrial growth and development. Although there has been some recent reversal in this trend, in terms of both population and sources of employment, the pendulum has long been unbalanced in favor of larger, urban-based labor markets. This contribution was even greater in the earlier decades of this century, when a much higher proportion of support for public education came from local revenues.

The impact of education on earnings varies significantly with the recipient and other factors known to influence earnings. Tweeten reports, for example, that *rural* white males lag about $1,000 in annual earnings behind *urban* white males.[33] Of this $1,000, about $400 can be attributed to differences in education. However, *rural black* males lag $7,400 in annual earnings behind *urban white* males. Nearly half this difference can be attributed to the effect of race, but $2,450 can be attributed to differences in education. For females, however, the impact of education is less; dramatic differences in earnings exist between rural *females* and urban *males*. The combination of sex and race accounts for about 70 percent of the $9,400 annual-earning differential between urban white males and rural black females. Differences in educational attainment account for only about 13 percent of that earnings differential.

Thus Tweeten concludes that, although there is evidence supporting the value of additional education in overcoming earnings differentials between rural and urban residents, that contribution is relatively small in relation to more persistent and overpowering influences of race and sex.

Despite the relatively small impact of additional education in influencing the earnings gaps between residential, racial, and sexual groups, there remains a significant problem of equality between the geographic location of those making the investment in education and the location where the beneficiaries choose to relocate that form of wealth. Although there are numerous ways to show the extent to which rural areas have contributed to a greater national concentration of wealth, perhaps none is more easily demonstrated than the geographic transfer of the earnings potential of investment in education.

Another dimension of the relationship between rural education and rural development concerns the reciprocal relationships between school and community in the rural setting. Although the impact and potential tend to be somewhat more particularistic, the school in most smaller rural communities represents the single largest public investment in the area, is the largest single employer of trained professionals, and is a major supplier of recreational and cultural activities for the community at large. Without the school, the community loses a major payroll, some of its leadership, an important calendar of community events, and a significant contributor to community identity. Beyond the costs and benefits, it is clear that rural people in many localities across the country recognize the value of their schools' location and have been willing to fight at length the prospect of losing this central institution. In Iowa, recognition of this prospect statewide led to the organization of People United for Rural Education (PURE) to carry on the battle for retaining their small schools in the state legislature and other public forums.

Although at the height of the school reorganization and consolidation movement of the 1950s and 1960s, rural resistance was generally viewed as a fight
against progressiveness, it has taken on a different complexion in recent years.
Despite the actual and presumed inadequacies of small rural schools, their supporting taxpayers and parents generally regard them as good and adequate, and
feel that whatever sacrifice might be made in terms of expanded curriculum
offerings is more than compensated for by the enhanced opportunities for student participation, individual attention, lessened problems with social control,
and emphasis on basics.[34]

Despite these more intangible social benefits of the presence of the school,
various programs and projects are gaining currency in rural areas that are building on the school-community relationship to enhance the school program and
simultaneously add resources and activities to the community. One such project
that has captured national attention is the Foxfire Corporation, inspired by the
leadership of Elliot Wigginton.[35] This project, which began as a local-high-school
oral-history exercise, has grown into a successful national commercial venture.
Besides that spectacular example, dozens of others are beginning to surface. One
small high school in Arkansas took over publication of the community commercial newspaper after the community had suffered a two-year lapse in publication of a local newspaper. These Arkansas high-school students, under the
direction of the school administration, publish a weekly community commercial
newspaper complete with grocery ads, social columns, local and national news,
classified ads, and reports of local government. Students serve as reporters,
advertising salesmen, and circulation managers; they execute layout and design,
photography, and printing. Not only are the students acquiring real vocational
training, but the community also benefits from a service that did not exist
before. The school does not expect to continue operation of the paper inde-
finitely. It intends to sell the enterprise to an interested and capable student as
soon as one emerges, spin off the enterprise, and develop some other needed
area of community service.

Increasingly, some rural schools faced with limited faculty resources and
shrinking budgets are turning to the community for supplementary faculty and
projects. This trend is taking a variety of forms. One such effort, going on in
rural Missouri for the past four years, involves contracting with local business
persons and artisans to provide vocational training to individual students.[36] The
basis for the relationship is a competency-based contract; the business person or
artisan clearly takes on the role of teacher, and the student receives graduation
credit, and acquires skills that may lead to employment. In addition to building
stronger school-community relationships, this method provides for a greatly expanded vocational offering in a situation in which it would not be economically
feasible to offer in-school training in more than one or two skill areas. The
student receives a certificate of competency specifying not only that he or she
has completed a training course, but also the specific skills and competencies the
student has acquired. Although a rural community or school is not likely to be

transformed by such efforts, they make a clear contribution to enhancing the program and well-being of the student, the school, and the community.

This view of the school as a potential contributor to community and rural development is gaining greater currency and has been embodied in a number of significant rural-school reform projects that have been undertaken in recent years. Some evaluations of these efforts are reviewed in the following section.

Recent Rural-School Reform Efforts

It is of interest that recent efforts at rural-school reform have been oriented significantly toward capitalizing on the potential of the relationship between the school and the larger community it serves. In a sense some of these efforts are being directed toward the earlier conclusion that no great gains in output or mobility are likely to be achieved by confining attention to the school—whether to its size, location, form of organization, or methods of instruction.

In a recent publication, Nachtigal evaluates fourteen different rural-school reform efforts ranging from generously funded projects of the federal government and foundations to some grass-roots efforts.[37] In his introduction, Nachtigal concludes that there have been three major themes in rural-school reform. The first of these, dating back to the turn of the century, still survives in various forms. That theme contended that the problem with rural education is that it is not urban; that is, the rural school itself is the problem. The second theme, Nachtigal suggests did not emerge until the heyday of school-consolidation efforts in the 1950s. This theme was the notion of the "necessarily existent" rural school—one for which consolidation was not a viable option because of excessive costs of space. The third theme grew out of the mass federal intervention of the mid 1960s. The substance of this theme was that the problems of education are generic. Nachtigal suggests that the results of his evaluation of fourteen recent reform efforts lead him to question the validity of the first and third of these themes.

Instead, Nachtigal builds a case for "accepting rural reality," which requires a more differentiated view of the rural school, its environment and circumstances—"one that allows and assists rural schools and rural communities to build on their strengths and overcome their weaknesses".[38]

Of the fourteen programs evaluated by Nachtigal, eight dealt with school-improvement variables within the educational system. These, he contends, were clearly based on generic assumptions about school improvement. However, six of the programs dealt with school-improvement variables outside the system. Especially noteworthy about those projects was the extent of school involvement with the community. One of the more widely acclaimed of these projects is in Staples, Minnesota, a locally initiated project that has evolved over the past twenty-five years, with the school becoming a major vehicle of social and economic development for the community at large.

A recent comprehensive evaluation of the Experimental Schools (ES) program conducted in ten different rural communities around the United States has been published.[39] This ambitious project, funded for five years, sought to evaluate the consequences of a federal investment program designed to improve the school system and, through the schools, to address a variety of community needs. One of the ten sites was also included among the fourteen programs evaluated by Nachtigal. The evaluation by Fitzsimmons and Freedman provides extensive documentation of the interactions that exist in rural communities and how these interactions influence community decisions and outcomes. They found that the school was one of the most highly interactive sectors of the communities they studied and, therefore, in a position to spread investment effects to other highly interactive sectors such as the economic base and local government. They concluded that the school, because of its centrality, should be in a key position to influence economic change and development in rural communities. However, they conclude that despite the centrality of the school, it lacks the power of enforcement necessary to be an effective agent of change.

The ES project was ambitious and clearly intended to involve the community and go beyond the school in the delineation of problems and development of courses of action. However, of the ES project, Nachtigal concludes that "federally imposed timelines and expectations of how proposal budgets should be constructed negated local community involvement."[40]

About all the projects reviewed, Nachtigal concludes that the single most important determinant of success or failure was the centrality of the problem definition. In those cases in which a high consensus was achieved concerning the relevance and worthiness of objectives between school and community, he found that projects were continued and useful; where that consensus was not achieved, projects ceased to operate when the funding ran out. He also concludes that there are some essential factors in project implementation: (1) there must be broad-based planning including community representatives; (2) implementation assistance must be provided for rural schools and communities to a greater extent than for urban projects; and (3) it is essential to build an institutional base if continuity is to be achieved when funding runs out or key participants leave.

These reform efforts and their extensive evaluations may become more prominent in the literature on rural education as time goes on because they represent a departure from the perspective that the school itself is the problem, and that its outcomes can be appreciably modified by relatively modest changes in the way it does business.

Conclusions

Whether they are called phases, transitions, or waves, it is clear that rural schools have undergone more significant and profound changes over the past fifty years than have urban schools. They made an almost total transition from one form of schooling to another in the name of improved education. However, unrefined differences in educational attainment of the rural population and performance of rural students on various achievement tests have led many to conclude that smaller rural schools are incapable of producing a quality of education equal to their metropolitan counterparts. However, recent, more refined, analysis suggests strongly that rural-urban differences in student performance are more attributable to factors beyond the direct control of the school than to the school's quality or amount of input.

Although rural schools increasingly have come to look and operate as urban schools do, severe factors remain that create a different set of opportunities and problems for them. Regardless of whether rural schools merely attempt to maintain a traditional program of schooling, or move in the direction of some of the recent reform efforts discussed, certain circumstances of the rural environment will influence attainment. The program of rural schools will especially have to cope with the rising costs of overcoming space. As transportation becomes a larger part of the operating budget, further consolidation will likely become an even less viable option than it has been in recent years. This may lead rural schools to experiment with methods of maintaining or enriching their programs without incurring additional travel for students. These experiments will probably include a greater sharing of teaching resources among schools, use of new information and computer technology, and even modification of traditional concepts of where learning occurs and who provides it.

In addition to the limitations imposed by space, rural schools are also typically in a situation in which close interaction between school and community is unavoidable. This proximity, and the corresponding reduced social space between the school and the population it serves, may continue in some cases to be viewed as part of the problem (as some of the literature cited in this chapter contended), or may come to be regarded as part of the solution. Building on the opportunities of the world outside the school may lead to expanding educational resources to provide a wider range of educational opportunities under conditions where traditional school programs would, of necessity, be limited. It may provide opportunities for more realistic educational experiences for students, to the possible benefit of both school and community.

The conclusion is that relatively little is to be gained from further attempts to convert rural schools into replicas of urban schools. But that is not to suggest that the programs and quality of education of rural schools should be consigned to second-class status. Rather, the circumstances of rural schools create problems and also provide opportunities for experimenting with alternative forms of education and educational innovations that may prove to be applicable to education generally. However, if creativity is to be a part of the solution, resource-limited rural schools will need assistance both in the form of greater tolerance for the problems and circumstances they face and in the form of greater financial and technical assistance.

Notes

1. Alvin Toffler, *The Third Wave* (New York: Bantam Books, 1980).

2. Edward P. Cubberly, *The Improvement of Rural Schools* (New York: Houghton Mifflin, 1912).

3. Henry J. Waters, "Introduction," in Marion G. Kirkpatrick, *The Rural School from Within* (Philadelphia: Lippincott, 1917).

4. Stephens J. Fitzsimmons and Abby J. Freedman, *Rural Community Development* (Cambridge, Mass.: Abt Books, 1981); Luther Tweeten, "Education Has Role in Rural Development," in *Rural Development Perspectives* (Washington, D.C.: U.S. Department of Agriculture, Economics, Statistics, and Cooperative Service, 1980).

5. Jonathan P. Sher, "Vocational Education in Rural America: Current Problems and Prospects," in *The Planning Papers for the Vocational Education Study,* Vocational Education Study Publication no. 1 (Washington D.C.: National Institute of Education, 1979).

6. William S. Carlsen and Faith Dunne, "Small Rural Schools: A Portrait," *High School Journal* 64(1981).

7. Stuart Rosenfeld, "A Portrait of Rural America: Conditions Affecting Vocational Education Policy," *Vocational Education Study,* Publication no. 6 (Washington, D.C.: National Institute of Education, 1981).

8. Frank A. Fratoe, *Rural Education and Rural Labor Force in the Seventies,* Rural Development Research Report no. 5 (Washington, D.C.: U.S. Department of Agriculture, Economics, Statistics, and Cooperative Service, 1978).

9. David B. Tyack, *The One Best System: A History of American Urban Education* (Cambridge, Mass.: Harvard University Press, 1974).

10. Gail Bass and Paul Berman, *Federal Aid to Rural Schools: Current Patterns and Unmet Needs,* R-2583-NIE (Santa Monica, Calif.: Rand Corporation, 1979).

11. Fratoe, *Rural Education.*

12. National Center for Education Statistics, *Condition of Education, 1976* (Washington, D.C.: U.S. Government Printing Office, 1976).

13. Christopher Jencks et al., *Inequality: A Reassessment of the Effect of Family and Schooling in America* (New York: Harper and Row, 1972).

14. Arthur Cosby and Ivan Charner, eds., *Education and Work in Rural America: The Social Context of Early Career Decision and Achievement* (Houston, Tex.: Stafford-Lowdon, 1978).

15. Jonathan P. Sher and Rachel B. Tompkins, "Economy, Efficiency, and Equality: The Myths of Rural School and District Consolidation" (Washington, D.C.: U.S. Department of Health, Education, and Welfare, National Institute of Education, 1976).

16. James Coleman et al., *Equality of Educational Opportunity* (Washington, D.C.: U.S. Government Printing Office, 1966).

17. Richard Raymond, "Determinants of Primary and Secondary Education in West Virginia," *Journal of Human Resources* 3(1968).

18. Sher and Tompkins, "Economy, Efficiency, and Equality."

19. William F. Fox, *Relationships between Size of School and School Districts and the Cost of Education,* Technical Bulletin no. 1621 (Washington, D.C.: U.S. Department of Agriculture, Economics, Statistics, and Cooperative Service, 1980).

20. Fred White and Luther Tweeten, "Optimal School District Size Emphasizing Rural Areas," in *American Journal of Agricultural Economics* 55 (1973):45-53.

21. Fox, *Relationships between Size of School.*

22. Jencks, *Inequality,* p. 256.

23. Arni T. Dunathan, "Midwest Schools Face Shortages of Good Teachers," *Kappan* (October 1979):122.

24. Ivan D. Muse and Loya Stonehocker, "A Study of Small Rural High Schools: Northwest Regional Vocational Laboratory" (Portland, Ore.: Rural School Study, 1973).

25. Daryl Hobbs, "Rural Education: The Problems and Potential of Smallness," *High School Journal* 64(April 1981):292-298; James Jess, "Developing Positive Parent and Community Involvement in the Schooling Process," *High School Journal* 64(April 1981):284-291; Fitzsimmons and Freedman, *Rural Community Development.*

26. Muse and Stonehocker, "Small Rural High Schools."

27. Martin Burlingame, "Win Some, Lose Some: Small Rural District Superintendents" (Paper prepared for presentation at the American Educational Research Association Annual Meeting, San Francisco, 1979).

28. Muse and Stonehocker, "Small Rural High Schools."

29. Carlsen and Dunne, "Small Rural Schools."

30. Cosby and Charner, *Education and Work.*

31. Ibid., p. 191.

32. Tweeten, "Education Has Role."

33. Ibid.

34. Stuart A. Rosenfeld, "Shaping a Rural Vocational Education Policy," *Vocational Education* (March 1980):7; Faith Dunne, "Reform and Resistance: An Examination of Rural School Improvement Projects in the United States" (Hanover, N.H.: Dartmouth College Department of Education, n.d.).

35. Elliot Wigginton, *Moments* (New York: Star Press, 1975); Gail A. Parks, "The Foxfire Concept: Experiential Education in Rural America," in Jonathan Sher, ed., *Rural Education in Urbanized Nations* (Boulder, Colo.: Westview Press, 1981).

36. Daryl Hobbs, "The School in the Rural Community: Issues of Costs, Education, and Values," *Small School Forum* 2(Spring 1981).

37. Paul M. Nachtigal, *Improving Rural Schools* (Washington, D.C.: U.S. Department of Education, Office of Educational Research and Improvement, National Institute of Education, September 1980).

38. Ibid., p. 33.

39. Fitzsimmons and Freedman, *Rural Community Development.*

40. Nachtigal, *Improving Rural Schools,* p. 31.

14 The Policy Implications of the Crisis Relocation Plan for Local Government

Sydney Duncombe

The evacuation of nonessential civilian population from urban target areas has been used in past wars to reduce civilian casualties. For example, children were evacuated from London to the English countryside during World War II. The current U.S. emergency plans go a step further in recommending the evacuation of nearly the entire population of high-risk areas in the event of imminent or actual nuclear war. Approximately 145 million U.S. residents live in these high-risk areas, according to one report, and approximately 80 percent of these people are expected to relocate.[1] To encourage orderly relocation, television stations have been asked to provide instructions in an emergency on where people are to go and what routes they are to follow. The evacuation would probably be triggered by a presidential declaration of national emergency, which is empowered under federal law if the president finds "that an attack on the United States has occurred or is anticipated" and that the national safety requires it.[2] The evacuation plan, called the *crisis relocation plan,* would give local governments—especially in rural counties—tremendous administrative responsibilities.

Why Crisis Relocation

The main purpose of crisis relocation is to reduce the number of casualties from nuclear blast, thermal radiation, and initial nuclear radiation in the major target areas in the United States. A 1-megaton blast could cause 100 percent casualties within 1.7 miles of impact; the blast and burn casualties would then diminish so that fewer than 11 percent would die and fewer than 40 percent would be injured 4.7-7.4 miles from the explosion.[3] With a larger nuclear weapon, casualties would increase. For example, a 25-megaton weapon burst in the air would extend the range of injuries to more than 15 miles from the blast and could cause 3,200,000 deaths and injuries in a large metropolitan area like Detroit.[4]

Crisis relocation is not intended to remove people from the risk of radioactive fallout. Although the fallout is heaviest close to the blast, it can cause deaths 300 miles or more downwind. It would be the responsibility of the host counties to protect evacuees from radioactive fallout.

203

There are two main civil-defense alternatives to crisis relocation in the event of an imminent nuclear war. One alternative is to encourage people in risk areas to find shelter in home basements and protected areas in commercial, industrial, and public buildings near their homes. This could be the only feasible alternative if there was not sufficient time for crisis relocation, but the result would be many millions of additional deaths near the blasts.[5] A second alternative would be to build thousands of blast-resistant fallout shelters in U.S. cities at an estimated cost of $70 billion.[6] Crisis relocation is considered in federal literature as a less costly and reasonably effective alternative.

The Federal Emergency Management Agency (FEMA) contends that 80 percent of the people of the United States could survive a nuclear war through a reasonably effective crisis relocation plan.[7] The next section of this chapter explores what is necessary for such a reasonably effective crisis relocation plan.

Program Implications of Crisis Relocation for Host Counties

In preparing to meet the needs of local residents as well as relocatees, a host county should have a plan that specifies not only the organizational responsibilities of a civil-defense command center, but also exactly what must be done in crisis relocation to secure the necessary food, water, supplies, and personnel for fallout shelters.

Counties need, and generally have, an emergency operating center that can be protected from fallout. Counties need a civil-defense staff that could be assembled within a few hours of a presidential declaration of emergency. This staff should include not only the county civil-defense director, but also key officials such as the county commissioners, city officials and police, fire fighters, and public-works personnel.

Host, as well as risk, counties require an adequate system, such as fire sirens and radio broadcasts, to warn residents of an imminent nuclear attack. To protect people against radioactive fallout, buildings within the county with sufficient protection must provide space for all relocatees as well as for host-county residents who do not have access to home-basement fallout shelters. If adequate space is not provided, there is danger that people without shelters may try to force their way into home-basement shelters and overcrowd public fallout shelters.

To avoid a potentially lethal dose of radiation, people within 200–300 miles of the blast could require enough food, water, and other supplies to remain in shelters from ten to fourteen days. More than a decade ago, it was common for civil-defense authorities to stock fallout shelters with food, medical supplies, and water containers. This policy has been discontinued, leaving county officials with the very difficult task of finding sufficient supplies on short notice.

The operation of a shelter with several thousand (or even several hundred) people for a ten- to fourteen-day period requires persons who have knowledge of shelter management. A well-prepared county should have programs for the selection and training of shelter managers.

Shelters need to be provided with emergency lighting, ventilation, and heating if normal electric service is interrupted. There will need to be sanitary facilities in shelters for cooking food, washing utensils, and disposing of human wastes. Doctors, nurses, medical facilities, and medical supplies should be available. A communication system not depending on telephone lines will be needed to link the fallout shelters to the county emergency operating center. The host county will have to maintain order, prevent looting, and keep traffic moving while people are trying to get to shelters. The county, or possibly other local governments, will not only have great responsibilities during a period of crisis relocation, but will also need to pay for or commander large amounts of food, supplies, or services. The success of the crisis relocation plan will rest largely on the shoulders of local officials (particularly county officials) in the many rural, semirural, and urban host counties throughout the nation.

Major Problems of Host Counties

I was part of a four-member team that included a county civil-defense director, an official of the Idaho Association of Counties, and an official of the Association of Idaho Cities. After a November 1980 survey of five northern Idaho counties that would receive evacuees from the Spokane County risk area, I reached the following conclusions about the problems these counties would face in implementing crisis relocation.

Shelter Space

Only one of the five counties studied, Latah, had adequate shelter space in public buildings for its own residents and relocatees. Nez Perce County had fewer than 13,000 shelter spaces for its own 33,000 residents and could not shelter an anticipated 28,000 relocatees without denying its own residents shelter. Shoshone County had a large number of potential shelter spaces in deep mines. However, some mines could not operate mine hoists and ventilating equipment if electric power were cut off, and other mines have ventilating equipment that could not be used because it would suck in contaminated air. The two remaining counties studied, Kootenai and Benewah, were not host counties but would undoubtedly be used by some Spokane residents with summer homes and friends in the area. Kootenai County has 6,000 public fallout-shelter spaces for

59,000 people and would probably receive heavy fallout from Spokane, which is directly to the west. Benewah County has too few fallout shelter spaces for its own population and would try to develop makeshift shelters in two railroad tunnels. Unless there is a massive effort to build new public shelters or upgrade home basements into shelters, lack of shelter space will cause severe problems in four of the five counties studied.

Water

Most of the pumps that operate municipal water supplies for public fallout shelters in the five counties would not work after nuclear explosions interrupted the northwest power-grid system. As a result, the only safe water supplies for most public shelters would be those in covered water tanks that gravity feed into city water systems. Latah County, with the best shelter system of the five counties, has 60,000 shelter spaces in the city of Moscow, but not a single generator that could operate any of the deep-well pumps that would have to supply the city if there were no electricity. In Shoshone County, relocatees who use the mines might have to drink water seeping into the mines and standing at the bottom of mine shafts. One city in the area, St. Maries, has a gravity-feed municipal water supply; but its creek-fed source would be contaminated by fallout. Lack of sufficient safe drinking water would be a critical problem for most public and home-basement shelters in the area.

Food

The national crisis relocation plan relies on food from commercial sources and food that relocatees carry with them. Most of the large food warehouses that serve northern Idaho are in the Spokane County risk area and could not be counted on as sources in an emergency since their employees would probably evacuate their families after a presidential declaration of emergency. Moreover, it is estimated that the typical Spokane relocatee could bring only one or two days supply of food in an emergency because of the need to carry clothing, sleeping bags, and other needed possessions in their cars. Food stores could be stripped of food within hours, leaving public officials with the problem of feeding county residents and relocatees. In Shoshone County, an anticipated influx of more than 60,000 relocatees might exhaust all county food supplies within three days. In the other counties, food supplies in stores, warehouses, and homes might last five days to a week. In several counties, particularly Latah and Nez Perce, utilization of unmilled wheat and dried peas is possible; but this requires some means of washing and cooking the wheat and peas. Lack of food will be a critical problem in all five counties.

Other Problems

None of the five counties had a sufficient number of physicians, nurses, and hospital beds to cope with an influx of thousands of people, some of whom may have severe radiation exposure and burns. There are relatively few trained shelter managers in the five counties. None of the five counties has a sufficiently large police force to assure maintenance of order and traffic control. Some progress has been made in the past year, particularly in Latah County, but not one of the five counties could be considered adequately prepared for crisis relocation if nuclear war occurs. Despite good work by county civil-defense personnel, it is possible that the public fallout-shelter system in all five counties would collapse within a few days.

I have been in contact with county civil-defense officials in two other states and found concern about implementation of crisis relocation. In Orange County, New York, food is a critical problem, with a county of 259,000 expected to feed more than 1 million relocatees from New York City. In Cascade County, Montana, shelter space and transportation routes are particularly critical. The Cascade County civil-defense director points out that many of the relocatees from risk counties would have to travel through missile fields, over a mountain pass with some of the coldest recorded temperatures in the nation, and over 100 miles on a route with gas stations up to 40 miles apart.[8]

The most serious of all the problems that host counties across the nation will face is housing relocatees in shelters that provide sufficient protection from fallout. A federal civil-defense manual states that about twice as many people live in risk areas as in host areas.[9] According to K.S. Gant and C.M. Haaland, much of the nation's shelter space is in large, aboveground facilities located in risk areas.[10] Lack of adequate numbers of home basements suitable as shelters, particularly in southern states, add to the problem. Gant and Haaland conclude that the public-shelter system now existing is not adequate for the needs of the U.S. population.[11] They believe that the crisis relocation plan will require many more shelters located in rural areas and small towns. Gant and Halland warn that host areas that cannot now provide shelter for their own population will find it extremely difficult to absorb relocatees from risk areas.[12] Provision of adequate shelter in host counties requires not only a fallout or home basement shelters, but also sufficient food, water, and supplies in the shelters for a ten- to fourteen-day shelter stay.

Conclusions

If county governments in host counties are to fulfill their expected mandate under the crisis relocation plan, they need much more financial help and technical assistance than they have been given to date. Funds for part-time civil-defense directors, training exercises once or twice a year, and an organizational plan are not enough. Some federal or state agency needs to get key food stocks out of central-city warehouses into host counties in a crisis before it is too late to move them. Some agency must purchase gasoline or diesel pumps and generators and give them to local government to assure adequate water supplies if the electric-grid system fails. Some agencies need to be able to stockpile medical supplies, medicines, and hospital beds for emergency hospitals. Many more shelters should be built in host counties that have insufficient shelter spaces for their own residents and relocatees. Many more shelter managers need to be enlisted and trained.

County governments and other units of local government do not have funds to pay these crucial preparation costs. They cannot pay the cost of feeding and caring for more than 100 million refugees. Yet legally and morally they cannot close their borders to millions of fellow Americans from high-risk counties.

The failure of host counties to be prepared for crisis relocation could mean the collapse of the public shelter system in most host counties, lawless mobs denied shelter forcing their way into home basements, and a casualty rate as high as 80 percent in many host counties.[13] Moreover, a foreign nation knowing the serious inadequacies in civil defense might be more tempted to risk nuclear confrontation when its own civil-defense system is much better prepared than our own.[14] Much of the current emphasis in defense spending seems to focus on increasing the destructive power of offensive missiles. Authorities such as T.K. Jones and W. Scott Thompson have questioned this, stating that it would be better to move from the present destruction-oriented concept of security to a survival-oriented or protection-oriented system.[15]

If the capability to implement the crisis relocation plan is not greatly improved, rural local governments may face an unprecedented crisis should relocation become necessary. Local officials in host counties are sitting on top of a volcano that they hope will never become active. Since the federal government has imposed this implied mandate, it should provide the funds and technical assistance to help local governments in rural America make this mandate work.

Notes

1. U.S. Federal Emergency Management Agency, *Questions and Answers on Crisis Relocation Planning* (Washington, D.C.: Federal Emergency Management Agency, 1980), pp. 2, 9.

2. *United States Code Annotated,* Title 50, Section 2291. A national emergency may also be proclaimed by a concurrent resolution of Congress.

3. Calculated from tables in U.S. Office of Technology Assessment, *The Effects of Nuclear War* (Washington, D.C.: Office of Technology Assessment, 1979), pp. 31, 32. This excludes deaths and illness from radioactive fallout.

4. Ibid., pp. 37–39.

5. U.S. Federal Emergency Management Agency, *Questions and Answers on Crisis Relocation Planning,* p. 8, states that if time does not exist for relocation, people would be asked to use the basements of larger buildings and home basements. They estimate a survival rate of up to 50 percent in this situation, compared with an 80-percent survival rate from an effective crisis relocation plan.

6. The Soviet government is reported to have built 15,000 blast shelters. By building our own blast shelters, we might increase the survival rate to 90 percent, according to a federal report. Ibid., pp. 5, 8.

7. Ibid., p. 5.

8. See William E. Murray, "Crisis Relocation, a View from the County Level," *County News,* 22 June 1981, p. 4.

9. Department of Defense, Defense Civil Preparedness Agency, *Guide for Crisis Relocation Contingency Planning: Overview of Nuclear Civil Protection Planning for Crisis Relocation* (Washington, D.C.: Department of Defense, 1979), pp. 2–4.

10. K.S. Gant and C.M. Haaland, "Community Shelters for Protection from Radioactive Fallout: Availability and Patterns of Probable Use," *Health Physics* (August 1979):222, 223.

11. Ibid., p. 223.

12. Ibid., p. 229.

13. I have concluded that the casualty rate would range from 50 to 80 percent in the five northern Idaho counties studied.

14. According to Department of State, *Special Report 47: Soviet Civil Defense* (Washington, D.C.: Bureau of Public Affairs, Department of State, 1978), the Soviet civil-defense organization has a staff of more than 100,000 full-time personnel. The report concludes that the Soviets believe that their present civil defenses "would improve their ability to conduct military operations and would enhance the USSR's ability to survive following a nuclear exchange" (p. 5).

15. T.K. Jones and W. Scott Thompson, "Central War and Civil Defense," *Orbis* (Fall 1978):711. T.K. Jones served with the Strategic Arms Limitation Talks (SALT) delegation during 1971–1974.

Part V
Agriculture and Rural Policy

15

Farm Structure and Rural Development

Frederick H. Buttel

Introduction: The Separation of Agricultural and Rural Development

"Rural development means more nonfarm jobs in rural areas."[1] —Don Paarlberg

The preceding statement by a distinguished academic and administrative personality in agriculture aptly depicts one of the most important barriers to formulating innovative policies for the nonmetropolitan segment of U.S. society: the rural-farm and rural-nonfarm components of the nonmetropolitan United States are considered analytically separate—clearly a reasonable and defensible posture—and autonomous—a more problematic assumption. This had led to academic and policymaking fragmentation. One group of academicians and policymakers—basically production economists and administrators of the commodity stabilization and foreign trade branches of the U.S. Department of Agriculture (USDA)—has come to specialize in agricultural development. A distinct set of persons—regional economists, community sociologists, and so forth—focuses on the socioeconomic problems of the nonfarm population. As a result, little attention has been paid to the mutual linkages between the development (and underdevelopment) of the farm and nonfarm components of the nonmetropolitan United States.

Several other observations further reinforce this point. First, Luther Tweeten, one of the most gifted contributors to the state of knowledge on nonmetropolitan America, is one of the few academicians to have undertaken extensive studies of both agricultural and rural-development policy. Yet it is significant that Tweeten's two most recent books—*Micropolitan Development*, which deals with rural economic development, and *Foundations of Farm Policy,* which is a comprehensive economic analysis of agricultural policy in the U.S.—show so little cross-fertilization of these two subject matters.[2] In particular, *Micropolitan Development* contains surprisingly little discussion of the impacts of agricultural structure and structural change on community or regional economic development. These two otherwise useful books thus represent a continued manifestation of the academic and policymaking separation of agricultural and rural development.

Reprinted by permission from *Farms in Transition,* 1982. Copyright © The Iowa State University Press.

The pervasiveness of this separation of inherently interrelated subject matters is further seen in statement on the recent small-community- and rural-development policy by the Carter administration.[3] This document clearly is a major step forward for people concerned with the socioeconomic development of the nonmetropolitan United States. Although we have had explicit statements of urban policy for over a decade, late 1979 marked the first time that an administration had done the same for rural America. Such a statement of policy provides an initial point of leverage by which the executive branch can be held accountable for its policy stances toward the rural sector. But although this small-community- and rural-development policy statement is important, it is significant that the statement almost entirely ignores the actual and potential interrelations of the farm and nonfarm sectors. In particular, there is no mention of how the administration's ongoing agricultural policies affect nonfarm people, or of how ongoing and proposed rural development policies might affect agriculture.

In fairness to Paarlberg, who is quoted at the outset of this chapter, it should be noted that these words were to some degree taken out of context. Indeed, later in the paragraph from which this excerpt was taken, Paarlberg does connect rural development (that is, nonfarm jobs-creating) policy with agriculture—more specifically, with part-time farming. Paarlberg argues that rural jobs creation will enhance the viability of part-time farmers, although he seems to ignore the possibility that the preservation of small- and moderate-scale farms might itself lead to more nonfarm employment. Paarlberg raises yet another important point: the hostility of the "farm lobby" (presumably the American Farm Bureau Federation and major commodity groups, in particular) to rural-development initiatives.[4] Large-scale farmers, in Paarlberg's view, see viable part-time farmers as unfair competition; one might also speculate that large-scale farmers are hesitant about jobs-creation programs that would place upward pressures on wages for hired workers. Nevertheless, Paarlberg's observations are crucial: the separation of agricultural and rural-development policy reflects the political realities of USDA decision making and the superimposition of these political realities on the land-grant-college research and extension complex.

The initial purpose of this chapter is to provide a highly abbreviated overview of available research on the interrelations of agricultural and rural development. This review of evidence emphasizes the connections between increasing farm size, mechanization, and rural community viability; but it will be argued that several other types of historical and contemporary research should be undertaken to provide a more comprehensive view of the development of rural America. Second, it will provide a brief critique of rural development practice in the United States, particularly that which prevails in academic and extension circles. Finally, it will explore the prospects for development of agricultural policies that would further the cause of rural development.

Before we proceed, it must be emphasized that the notion of rural development will be employed in two distinct but related senses. The first use of the term will be to depict the actual historical pattern of social and economic change in rural communities and regions. In this first sense, *rural development* essentially means the degree of capital accumulation and its retention in rural regions. Likewise, rural regions that fail to undergo capital accumulation or that experience the extraction of accumulated capital (for example, profits from absentee-owned enterprises being invested elsewhere, or adverse terms of exchange for farmers that result in decapitalization) can be called *underdeveloped*. The second use of the term *rural development* will be to depict the ongoing and potential public policies through which the social and economic condition of rural people can be improved. This second concept of rural development thus pertains to the theory and strategy of the profession that has come to be known as rural development.

Farm Structure and Rural-Community Viability

As noted in an earlier article with William L. Flinn,[5] a substantial number of pioneering rural sociologists were concerned that the course of U.S. agricultural development in the twentieth century was uneven in its impact on rural people.[6] Many of these rural sociologists noted that the development of agriculture led to the underdevelopment of rural communities. Nevertheless, this critical posture toward agricultural development largely abated during the 1950s and 1960s as most rural sociologists began to accept implicitly that the course of structural change in agriculture was not only inevitable but also, on balance, in the public interest.

Much of this consensus about the desirability of structural change in agriculture began to crumble in the 1970s. The stagnation of per-acre yields for most major crops, rapid food-price inflation, concerns about the plight of migrant farm workers and family farmers, high levels of soil erosion, disclosure of some of the antisocial tendencies of agribusiness firms, and a number of related factors led to a widespread questioning of the social and technical bases of modern U.S. agriculture. It was in this last decade that Goldschmidt's studies of the consequences of agricultural structure for rural-community viability were rediscovered, leading to a number of studies that replicated Goldschmidt's observations in the Central Valley of California during the 1940s.[7] Rodefeld was probably the first to blaze this new trail of inquiry.[8] Although this emerging crisis in U.S. agriculture had a considerable impact on the academic community, it is also important to note that nonfarm public-interest groups were instrumental in bringing the issue of community consequences of farm-structure change before the public-policy arena. Although Goldschmidt's work has some major theoretical and methodological shortcomings, it has been one of the most fertile sources of hypotheses for social-science research on agriculture during the 1970s.[9]

Summary of Empirical Results

Most research in this area has focused on the impacts of change in the size and number of farms on community characteristics. Several studies also consider the degree of corporate ownership of farms as a major structural characteristic of agriculture, although most researchers utilizing this variable have relied on census data and acknowledged the limitations of census procedures for estimating the prominence of corporate operation of farms.[10] In addition, the size and number of farms and the degree of corporate ownership of agricultural production units are usually considered to be closely bound up with mechanization or technological change in agriculture.[11] This correspondence of structure and technology—particularly mechanization—is reasonable in most respects. U.S. agricultural development during the nineteenth century and most of the twentieth was accompanied by labor scarcity and high wages (relative to other advanced societies). Thus the increased scale of agricultural operations was facilitated and accompanied by the displacement of family labor with mechanical technologies, rather than by the consolidation of large farms utilizing hired labor.[12] It should be recognized, however, that in several regions of the United States—particularly California—mechanization followed, rather than led to, increased farm size and reduced size of the farm population. Already existing large farms in California, many dating back to the Spanish land grants, employed large numbers of hired workers during the early decades of the twentieth century who only later, primarily during the 1960s and 1970s, were displaced with labor-saving machinery.[13] Nevertheless, the discussion that follows treats the size and number of farms, the degree of corporate ownership and operation of farms (large-scale industrial farming), and the degree of farm mechanization as a singular dimension of structural change in agriculture—an assumption that has been borne out in a variety of subnational and cross-national studies.[14]

The issue of the rural-development or underdevelopment consequences of increased scale and mechanization in agriculture is obviously quite complex. For example, it is apparent that the consequences of scale and mechanization vary greatly across different socioeconomic contexts. The nature of agricultural production, the viability of the regional or local economic base, the level of industrial development, and the class relations among agriculturalists are important contextual factors that have not been systematically taken into account by researchers.[15] Thus any summary of this literature must be posed in terms of general tendencies rather than as deterministic statements.

With this caveat in mind, it can be noted at the outset that social-science research on the interrelations of agricultural and rural development has had two major characteristics. First, agricultural structural variables are taken to be independent variables. Second, this research investigates the impact of agricultural structure (or change in agricultural structure) on change in the numbers and socioeconomic characteristics of farm personnel, and on change in the characteristics—especially population size and employment levels—of rural communities. Despite these similarities, the actual research methods have been quite diverse. These have included Goldschmidt's anthropological methods,[16] the analysis of sample survey data,[17] the analysis of census data,[18] and linear programming.[19] Heffernan notes that despite the diversity of methods employed in this literature, the results have been remarkably consistent.[20] The results basically support the "Goldschmidt hypothesis"—that the increased size, reduced number, increased mechanization, and increased corporate operation and ownership of farms tend to lead to the socioeconomic decline of rural communities and regions.

The most obvious and important consequences of the dimension of structural change in agriculture considered in this chapter are declines in the size of the farm work force (including farm operators, managers, farm-family laborers, and hired laborers) and in the size of the farm population (members of the farm work force plus their families). Mechanization is the most immediate cause of these declines. A second consistent observation is that decline in the size of the farm work force and farm population is accompanied by shifts in their characteristics. The degree to which agricultural regions experience increasing farm size, reduced numbers of farms, increased mechanization, and increased prevalence of large-scale industrial farming tends to be inversely associated with the prevalence of family labor (owner-managers plus unpaid family labor) and positively associated with the proportion of hired labor in the farm work force. The implication that is usually drawn is that an increased prevalence of hired labor will have undesirable effects on the rural social structure and on rural-community viability. Because of the increased proportion of hired labor, a number of studies have indicated that structural change in agriculture will be accompanied by shifts toward inequality or concentration of landownership; lower educational backgrounds; lower job and residential stability; lower levels of per-capita income; and lower levels of participation in community institutions such as voluntary organizations, churches, and the political system.[21] This research thus suggests that aside from the clear economic gains captured by a shrinking group of large-scale farmers, the overall consequences for the farm population as a whole will tend to be adverse.

Most of these observations have been confirmed by research at the community level. These effects appear to be greatest in rural communities that are relatively small, in communities located in the relatively unurbanized "agricultural interior," and in communities where inequality in the distribution of community resources such as education has left dislocated farm personnel poorly prepared to enter the urban labor force.[22] Nevertheless, the key observation at the community level of analysis is that the rate or extent of farm structural change has consequences for the socioeconomic viability of rural places. Most important, declines in the size of the farm work force and farm population lead to declines in the population of rural communities and trade centers greater than the initial loss of farm personnel and their families.[23] This exaggerated decline in the population of rural communities has been attributed to the fact that a declining farm population undermines the sales and eventually the survival of retail merchants and service-providing enterprises in rural trade centers.[24] Historically, this trend has been aggravated further by the constantly increasing level of sales necessary to support small business operations.[25] Thus the overall consequence is a tendency for farm structural change to set in motion a downward multiplier or spiral of decline in rural-community economic activity.

A number of related impacts of rural-community viability have been documented. These include declining community tax bases and resultant fiscal and cost-efficiency problems in community-service delivery and declines in service availability.[26] Another set of studies concludes that the trend toward large-scale, mechanized, absentee-owned agricultural enterprises is associated with adverse consequences in terms of community social participation and satisfaction with community life.[27] It should be noted, however, that these studies are all cross-sectional in nature and fail to provide needed longitudinal evidence that is generally available for the other consequences of large-scale agriculture discussed previously.

It should be emphasized that the results of the research that has just been reviewed should be interpreted in probabilistic terms or in terms of tendencies. Obviously, a rural community close to a major population center or a rural community undergoing rural industrialization will experience increases in population and economic activity regardless of the degree of structural change in the community's agriculture. These generalizations should be understood to be subject to qualifications associated with the context in which structural change in agriculture occurs.

The research reviewed herein has a number of implications for rural-development policy. A minimal or "weak" implication is that rural-development initiatives that ignore ongoing trends in the agricultural sector will be ineffectual. The "strong" implication is that social policies that encourage or support small-scale agriculture are necessary to ensure the viability of rural communities in the United States.[28] The viability and desirability of each of these policy postures will be examined in more depth later.

Limitations of Existing Research on Agricultural and Rural Development

Research centering around the Goldschmidt hypothesis has been seminal and has fostered a much-needed reassessment of agricultural and rural policy. At the same time, this literature has a number of limitations that prevent a broader understanding of agricultural and rural development and of the policy-formulation process itself. Three such limitations will be emphasized here:

1. the singular direction of imputed casuality—that change in agricultural structure causes change in the development or underdevelopment characteristics of rural communities;
2. the ahistorical nature of this line of research;
3. the theoretical unsophistication of this literature.

The obvious fact that agricultural and rural development are mutually interrelated, although the major available studies tend to see only agricultural structure as the independent variable, is a clear deficiency in this line of research. The major void in this literature is a consideration of how the development or underdevelopment of rural communities and regions affects the structure of agriculture. Essentially the only exploration of this topic is the commonplace observation that increased employment generation—for example, as a result of rural industrialization—will enhance the viability of part-time farming and increase the incomes of farm families. What is lacking is a comprehensive study of the mutual interrelations of structural change in agriculture and in rural communities and the policy consequences of these interrelations.

As an example of this type of reasoning, one might posit that rural America has experienced two overarching trends during the past two centuries. The first of these has been the substitution of capital (and later energy) for labor in agriculture. In more specific historical terms, U.S. agriculture has experienced several periods of social and technical development. The first was the widespread adoption of horse-drawn, labor-saving technologies during the 1850s. The second was the surge of tractor and tractor-related mechanization during the first several decades of the twentieth century, and the third was the simultaneous surge of large-scale-machinery mechanization and biochemical-technology adoption during the post–World War II period.

The second overarching trend has been the elaboration of spatial differentiation and regional polarization. All capitalist-industrial societies, including the United States, have been characterized by regional inequality, with poor or underdeveloped regions typically being rural or nonmetropolitan in nature and privileged regions being urbanized and/or industrialized.[29] Although there is evidence that such regional disparities in the United States have exhibited some amount of convergence during the past decade,[30] the regional pattern of economic polarization set forth early in U.S. development has remained remarkably persistent.

How have the substitution of capital for labor in agriculture and the elaboration of regional polarization been mutually related? Under what conditions has agricultural development (or the relative lack of such development) led to regional decline or viability? Under what conditions does rural regional decline lead to changes in agriculture? These are the types of questions that the available literature is generally unable to answer and that demand systematic inquiry.

The necessary historical dimension for this area of research is implicit in comments on the restricted view of causality in studies of agriculture and the rural community. These studies, though extremely valuable, tend to ignore the ways in which historical trends in the economy and the society shape the inter-relations between agricultural and rural development. This lack of historical depth parallels the restricted theoretical sophistication of most of this research. The following discussion focuses on how some of these historical and theoretical issues can be addressed more meaningfully.

In basic terms, the historical and theoretical limitations of this body of re-search reflect the fact that we have not asked the big questions. It is ironic that U.S. social scientists tend to have a better historical understanding of the de-velopment of third-world countries than they do of their own. In fact, some of the very interesting questions asked by social scientists concerned with third-world development could be profitably applied to the U.S. context. The follow-ing are illustrative of some of the historical-theoretical issues that must be grappled with in order to understand fully the major trajectories of change in agriculture and the larger rural economy.

Researchers from a variety of theoretical postures have noted that indus-trialization tends to be accompanied by, and at least partially premised on, the extraction of surplus from agriculture.[31] In other words, agriculture tends to be "squeezed" during the initial industrial-development process, leading to the temporary if not permanent underdevelopment of rural regions. Although there have been no thorough studies to document the point, it would appear that such a process characterized the United States at least from roughly 1865 to 1896. Product prices—especially for the major food crops and feed grains—tended to be low, whereas factor or input prices—especially for machinery, transport, and credit—tended to be high, presumably leading to extraction of capital via un-equal terms of trade.[32] The extent to which such extraction of capital from agriculture in the first world continues to occur has only recently become an issue, but unfortunately this is largely confined to European scholars centered around the *Journal of Peasant Studies*.[33] Nevertheless, some very important issues for rural development concern the extent, if any, to which capital is ex-tracted from agriculture (and from which categories of agriculturalists), and how this extraction of capital affects the nonfarm portion of the rural economy.

A second crucial issue pertaining to farm structure and rural development that has received insufficient attention is the evolving nature of backward and forward linkages from the agricultural sector to industry. Perelman points out how U.S. agricultural development after the Revolutionary War occurred largely along commercial lines.[34] Farmers were in essense forced to be commercial and to sell surplus products on the market because of debt, high prices paid for land because of land speculation and government policy, taxation, and state subsidization of the transportation network for distribution of raw materials and manufactured commodities. Cochrane further points out that backward linkages with input providers and forward linkages with eastern markets accompanied this commercial impulse and provided considerable stimulus to the development of U.S. industry.[35] Of course, this stimulation by commercial agriculture of U.S. industry had a particular spatial configuration. Virtually all industry was located in the East prior to the Civil War, and the majority of industrial development prior to World War II was concentrated in the Northeast and Midwest.[36] Until thirty years ago the elaboration of backward and forward linkages between agriculture and industry was, therefore, of a sort that would convey minimal benefits to the nonfarm rural economy. However, the spatial context of industrial location and employment generation began a decided shift in the post–World War II period, primarily during the 1970s. It was during this period that nonmetropolitan industrialization and turnaround migration began in earnest, thereby potentially changing the distribution of benefits from backward and forward linkages with agriculture between metropolitan and nonmetropolitan regions. One might put this in slightly different terms: if it had not been for the conditions (the "urban crisis," the search for cheap labor by corporate enterprises, and so forth) that fostered nonmetropolitan industrialization and the rural population turnaround and counterbalanced the dislocating tendencies of structural change in agriculture, the condition of the larger rural economy might have been considerably worse—if not desperate. The chief policy implication is that a generally buoyant economy, plus shifts in employment generation and industrial location, may have concealed the largely adverse consequences of change in agriculture; thus if for certain reasons (such as the reduced power of major industrial unions and reduced wage rates in the now declining industrial cities) industry begins to reconcentrate, the rural U.S. economy could find itself quite vulnerable.

Another historical-theoretical issue that has recently come to the attention of European scholars but has largely been ignored by U.S. researchers is the question of the degree to and the conditions under which capital accumulation in agriculture leads to or blocks capital accumulation in the larger economy. Our own history suggests that rapid industrial development occurred without major capital accumulation in agriculture. Presumably, as implied earlier, capital for urban-industrial expansion was (partially) extracted from agriculture through unequal terms of exchange, causing U.S. agriculture prior to 1900 to exhibit only small increases in fixed-capital formation. The pace of capital accumulation in agriculture has obviously quickened since World War II, apparently leading to a high rate of capital formation in the agricultural input and output industries. Again, presumably agriculture became insignificant as a source of investment capital, and a number of technological innovations (particularly large tractor and tractor-related machinery and biochemical inputs) permitted a pattern of capital accumulation in agriculture that was compatible with or did not detract from capital formation in industry. Indeed, capital accumulation in industry may have become as premised on capital accumulation in agriculture during the present conjuncture as it was on the decapitalization of agriculture during the late nineteenth century.

A more specific issue for our purposes is how these shifting patterns of capital accumulation within and between agriculture and industry have affected the course of rural development and underdevelopment. Capital accumulation in agriculture may be seen to have two potentially contradictory impacts on rural development. On the one hand, apparently during the initial stages of rapid capital accumulation in agriculture (the so-called golden age of agriculture from 1900 to 1920 or 1910 to 1914, depending on how one dates it), rural regions tend to benefit from the prosperity of agriculture. However, capital accumulation in agriculture, as Cochrane points out, is likely to be a socially and economically uneven process.[37] Some farmers are more successful in doing so than others, and this accumulation process becomes marked by increasing stratification or differentiation among farmers. What Cochrane has called the treadmill of technology thus leads to "cannibalism"—larger, more aggressive farmers outcompeting and purchasing the lands of their less successful neighbors—and to the decline of rural communities and regions as discussed previously.[38]

A final issue that will be considered here is the role of "articulation/disarticulation" in shaping the viability of rural communities and regions. Again, it is interesting that these concepts were initially employed to understand the rural-development problems of third-world nations.[39] They are just now being reintroduced into the domestic rural-development literature.[40] *Articulation* refers to the extent to which the production activities of a region have backward and forward linkages with producers and consumers in that same region; *disarticulation* refers to the degree to which such linkages are absent. Articulation can be seen as the flip side of comparative advantage and specialization. As regions become specialized in particular production activities because of comparative advantage and other factors, those regions specialized in the production of raw materials tend to undergo disarticulation. The raw-materials-specialized regional economy becomes an export enclave, and disarticulation leads to the diminution of multipliers of economic activity.

Historically, U.S. rural regions have undergone a transition toward disarticulation as they have tended to become specialized in the production of food and raw materials that are consumed and transformed elsewhere, and for which inputs are supplied by extraregional firms. One might argue that the small size of local and regional multipliers is what made the impacts of increasing farm size, decreasing size of the farm population, increased mechanization, and the rise of larger-than-family agriculture so destructive for rural communities and regions during the immediate post–World War II period.

A number of factors—including but not limited to the urban crisis and the energy crisis—have begun or are beginning to modify the disarticulating tendencies of rural regions and have led to a more diversified rural economy. The urban crisis (especially the unattractiveness for industry to invest in old industrial cities and for urbanites to retain metropolitan places of residence) has led to deconcentration of industrial location and population distribution. The energy crisis has begun to undercut regional comparative advantage as rising energy costs make long-haul transportation of bulky commodities increasingly expensive. This latter phenomenon is becoming increasingly apparent in agriculture. Agricultural economists in the Northeast, for example, are now saying that lettuce, tomatoes, and other commodities can now be grown competitively in the region. If energy prices continue to escalate and long-haul transportation becomes more expensive, this may signal a shift toward regionally based food systems that will have beneficial effects for rural development in terms of greater articulation and multipliers of economic activity.

In sum, the connections between farm structure and rural development have not been explored to the fullest extent possible. The fact that the general trends in agricultural development in the post–World War II period have tended to exert substantial impacts on rural *underdevelopment,* all other things being equal, is of vital importance for developing sounder policy approaches. However, the foregoing discussion has attempted to suggest as well that this policymaking activity cannot adequately be conducted in a vacuum without knowledge of the historical development of the larger economy and the relations between agriculture, the nonfarm rural economy, and the industrial sector.

A Critique of U.S. Rural-Development Theory and Policy

Rural development (or community-resource development) has for over a decade been a recognized academic specialty in colleges of agriculture and extension divisions, and a recognized policy specialty in the U.S. Department of Agriculture. At this point it seems useful to reflect on rural-development theory and policy in terms of the considerations raised in the foregoing sections. Rural-development theory and policy can be criticized not only for what they do, but also for what they fail to do. This brief critique is intended to be neither exhaustive nor uncompromisingly critical; rather, my purpose is to indicate how academic and political orthodoxies have led rural-development initiatives to be less effective than they otherwise might have been.

Rural-development theory and practice basically fail to do two things. First, as emphasized at the outset, rural development is usually conceived of in terms of an autonomous, nonfarm rural economy; the important influence of structural change in agriculture on rural development and underdevelopment thus is typically ignored. Second, rural-development theory and practice are often undertaken with an assumption that the rural community is a self-contained entity. This flaw is most prevalent among rural sociologists. As a result, the regional context—patterns of regional disparity and convergence, resource flows within and between regions, and so forth—of rural development is often ignored. Basically, then, rural-development theorists and practitioners tend to neglect the two overarching trends—structural change (substitution of capital for labor) in agriculture and the deepening (and, more recently, the modest narrowing) of regional disparities—that have affected the rural economy and society.

The lacunae of rural-development theory and practice can also be understood in terms of what rural-development specialists typically focus on. Rural development in the U.S. currently has four major foci: (1) rural industrialization; (2) encouragement of export-led, specialized rural economies; (3) community-leadership development; and (4) an emphasis on citizen consumption (that is, service delivery) rather than citizen production. Each of these four major aspects of rural-development theory and policy will be explored in turn.

Rural industrialization has undergone such a compelling critique by others that a restatement of these criticisms is unnecessary here.[41] At a general level, it appears that "smokestack chasing" is relatively ineffectual as a rural-development tool for several reasons. First, there just are not enough rural smokestacks to go around to lead to the meaningful development of all or most rural communities in the United States.[42] Second, the tax breaks that result from intercommunity competition for industry typically lead to community fiscal strains in providing the necessary added services, such as public works, schools, and police and fire protection. Third, rural industrialization usually involves massive "leakages" from the community, so that the host community cannot usually count on capturing the majority of benefits from industrial investment. Finally, rural industrialization often tends to result in the further marginalization of already marginal groups, such as the uneducated and the elderly. As rents, taxes, and other living costs increase, economically marginal groups may even find it necessary to leave the community. These, plus a host of other problems, argue against rural industrialization as a primary strategy to achieve rural development.

A second important contemporary strategy of rural development has been to encourage development along the lines of export specialization, usually in the area of nonagricultural raw materials. Typically, external capital is encouraged to invest in a local extractive industry such as timber or minerals. This trajectory of rural development is limited by two circumstances alluded to earlier. The first concerns the fact that export-led growth will lead to disarticulation and low multipliers of economic activity. The stark reality of eastern Kentucky coal regions exhibiting the conspicuous consumption of millionaires driving Cadillacs while the majority of the population continues to live at or near poverty levels is dramatic evidence of how export-led growth is not balanced or desirable growth. A second limiting condition is energy scarcity, which promises to make remote sources of raw materials increasingly uncompetitive because of escalating energy and transportation costs.

Community-leadership development is perhaps the most central focus of sociologists concerned with rural development. Leadership-development strategy is premised on an assumption that the limiting factor in rural development is unprofessional and technically underqualified leadership, which, given the necessary information and training, will be able to stimulate local economic development. Although this observation is undoubtedly true in many contexts, rural-development specialists often fail to recognize the power of the master trends—structural change in agriculture and regional polarization—that affect the economic viability of rural regions. At best, aggressive community leadership will be able to attract additional federal grants and will enable a handful of communities to attract economic activity that otherwise would have gone to other communities. At worst, community-leadership development may intensify the competition between rural communities over the handful of smokestacks that locate in nonmetropolitan regions each year, perhaps causing the community to suffer from excessive industrial tax concessions and limited capacity to provide essential services. Community-leadership development fails to address the major social and economic forces that have led to inadequate development of rural areas in the United States.

The Carter administration's statement on small-community and rural-development policy is prominent evidence of the emphasis that federal rural-development authorities place on consumption and service delivery.[43] To be sure, availability of services is a singularly important indicator of the extent of rural development, and federal assistance to rural areas in service delivery is welcome. However, this rural-development strategy promises to be vulnerable along with the larger welfare-state apparatus of which it is a part. Federally subsidized services in rural areas could well be the first to be dismantled, because of their high per-unit costs, as political pressure escalates on the transfer-payment segment of the federal budget. Many rural communities, premising their local budgets on the availability of federal funds, could face tremendous fiscal problems if these props were taken away. More fundamentally, however, the limitation of a consumption- and service-oriented approach to rural development is that it fails to consider necessary realignments in production institutions. The only enduring road to increased income and consumption lies through meaningful involvement in production. Hence, rural development ultimately should be conceived of in terms of change in production institutions.

Toward Agricultural Structure Policy for Rural Development

The previous discussion has reiterated the frequently heard claim that a structural policy encouraging small-scale family farms would be a potent rural-development policy as well.[44] Thus there emerges the practical question of whether it is possible for agricultural policy to be shaped in ways that contribute to rural-development objectives. Unfortunately, these prospects do not seem particularly good. As Robinson has noted, structural policies that would lead to reduced farm size and associated characteristics would likely be politically infeasible,[45] whereas politically acceptable policy changes would tend to be ineffectual in influencing change in agricultural structure.[46]

Given that there has never been serious discussion in the United States about controlling the land market (and because the land market may be a more pernicious cause of social dislocation in agriculture than federal commodity programs), the range of instruments for federal administrators to affect agricultural structure is limited.[47] These instruments are basically confined to commodity programs, tax policy, credit policy, and production controls. Other policy strategies—such as enforcing the original intent of the 160-acre limitation on federally irrigated land of the Reclamation Act of 1902—would have some beneficial effects, but these effects would be quite localized. Basically, federal structural policy, if it is to have major impacts on structure, would have to embody strong, overt disincentives to large-scale agriculture. Commodity programs would need to have stringent payment limitations with the effect of withholding subsidies for large family farms (that is, owner-operated farms with gross sales substantially above the national mean), larger-than-family farms, and corporate/large-scale industrial farms. Tax policy would need to be changed to place, in effect, a confiscatory tax on capital gains and to limit severely tax avoidance through liberal depreciation rules and other tax loopholes. Credit policy would have to be reoriented in terms of federal credit subsidies for newly entering or small farmers, while forcing large farmers to rely on the private credit market. In sum, federal structural policy must overtly penalize large producers in order to achieve a dedevelopment or devolution of U.S. agriculture, assuming that policies to intervene in the land market continue to be eschewed.

Minimal familiarity with the process of agricultural-policy formulation suggests that none of these policy instruments is remotely viable. Not surprisingly, organizations of large farmers (in particular, the major commodity groups and the American Farm Bureau Federation) are quite influential in shaping federal agricultural policy (or more precisely, in vetoing policy provision that are not in their interest).[48] Devolutionizing policies would, of course, be anathema to these groups; and political support for such initiatives would have to be found among other socially powerful organizations. Although small farmers could be expected to provide some support for these initiatives, the bulk of the political burden will fall on nonfarm groups. At present, these nonfarm groups appear to be fractionalized. The "hunger lobby" is primarily concerned with expanding food-aid programs and reducing the price of food to the consumer. Environmentalists would increase the price of food by raising the price of heretofore underpriced inputs such as water and energy. Farm-worker support groups essentially hope to do the same through their goal of increasing the wages of hired farm laborers. As a result, nonfarm public-interest groups have competing interests and goals that cannot easily be amalgamated in support of small farmers and rural development.

In addition, general political pressures would complement large-scale farmer resistance to progressive structural policies. A milieu of fiscal austerity, for example, makes additional federal expenditures on income supports for small farmers unlikely. The prevailing political climate regarding "tax reform" suggests that, if anything, capital-gains taxes will be *decreased* and investment tax credits and other loopholes *increased* to encourage capital formation in industry. Subsidized credit for small farmers in an era of general capital shortages and sentiment for targeting scarce credit to certain sectors of industry also seems unlikely. Basically, then, the possibilities for progressive national structural policy toward agriculture seem remote, even given the powerful arguments that can be marshaled for such policies on the grounds of rural development and rural-urban equity.

As alluded to previously, there is one potential national-policy tool—control over the land market—that could have substantial impacts on agricultural structure and could lead to rural-development benefits. Among the developed capitalist societies, the United States stands out as virtually the only nation with no state control over the private market in agricultural or rural land. The operation of the land market clearly is one of the major mechanisms that has led to increased farm size, fewer farms, greater mechanization, and increased operation of farms by larger-than-family or large-scale industrial-production units.[49] An unregulated land market, in conjunction with a tax system that encourages speculative investments, makes farmland attractive for nonfarm investment. In addition, the benefits of federal commodity and credit programs tend to become capitalized in the price of land. This directly subsidizes nonmanaging landlords, directly penalizes tenants through higher rents, and indirectly penalizes owner-operators through higher taxes and interest payments.[50] To repeat the observation made earlier, the operation of the private market in agricultural land is perhaps the key force that augments the "treadmill of technology" and leads to differentiation among agriculturalists and the marginalization of the small producer.[51]

Unfortunately, little public attention seems to be focused on the land market and how it might be controlled in the interest of small- and moderate-scale farmers and the majority of the nonfarm population. By contrast, several European countries have established mechanisms whereby the state has veto power over land transactions other than intergenerational ones. In certain cases this veto power is extended to prevent sales of farms to nonfarm persons or to farmers who already own considerable agricultural land. In Western Europe, in fact, the land question has come to be recognized as being of sufficient importance to the viability of the rural social structure that otherwise mainstream agricultural economists are going so far as to advocate nationalization of agricultural land in the interest of conservation, economic efficiency, and rural development. Clearly, this latter option seems so remote as to exclude it entirely from the upcoming policy agenda. Nevertheless, significant structural change in agriculture in the direction of less concentration of land and less marginalization of the small- and moderate-scale producer will likely require substantial public intervention in the land market along the lines discussed earlier.

Local Dimensions of Agricultural and Rural-Development Policy

This discouraging picture of the prospects for progressive agricultural and structural policy should not imply that there are no strategies for dealing with problems of structure and rural development in the United States. But the major policy avenues open at present are primarily local in nature. This is not to exaggerate the efficacy of local strategies; their implementation in each neighborhood, community, county, and state is problematic. Nevertheless, local initiatives of the type depicted seem at present to have greater promise than national structural policy to affect the agricultural and nonfarm rural economies beneficially. Three such strategies will be briefly summarized here: (1) multifamily group farming, (2) community land trusts, and (3) establishment of localism in the food system. Although there are other possible local strategies, these three seem the most promising in terms of altering the major forces for structural differentiation in agriculture and underdevelopment of rural regions and communities.

Most economies-of-scale studies show that the principal differences in efficiency between small- and large-scale farms are due to machinery costs. Thus institutional modifications that enable small farms to reduce their machinery costs could be extremely important in enhancing the viability of small-farm operations. Encouraging data for this argument come from research on multifamily group farming in Saskatchewan, which indicates substantial savings in machinery costs for farmers who share equipment with their neighbors.[52] This research suggests that group farming can enable smaller operations to take full advantage of economies of scale without each family having to invest in separate sets of machinery. This Saskatchewan research also indicates that group farming and cooperative use of farm-production resources allow these family farmers to farm their land more intensively; machinery and equipment sharing enables these farmers to undertake livestock enterprises that would otherwise have high per-unit costs. Because of the high level of livestock production (by comparison with matched sets of farmers not participating in group farming), group farms exhibited increased use of animal manure (and reduced use of chemical fertilizers) and better erosion control. Small- and moderate-scale farmers involved in group farming may be able to benefit from economies of scale and to take advantage of any differential benefits that these farms might potentially receive from federal commodity programs.

With no federal policy in sight for control of the land market, community land trusts appear to be the most promising mechanism to deal with the pernicious effects of the market. A community land trust is a nonprofit corporation with an elected board of trustees and, usually, open public membership from the community. The community-land-trust mechanism involves farmers and forest landowners selling the development and transfer rights to their land to the land trust, in exchange for use rights and insulation from the effects of land speculation and inflation. The land trust retains title to the land and removes the land from the speculative market, while the land is leased to individuals, families, cooperatives, public agencies, or other groups as a lifetime (or inheritable) ninety-nine-year lease. The board of trustees has the power to decide appropriate uses for the land and to terminate leases if the board feels the land is being misused. The logic behind the land trust is to enable farm families to capture the increasing value of landed property, as their rents decrease relative to those prevailing on the private land market, and to employ it for public purposes, rather than have this value be appropriated by absentee owners or land speculators. Clearly, the major limitation to community-land-trust ventures is initial funding with which to launch the venture. Securing public loans for initiating land trusts, along with providing organizational and technical assistance, would be extremely useful agricultural and rural-development strategies.

The final local strategy for agricultural and rural development involves the encouragement of localism in the food-delivery system. It was noted earlier that rising energy prices and increasing costs of irrigation, fertilizers, transportation, and centralized food processing portend an unprecedented despecialization of the food-production and -delivery system. Although it is likely that these changes will occur regardless of public-policy intervention, the flow of benefits can be hastened through activities that build local food-delivery systems. Reestablishing local marketing options, however, will not always be a simple matter. Martinson and Campbell, for example, document the historic demise of local terminal and auction markets for most farm commodities and the fact that farm products now increasingly must be sold directly to processor or distributor firms through private negotiations or forward contracts.[53] Local-market development will generally tend to be a sizable undertaking.

Despite the prevailing orthodoxy that suggests that scale economies foredoom local-market institutions, the past decade has witnessed a remarkable increase in direct marketing of fresh produce in most regions of the country, particularly in the Northeast. Further, increased attention is being paid to establishment of community- or regional-based food-processing ventures such as community canneries and grain-processing facilities.[54] Generally these food-processing ventures are undertaken by community- or employee-owned enterprises such as community-development corporations. These local processing and marketing ventures promise to enhance rural development and diminish the dislocations from structural change in agriculture in several ways:

1. by providing additional markets for smaller farmers who have the surplus labor to allocate to the production of a diversity of high value or specialty crops,
2. by directly and indirectly providing additional employment in the community;
3. by retaining locally generated profits in the community because of the community- or employee-owned character of these enterprises;
4. by leading to greater articulation of the local rural economy through the fostering of greater backward and forward linkages from the farming sector to other community enterprises and consumers.[55]

Again, like group farming and community land trusts, the establishment of greater localism in food delivery can be greatly facilitated by funding from local units of government and by technical assistance from extension and community-resource-development personnel.[56]

Summary

This chapter has attempted to present the case for a closer integration of agricultural and rural-development policy. Available research strongly indicates that the structural changes in agriculture that have accelerated since World War II have tended to undermine rural-community viability and have led to rural underdevelopment. At the same time, prevailing rural-development strategies have proved to be limited. However, the obvious implication of these findings—that there should be agricultural-structure policies to reverse these historic changes—must be tempered by political realities. It seems unlikely that sufficient political coalitions can be forged to support such structure policies over the strong objection of privileged agricultural producers. Therefore, analogs of federal structure policies can best be pursued at the local level at the present time.

These prescriptions for the reconceptualization of rural-development policy must be interpreted in terms of desirable tendencies or directions, rather than in terms of absolutes. A total localization of community or regional food-delivery systems is as impractical as the highly centralized systems they are intended to supplant. A rural region in Kansas can no more produce all its own food than multinational food corporations can reduce the energy friction of space in an energy-scarce world. Nevertheless, there is an urgent need to reconsider rural-development orthodoxies and to cast new light on these problems. Considerable research is needed to guide the theoretical and practical design of new rural-development initiatives. This research must be historically informed and sensitive to the multiple interactions between agricultural change and rural development. Further, the pursuit of such research and policy provides a creative way to address the "new agenda," as Paarlberg describes it.[57] Unfortunately, as Paarlberg fears, the new agenda is at present too diverse and fragmented to be coherently addressed by federal authorities. This is where university and locally based rural-development personnel with financial, logistical, technical, and ideological support from federal personnel can step in and play a significant role in the rural-development process.

Notes

1. Don Paarlberg, *Farm and Food Policy: Issues of the 1980's* (Lincoln: University of Nebraska Press, 1980).

2. Luther Tweeten, *Foundations of Farm Policy*, 2nd ed. (Lincoln: University of Nebraska Press, 1979); Luther Tweeten and George L. Brinkman, *Micropolitan Development* (Ames: Iowa State University Press, 1976).

3. Carter administration, *Small Community and Rural Development Policy* (Washington, D.C.: The White House, 1979).

4. Paarlberg, *Farm and Food Policy.*

5. William L. Flinn and Frederick H. Buttel, "Sociological Aspects of Farm Size: Ideological and Social Consequences of Scale in Agriculture," *American Journal of Agricultural Economics* 62(1981).

6. John H. Kolb and Edmund S. de Brunner, *A Study of Rural Society* (Boston: Houghton Mifflin, 1952).

7. Walter Goldschmidt, *As You Sow* (Glencoe, Ill.: Free Press, 1947); idem, *As You Sow: Three Studies in the Social Consequences of Agribusiness,* (Montclair, N.J.: Allanheld, Osmun and Company, 1978).

8. Richard D. Rodefeld, "The Changing Occupational and Organizational Structure of Farming: Implications for Farm Work Force Individuals, Families, and Communities" (Ph.D. diss. University of Wisconsin, Madison, 1974).

9. Kevin F. Goss, "Review of Goldschmidt, *As You Sow*," *Rural Sociology* 44(1979):802–806.

10. Currently available longitudinal census data on "corporate" farms lump closely held, family corporations and nonclosely held, large-scale industrial corporations together in the same category. See Rodefeld, "Changing Occupational and Organizational Structure," for the implications of this aggregation problem. Also see Richard D. Rodefeld, "Trends in U.S. Farm Organizational Structure and Type," in R.D. Rodefeld et al., eds., *Change in Rural America* (St. Louis, Mo.: C.V. Mosby, 1978).

11. Richard D. Rodefeld, *The Direct and Indirect Effects of Mechanizing U.S. Agriculture* (Montclair, N.J.: Allanheld, Osmun and Company, 1980).

12. Willard W. Cochrane, *The Development of American Agriculture* (Minneapolis: University of Minnesota Press, 1979).

13. E. Phillip LeVeen, "The Prospects for Small-Scale Farming in an Industrial Society: A Critical Appraisal of *Small is Beautiful*," in R.D. Dorf and Y.L. Hunter, eds., *Appropriate Visions* (San Francisco: Boyd and Fraser, 1978).

14. Frederick H. Buttel and Oscar W. Larson III, "Farm Size, Structure, and Energy Intensity: An Ecological Analysis of U.S. Agriculture," *Rural Sociology* 44(1979):471-488; Frederick H. Buttel, "Agricultural Structure and Energy Intensity: A Comparative Analysis of the Developed Capitalist Societies," *Comparative Rural and Regional Studies,* Occasional Paper no. 1 (1979).

15. David Brown, "Farm Structure and the Rural Community," in *Structure Issues of American Agriculture,* Agricultural Economic Report no. 438 (Washington, D.C.: Economics, Statistics, and Cooperative Service, U.S. Department of Agriculture, 1979).

16. Goldschmidt, *As You Sow: Three Studies.*

17. Rodefeld, "Changing Occupational and Organizational Structure"; William P. Heffernan and Paul Lasley, "Agricultural Structure and Interaction in the Local Community: A Case Study," *Rural Sociology* 43(1978):348-361.

18. Craig K. Harris and Jess C. Gilbert, "Large Scale Farming, Rural Social Welfare, and the Agrarian Thesis: a Re-examination" (Paper presented at the annual meeting of the Rural Sociological Society, Burlington, Vt., August 1979); Isao Fujimoto, "The Communities of the San Josquin Valley: The Interrelations among Farming, Water Use, and Quality of Life" (Unpublished paper, Department of Applied Behavioral Sciences, University of California, Davis, 1977).

19. Steven T. Sonka and Earl O. Heady, "Farm Size, Rural Community Income, and Consumer Welfare," *American Journal of Agricultural Economics* 56(1974):534-542.

20. William D. Heffernan, "Sociological Dimensions of Agricultural Structure in the United States," *Sociologia Ruralis* 12(1972):481-499.

21. Rodefeld "Changing Occupational and Organizational Structure"; Hefferman, "Sociological Dimensions"; Hefferman and Lasley, "Agricultural Structure."

22. Philip M. Raup, "Some Questions of Value and Scale in Agriculture," *American Journal of Agricultural Economics* 60(1978):303-308.

23. Kevin F. Goss and Richard D. Rodefeld, "Farming and Place Population Change in Michigan, 1930-1970" (Paper presented at the annual meeting of the Rural Sociological Society, Madison, Wisconsin, August 1977).

24. Sonka and Heady, "Farm Size"; Olaf F Larson, "Farming and the Rural Community" in A.H. Hawley and V. Rock, eds., *Rural Renaissance and Urban Phenomena* (Chapel Hill: University of North Carolina Press, 1981).

25. Bert L. Ellenbogen, "Service Structure of the Small Community: Problems and Options for Change," in *Communities Left Behind* (Ames: Iowa State University Press, 1974).

26. Paul W. Barkley, "Some Nonfarm Effects of Change in Agricultural Technology," *American Journal of Agricultural Economics* 58(1978):812-819;

Fujimoto, "Communities of the San Joaquin Valley"; Small Farm Viability Project, "The Family Farm in California" (Report to the State of California, Sacramento, 1977); Steven T. Sonka, "Consequences of Farm Structural Change" (Report prepared for the Project on a Research Agenda for Small Farms, National Rural Center, Washington, D.C., 1979).

27. Oscar B. Martinson, E.A. Wilkening, and Richard D. Rodefeld, "Feelings of Powerlessness and Social Isolation Among 'Large Scale' Farm Personnel," *Rural Sociology* 41(1976):452–472; Heffernan, "Sociological Dimensions"; Heffernan and Lasley, "Agricultural Structure"; Rodefeld "Changing Occupational and Organizational Structure."

28. Sharon Powers, Jess Gilbert, and Frederick H. Buttel, "Small Farm and Rural Development Policy in the United States: Rationale and Prospects," in *Rural Research in USDA,* Hearings before the Subcommittee on Agricultural Research and General Legislation of the Committee on Agriculture, Nutrition, and Forestry, U.S. Senate, 95th Congress, Second Session (Washington, D.C.: U.S. Government Printing Office, 1978).

29. Stuart Holland, *Capital against the Regions* (New York: St. Martin's Press, 1976).

30. Kenneth Fox, "Uneven Regional Development in the United States," *Review of Radical Political Economics* 10(1978):68–86.

31. Alain de Janvry, "Nature of Rural Development Programs: Implications for Technology Design," in A. Valdes, G.M. Scobie, and J.L. Dillon, eds., *Economics and the Design of Small-Farmer Technology* (Ames: Iowa State University Press, 1978).

32. Cochrane, *Development of American Agriculture.*

33. Harriet Freidmann, "Household Production and the National Economy: Concepts for the Analysis of Agrarian Formations," *Journal of Peasant Studies* 7(1980):158–184.

34. Michael Perelman, *Farming for Profit in a Hungry World* (Montclair, N.J.: Allanheld, Osmun and Company, 1977).

35. Cochrane, *Development of American Agriculture.*

36. Barrington Moore, Jr., *Social Origins of Dictatorship and Democracy* (Boston: Beacon, 1966).

37. Cochrane, *Development of American Agriculture.*

38. Ibid.

39. de Janvry, "Nature of Rural Development Programs."

40. David M. Gordon, *The Working Poor: Toward a State Agenda* (Washington, D.C.: Council of State Planning Agencies, 1979).

41. Gene F. Summers et al., *Industrial Invasion of Nonmetropolitan America* (New York: Praeger, 1976).

42. Michael F. Nolan and William D. Heffernan, "The Rural Development Act of 1972: A Skeptical View," *Rural Sociology* 39(1974):536–545.

43. Carter administration, *Small Community and Rural Development Policy.*

44. Frederick H. Buttel, "Agricultural Structure and Rural Ecology: Toward a Political Economy of Rural Development," *Sociologia Ruralis* 20:(1980): 44–62; Powers, Coilbert, and Buttel, "Small Farm and Rural Development Policy."

45. Kenneth C. Robinson, "The Structure of Agricultural Production in North American Alternatives for the Future" (Unpublished manuscript, Department of Agricultural Economics, Cornell University, 1980).

46. It should be noted that there is an emerging consensus that small farms (those with gross annual sales of $20,000 or less) are becoming more persistent in comparison with their rapid rates of decline in the 1950s and 1960s. Two factors seems particularly important in accounting for the persistence of these small farms: (1) off-farm employment as a supplement to meager farm incomes, and (2) the tendency for small farmers to be more insulated than large farmers from the effects of energy-price increases because they employ smaller amounts of energy-intensive inputs such as fertilizers or pesticides (Perelman, *Farming for Profit*). Indeed, the emergent structural weakness of U.S. agriculture as the 1980s unfold appears to be the vulnerable status of moderate-scale family-labor farms that are largely dependent on agricultural income. These moderate-scale farms are especially subject to instability in factor and product markets. This vulnerability of moderate-scale farms is increasingly referred to as the problem of the "disappearing middle." See Neal Walker, "Issues Involved in Formulating a Structures Policy for U.S. Agriculture" (Paper presented at the Southern Agricultural Economics Association meetings, Hot Springs, Arkansas, February 1980).

47. William P. Browne and Charles W. Wiggins, "Interest Group Strength and Organizational Characteristics: The General Farm Organizations and the 1977 Farm Bill," in Don F. Hadwiger and William P. Browne, eds., *The New Politics of Food* (Lexington, Mass.: Lexington Books, D.C. Heath and Company, 1978).

48. Robinson, "Structure of Agricultural Production."

49. Flinn and Buttel, "Sociological Aspects of Farm Size."

50. Cochrane, *Development of American Agriculture.*

51. Frederick H. Buttel, "Agriculture, Environment, and Social Change: Some Emergent Issues," in F.H. Buttel and H. Newby, eds., *The Rural Sociology of the Advanced Societies* (Montclair, N.J.: Allanheld, Osmun and Company, 1980).

52. Michael Gertler, "Resource-Management Implications of Group Farming in Saskatchewan" (Paper presented at the annual meeting of the American Association for the Advancement of Science, Toronto, January 1981).

53. Oscar B. Martinson and Gerald R. Campbell, "Betwixt and Between: Farmers and the Marketing of Agricultural Inputs and Outputs," in F.H. Buttel and H. Newby, eds., *The Rural Sociology of the Advanced Societies* (Montclair, N.J.: Allanheld, Osmun and Company, 1980).

54. Carolyn Britt and Tom Walker, with Michael Schaaf, *Jobs and Energy in New England: Food Processing and Marketing* (Bath, Me.: Coastal Enterprises, Inc., 1978).

55. I have referred to this emergent form of rural development theory and practice as *import substitution*. Import substitution pertains to rural-development strategies based on increased local production of commodities that formerly were imported by a community or region. Food is the obvious starting point for import substitution, since: (1) most rural regions already engage in substantial agricultural production, and (2) food imports represent a sizable proportion of rural regions' cash flows. However, import substitution can potentially take root in the provision of several other commodities, including energy (for example, in the form of fuel-wood cooperatives); housing (as in the provision of building materials from local sources); and other areas, depending on the nature of the local resource base. The basic rationale behind import substitution is local production, where economically feasible, of those commodities imported from other regions, thereby augmenting regional disarticulation and increasing local multipliers. Frederick H. Buttel, "Rural Resources and the Environment," in Don A. Dillman and D.J. Hobbs, eds., *Rural Sociology: Research Issues for the 1980s* (Boulder, Colo.: Westview Press, 1982).

56. An additional local strategy that might be mentioned is to encourage experiment-station research geared toward energy-cost minimization on modest-scale farms. This type of research would tend to build on the cost minimization adaptations that small farmers typically pursue. (Larger farmers generally pursue cost minimization through farm-size expansion to spread the fixed cost of machinery investments over larger acreages, rather than through minimization of nonmachinery variable costs.) The development of low-energy, low-cost agricultural-production techniques would thus tend to build on the strengths of small producers (excess labor) and to minimize their weaknesses (lack of investment capital). Finally, it is important to note that the development of such low-energy agricultural-production techniques would undoubtedly be based on crop rotations, which dovetail quite well with the increased diversity in agricultural production necessary for more localism in the food-delivery system.

57. Paarlberg, *Farm and Food Policy*.

Indexes

Name Index

Subject Index

About the Contributors

Ralph Baker is professor of political science at Ball State University. He is coauthor of *The Criminal Justice Game: Politics and Players* and coeditor of *Determinants of Law Enforcement Policies* and *Evaluating Alternative Law Enforcement Policies.* He has also contributed to articles in *Law and Public Policy, Police Administration Review,* and the *Policy Studies Journal.* Professor Baker's major research interests are the politics of the criminal-justice system and public law.

Calvin L. Beale is a demographer and senior analyst with the Economic Research Service, U.S. Department of Agriculture (USDA). He has focused his work on interpretations of rural and small-town population patterns for the USDA since 1953. Before that he worked for the Bureau of the Census. His large number of articles, chapters, and monographs have made him the most widely respected rural demographer in the United States. He is also coauthor of *Economic Areas of the United States.*

Lewis G. Bender is an associate professor of political science and coordinator of the Masters of Public Administration Program, Eastern Michigan University. He has written several articles on substate regionalism and contributed to numerous professional conferences.

Edward J. Blakely is assistant vice-president, Academic Personnel Systemwide, and professor of city and regional planning at the University of California, Berkeley. He is also a consultant for several international agencies on problems of economic and social development, as well as the author of several books, articles, and monographs, including *Toward a Theory of Training People for the War on Poverty.* He is coauthor of *Rural Communities in Advanced Industrial Society* and corecipient of a Ford Foundation grant to examine population growth and economic change in four states with large rural areas.

Ted K. Bradshaw, research sociologist and editor of *California Date Briefs* at the Institute of Governmental Studies, University of California, Berkeley, has written many articles and papers on California's economic development, educational system, government agencies, changing energy institutions, and policy issues. He is coauthor of *Rural Communities in Advanced Industrial Society* and corecipient of a Ford Foundation grant to examine population growth and economic change in four states with large rural areas.

Frederick H. Buttel is associate professor of rural sociology at Cornell University. He is coeditor of *The Rural Sociology of the Advanced Societies: Critical*

Perspectives; coauthor of *Environment, Energy, and Society*; and author or co-author of fifty articles and book chapters on agricultural structure, rural development, energy and environment, and related topics.

Lynn M. Daft is a senior associate with Schnittker Associates, an economic consulting firm in Washington, D.C. Before assuming this position, he served in a number of capacities in the federal government, including positions at the White House, the Office of Management and Budget, the Congressional Budget Office, the U.S. Department of Agriculture, the Office of Economic Opportunity, and the National Advisory Commission on Rural Poverty. His Ph.D. training is in agricultural economics.

Jan E. Dillard is a policy analyst for WAPORA, Inc., a private environmental and economic research consulting firm. She has been involved in various research projects regarding the implications of controls on land uses by various levels of government, and she recently completed a study of the effectiveness of various environmental-protection programs in the Environmental Protection Administration's Region IV. Her current research concerns the impact of interest groups on the adoption of state land policies.

John Dinse is assistant professor of political science at Central Michigan University. His primary fields are political theory and U.S. political thought. He became interested in public administration and policy in order to develop and teach a course that seeks to show the relevance of political theory to public administration. His research interests include the U.S. Left and the philosophy of science as well as public administration and policy problems.

Sydney Duncombe is professor of political science and director of the Bureau of Public Affairs Research at the University of Idaho. He has worked in budgeting and management analysis in the states of New York, Ohio, Washington, and Idaho and has served as budget director of the states of Ohio and Idaho. He is the author of *County Government in America, Modern County Government,* and numerous articles on state and local government.

Daniel M. Ebels is an assistant professor at Calvin College and on the board of directors of a local housing agency. His research and publications are primarily in the area of municipal capital markets and applied fiscal policy.

William L. Flinn serves as director of Mid-American University and professor of agricultural economics and rural sociology at The Ohio State University. His many publications on rural life and widespread professional interests have culminated in his election as president of the Rural Society Association.

Paul Michael Green is director of the Institute for Public Policy and Administration and professor of public administration at Governor's State University, Lake Forest South. He also serves as a township supervisor, a position ideally suited to his research interest in local government and politics. In addition to publishing in the field of local politics, he is involved as an author of Illinois reapportionment material as part of a national project.

Daryl J. Hobbs is professor of rural sociology and director for rural development at the University of Missouri–Columbia. He has served as chairperson of the departments of Sociology and Rural Sociology at the University of Missouri and recently served as president of the Rural Sociological Society. He has published numerous articles on rural education and has been involved as a consultant on rural education to the National Institute of Education, the Mid-Continent Regional Education Laboratory, the National Rural Center, and ERIC/CRSS. He is coeditor of *Rural Society: Issues for the 1980's*.

Fred A. Meyer, Jr., is associate professor of political science at Ball State University. Professor Meyer is coauthor of *The Criminal Justice Game* and coeditor of *Determinants of Law Enforcement Policies* and *Evaluating Alternative Law Enforcement Policies*. He has also contributed to articles in *Law and Public Policy, Police Administration Review,* and the *Policy Studies Journal.* His major research interests are the politics of the criminal-justice system and urban politics. He is editor of the *Indiana Journal of Political Science.*

Harriet Newburger works as an economist in the Department of Housing and Urban Development's Office of Research. She has coauthored an article in the *American Economic Review.* Her current research interests include small-city community development and racial discrimination in U.S. housing markets.

Alvin D. Sokolow is associate director of the Institute of Governmental Affairs and associate professor of political science at the University of California, Davis. He directs a program of research and public service on policy, politics, and government in small and especially rural communities. He is coauthor of *Choices for the Unincorporated Community* and of a textbook on California government and politics, as well as author of numerous journal articles, monographs, and papers on rural politics and state legislative behavior.

About the Editors

William P. Browne, professor of political science at Central Michigan University, is author of *Politics, Programs and Bureaucrats,* as well as over twenty published articles, book chapters, and monographs related to public policy and interest-group politics. He previously coedited a *Policy Studies Journal* symposium focusing on agriculture policy, and two related books, *The New Politics of Food* and *The Role of U.S. Agriculture in Foreign Policy.*

Don F. Hadwiger, professor of political science at Iowa State University, has authored, coauthored, or coedited five books on agriculture policy and politics as well as a *Policy Studies Journal* symposium on agriculture policy. In addition to writing over a dozen articles on rural policy and agriculture, he has worked with both the USDA and congressional agriculture committees.